Where the Wolf Lies

A Novel

T Y L E R   F L Y N N

Where

the

A Novel

Wolf

Lies

THERE'S A WOLF IN ALL OF US...

PAPILLON
PRESS

Tyler Flynn
Where the Wolf Lies
Copyright © 2019 Tyler Flynn

Imprint of Papillon Press
Instagram: @TylerFlynnBooks

Twitter: @TylerFlynnBooks
Tylerflynnbooks.com

IBSN eBook: 978-0-578-47229-4
IBSN Hardcover: 978-0-578-47230-0
ISBN Paperback: 978-0-578-49733-4

Entre Chien et Loup

This is a French idiomatic expression, which literally translates to "between dog and wolf." The expression captures the hour between day and night when it becomes difficult to distinguish things, such as a dog from a wolf. However, the French use the expression when speaking about something, or someone that is mysterious, or caught between two ideals. *Entre chien et loup* means the comfort of familiarity versus the doubt of the unknown, hope versus despair, and safety versus danger, where one becomes nearly indistinguishable from the other. That, some French say, is where the wolf lies.

For my wife Marie.

Je t'aime pour toujours.

1

All great cities are built on rivers.

Paris on the Seine, New York on the Hudson, Cairo on the Nile. London, on the banks of the Thames, is no different.

The wet streets of the old city glistened in the midmorning sun. The rain from the night before, and the day before that, never gave the puddles a chance to dry. However, the nicest day of fall had arrived; it hadn't yet rained that morning, but the air was heavy with the promise of a storm to come.

The ancient city on the Thames moved at a bustling pace. Tourists flocked to the capital filling the streets, museums, shops and alleyways. Cafés were packed with the morning crowd; locals chatted about the weather and shared laughter as the morning passed by.

Igor Romanski didn't have the time to sit at a café. He strode east along the river after having crossed the Millennium Bridge. His thick-soled black derbies, which many Londoners wore thanks to the ever-present threat of rain, were uncomfortable but necessary. He wore a long navy-blue Sunspel car coat—collar turned up against the cool breeze coming off the river— with dark jeans and a blue jumper. A leather backpack was slung over his broad shoulders. Igor's wide face framed his restless gray eyes. With a name like Igor in a Western country, he had to work diligently to fit in with the class in which he operated in England.

He hustled towards Borough Market, which on a Friday morning would be buzzing. There, people could buy baklava from a Turkish deli, or fresh Stilton from Cornwall, or even *pied de cochon*—pigs' feet—cured and brought in from Spain. The European Union allowed different cultures to collaborate, and nothing exemplified that better, perhaps, than the market. Igor smirked at the irony. *If only they knew what I was doing.*

He entered the market from the west, glancing into dark alleys flanking his route. Igor navigated past them, as he had done dozens of times before, entering from Park Street, past The Anchor pub. There, he peered into the reflective, smoked-glass windows of his landmark to see if he had been followed. Pleased he hadn't been, Igor passed under the high railroad tracks as the sun, fighting an endless battle with the stubborn English sky, disappeared from view.

Igor surveyed the collection of stalls converted to storefronts, surrounded by steel beam pillars painted British racing green. Signs identified the various shops, where one could find almost anything: potpies, Indian spices, fresh eggs, and fish caught that morning. The stand to his right was piled high with brightly colored fruit and vegetables in greens, burnt yellows, and shiny reds. An elderly couple caught his eye as they crossed in front of him distractedly, causing him to abruptly stop walking. The man hunched over, weakened by age, shuffled along, and held the hand of his wife. Igor clenched his jaw in an effort to suppress his desire to whip them to hurry on and sought out another path.

His mobile buzzed in his coat pocket. A text message from a number he didn't have in his contacts.

Is it done yet?

Igor silently cursed the impatience of his partner.

I will make contact when it's finished.

He fired the message off, presuming that would be the end of the conversation. The phone buzzed another time.

Make sure everything is ready. Soon we will have a new guest to entertain.

Igor grunted and tucked away his phone. He couldn't afford to linger on the ambiguity because he had a job to do. But who was the new guest? Another target or a potential client? He gritted his teeth and refocused on the task at hand.

He proceeded further through the right side of the market, maneuvering with his hands stuffed deep in his pockets. To any shop owner or onlooker, he was hidden in plain sight. Conceivably, he was a man out buying ingredients to make a romantic dinner at home, or, judging by his smart dress, he was a chef from a nearby restaurant picking out fresh produce. Igor didn't care what strangers thought as long as he wasn't memorable. That was the key. He wanted to blend in amongst the crowd, and for that reason he'd chosen the market.

Igor slowed his pace and feigned interest at an Italian olive-oil shop. Light-colored wooden barrels were arranged around the inside of the store, creating a woodsy, musky aroma. A small bread basket sat on the counter for curious customers to try the product. Igor turned his head cautiously, allowing his shoulder to creep upwards, blocking the bottom half of his face, and looked back down the way he came. The elderly pair were still shuffling through the market, but nothing seemed out of the ordinary. Satisfied he wasn't being followed, he continued on.

Who was the new guest? He strained to push the thought from his mind. He had to focus. The market was just about to hit the peak of its busiest hour—midday—when the lunch rush came.

He walked for a bit and then ducked into a cheese shop. An older woman sat behind the glass case that kept the cheeses cold. There were a few people in the shop, amongst them a young woman with a bright yellow raincoat who picked up small boxes of Camembert, opening them and prodding them with her fingers. The shopkeeper trudged over to help her, speaking fast in broken English—*probably German*, Igor thought. He climbed up two wooden stairs that creaked with displeasure under his weight and went towards the back of the shop. There, he peered into the cold case at the blue cheeses from all over Europe.

Igor peeked over his shoulder at the shopkeeper who was busy discussing the best texture for Camembert—"Was it to be enjoyed tonight, madam? Perhaps tomorrow?"—and decided she was well occupied. He walked back to the front of the shop, his heavy derbies thudding across the wooden floorboards but again he was paid no attention, which was ideal because straight ahead was the shop that was his true destination all along.

The store's red sign displayed the name "Vin Merchants." The sign was adorned with light oak paneling that covered the standard green steel beams of the market. Two oak wine barrels framed the cramped entrance. The shop was divided in two by wooden wine crates stacked on top of each other to waist height. In the back-left corner, a man was behind the counter. He was bald, with a shiny pink head and small green eyes that were occupied by his clipboard.

Igor ventured in the shop, grabbed a bottle, and studied the label, spinning it in his hand carefully to read the back.

The shopkeeper peered at Igor over the top of his reading glasses.

"Anything I can help you with, sir?"

Igor stared at the man for a brief second, shrugged his shoulders, and scanned the wines against the wall. "I am looking for a special bottle." Igor's English was polished; the Russian accent he grew up with had been buffed away by years of effort.

"Well, I'm happy to help. A particular style maybe?" The man set the clipboard on the counter.

"Yes, I am looking for a bottle of 1997 Bordeaux, preferably Château Giscours."

Igor let his request hang in the air, studying the thinly veiled pained look on the shopkeeper's face. He leaned over, his elbows resting on the counter, and blew a huff of air.

After a moment, the shopkeeper smiled. "Now that is indeed a rare bottle. Unfortunately, I have to tell you that it isn't possible to find, nor would you want to. 1997 was a disastrous year in the Médoc. It rained during the entire harvest. And Château Giscours was not, as you would say, a sought-after château back then. Actually, a Dutch businessman purchased the château in '95. He revamped everything, but it took many years to make it the prestigious winemaker it is today. Could I offer another suggestion?"

While the man spoke, Igor strolled about the shop, vaguely listening to the story. On the wall he found a 2012 Château Malescot St. Exupery. He held it up with both hands, cradling the bottle like a newborn. He looked up to find the shopkeeper staring at the bottle, then up to meet his eyes.

Igor shrugged. "Perhaps I was mistaken. I was simply asking for a friend." He walked to the counter and could feel the man's eyes on him. "But I would like this bottle to have for my dinner tonight. Would you recommend it?"

The man straightened and cleared his throat. "Certainly, but..." he bent below the counter and pulled out a bottle; its dark glass hiding its contents. "...While the bottle you picked is great, might I recommend this one as well?"

"That's kind, thank you." Igor saw the shopkeeper had a bead of sweat on his forehead, displaying the same nervousness he did every time Igor came.

Igor thumbed through his wallet, making sure to find the card corresponding with the account he was layering the illicit money from. The shopkeeper rang Igor up and gave him a receipt for the exorbitantly overpriced wine with a gruff nod. Without another word, Igor left the shop with his two bottles of wine in his backpack.

He walked eastward past Southwark Cathedral, its Gothic architecture and small size out of place next to the market. He avoided the cool breeze coming off the River Thames, but only for a short distance, before ascending the stairs leading up to London Bridge.

Igor had always dreaded the next part, but it was a small price to pay and a necessary precaution. Only time was lost. The winding way home had taken him on two different Tube lines, two buses, and a meandering half-mile walk, until he reached South Kensington.

Igor had filed out of the dark Underground station and spilled onto the sunlit streets, passing several *boulangeries*—thanks to the French neighborhood—with long queues as he walked towards his building. Having finally arrived back, he climbed the narrow flight of stairs and opened his apartment door. The door creaked, as if giving a sigh of relief that Igor had returned home. The work was done—the hardest part, at least. He laboriously took off his heavy shoes and went into the kitchen to boil the kettle for a cup of tea, one of a few English habits he'd picked up.

The apartment was dark, with the only light coming from the sliding glass doors that led to a small balcony overlooking the tiny parcel of land with three trees and a bench deemed a park by the city. The walls were a tired khaki, and a blue velvet sofa occupied the living room, while the kitchen was confined. But he didn't mind; he rarely stayed here.

While the kettle boiled, he made for his bedroom, which was only large enough for a bed. The apartment certainly wasn't home. He'd nearly forgotten where that really was, if anywhere. Having a home was a privilege he wasn't allowed in his line of work.

Igor tossed his backpack on the bed and, from underneath it, dragged out the large duffel bag hidden behind the golf clubs he never used. He took out the IBM laptop and dutifully went to work replacing the battery, inserting the tiny screws into their proper holes. The laptop came to life with a small chime. Igor plugged in the internet router, then opened a dummy Gmail account and typed out a lengthy password with great care.

In a blank email, he recalled the drop earlier in the day and relayed the message via the agreed code.

Order was filled today. They didn't have the 97 you asked for.

It was a safe signal; no one had been prying around the shop.

He grabbed the bottle the shopkeeper had given him and spun it around to look at its contents under the light. The dark-green glass obscured the rolls of banknotes inside. *Now,* Igor thought, *I have enough for the job.*

He suddenly recalled the vague text messages, the various questions left unanswered in his mind, but he would find out soon enough.

Everything is ready for next week. I look forward to meeting our new guest.

Igor saved the email as a draft so no electronic trail would be left. He double-checked that it had been saved and turned off the computer. The person for whom the message was intended would see the draft when they signed in later. He detached the battery, then carefully put the computer back into the duffel bag and under the bed.

A loud, piercing whistle came from the kitchen: the kettle was boiling.

2

Paul Hart navigated the New York City commuters as he made his way through World Trade Center station. The subway from his Midtown apartment to Wall Street took thirty minutes but usually offered him the opportunity to think about the lonely night before, or the promise of the coming day ahead. On days he wasn't feeling contemplative, there was always the entertainment of his fellow riders.

He passed through the Oculus and up to the World Trade Plaza and headed across Vesey Street to his office. It was a tepid fall day, and a breeze from the Hudson made its way across the lower part of Manhattan.

The elevator doors opened to the twenty-eighth floor, and Hart stepped out onto the cream-colored carpet. "Calhoun Capital Group," hung on a dark-wood wall in steel lettering. The design was an effort to put clients at ease. *Yes, you can trust us with your money.*

Hart's days at the office were mundane. He never found himself in the midst of a crisis, or in a fierce debate with a colleague, but occasionally, if he came in early enough, there were croissants in the kitchenette. On the other hand, the hours could be long, coupled with the thankless task of managing other people's money. The lack of a life outside of work made him at times question his current arrangement. Then again, he reasoned, work was called work for a reason; might as well get dressed up and paid well for it.

Hart passed the receptionists every morning on the way to his desk. The overworked and underpaid ladies were always eager to greet him with warm smiles. He was handsome, less than six feet, but carried himself with the resolve of a taller man. His hair in recent years had darkened to a golden-honey color and was casually swept about by a quick brush of his hand in the morning. He had observant blue eyes and usually had a light scruff of stubble.

He reached his desk and set his bag down in the desolate cubicle. There were no family photos or pictures of pets, although he'd been thinking of rescuing a shelter dog. Hart had been asked by colleagues countless times why he didn't decorate his desk with sports schedules or family photos, and usually he'd be diplomatic and say he wasn't a decorative type. His real reason, however, was simple. Why decorate an office space if it wasn't going to be your last? His cubicle was near the corner office of his boss, so a watchful eye could be kept on him at all times. But nevertheless, his current cubicle was not his envisioned final destination. He wanted to own the corner office someday, and once he was there, he would hang all the family photographs his heart desired. But first he needed to have someone to help him start with that imaginary family. What was harder, getting the corner office or filling it with pictures of a family? Hart slumped in his chair and stared at his computer screen. The thought was too weighty to ponder before 8 a.m. He needed coffee—and several strong cups of it.

He momentarily entertained going to get coffee from the break room but decided against it, since he'd have to pass but James Hutchens' office, the managing partner of Calhoun Capital. Instead, longing for coffee, Hart logged into his computer, using his ID badge and his eight-digit pin code. The firm took security seriously, and his ID badge would change codes every twenty seconds and never repeated a code twice. When working with other people's money, Hart wasn't surprised with the lengths companies went to provide security.

Once his computer had stirred, his inbox chimed several times, reminding him of several rather laborious meetings in his schedule. At 10:00 a.m. he was to attend a meeting with a portfolio manager and an irksome client, and by 11:30 a.m. he had to print off several thirty-page pamphlets for a presentation for which he had prepared but would only sit in on. However, curiously, his entire afternoon after 1:00 p.m. was blocked off, with only "See James" in the subject line.

A knock on the siding of his cubicle caused his heart to skip a beat.

"Sheryl, you have to stop sneaking up on me like that." Hart grinned, half-amused and half-perturbed.

"Well, I wanted to say hello before the boss came in. Is that so wrong?"

Sheryl was in her mid-forties but managed to look in her thirties thanks to religiously attending early-morning Pilates. She'd been Hutchens' assistant for as long as Hart had worked at Calhoun.

Hart smiled. "Absolutely not. To what do I owe the pleasure this morning?"

"James is coming back from Florida this morning and may come in a few minutes late, but I wanted to give you a heads-up. He has a request, but I can't tell you what. Just be prepared." She smiled at Hart, looking him over.

Hart nodded. He didn't know what it was, but Sheryl had seen fit to give him a heads-up, which she never did. "Thanks, Sheryl. I guess I owe you one."

"No, you don't." She reached over the cubicle and handed him a plate with a bagel and a cup of coffee. "You owe me two, actually." She gave a devilish grin and disappeared before Hart could say thank you.

"How was Florida?" Hart asked as he walked into the office.

"Florida?" Hutchens seemed confused and touched his face. "Oh, the tan. Yes, a quick golf trip with some friends, you observant son of a bitch." Hutchens cleared his throat and sat up in his chair.

A longtime East-Coaster, Hutchens had become immersed with the financial elites and wore their uniform—generously cut double-breasted suits and shiny loafers—at least three days a week. He had thinning silver hair and stood like a bear, with his six-foot-four frame and habit of tucking his hands into the back of his waistband, leaning backward as if readying himself to burst out in laughter or rage.

"Actually, I just said hi to Sheryl when I was walking in. She mentioned you flew back this morning." Hart was pleased to have thrown his boss off-balance and proceeded to take a seat in one of the two large red leather chairs facing the desk.

The office was ornately decorated, but its greatest quality was the view, looking west over the Hudson. The office was designed to stun potential clients, and it easily fulfilled its duties. Dark mahogany bookshelves lined the room, the carpet hunter-green with gold flowery specks, and there was a tall credenza filled with pictures of his family and celebrities.

"Paul, this will only take a few minutes, but I wanted to personally bring you up to speed." Hutchens made his way over to the window. He peered down at the street for a moment. "I have a job for you."

Hart, who was still absentmindedly writing the date at the top of the notepad on his lap, looked up at his boss with his best poker face. Best to know what is being asked of you before accepting. It had become his policy with his impulsive boss.

"We have a client that is relatively new, been with us for a little under a year." Hutchens ambled over to his desk and, with his large paw-like hands, lowered himself into his leather chair with a thud. He smacked the space bar to wake up his computer.

As the screen flickered to life, Hart sat back in relief. He'd only been formally called into the office twice. First, when he was hired, and the second time was for a necessary but awkward assurance that his job was safe, which he never quite believed. Hutchens pivoted the monitor on the desk and pointed to a picture, obscuring it with his enormous leather-strapped Breitling watch.

Hart studied the photo of a man who looked to be mid-fifties, with slicked back salt-and-pepper hair and a neatly trimmed beard. He wore a blue blazer over an oxford shirt and light-khaki pants, and had an amenable smile while walking through a row of vines.

"This man is Claude Renard. I know you don't recognize him," Hutchens grunted. "He is CEO of a French agricultural firm specializing in farming equipment. Based out of Paris. All roads lead to Paris." Hutchens chuckled softly and received the compulsory *I work for you* smile from Hart. "He is amongst the wealthiest businessmen in France, but thanks to Renard Industries being privately held and operating under a holding company, he is not well known to the public. He has a penchant for privacy."

Hutchens leaned back in his chair. "His father started this small agricultural equipment company in the late eighties. The international economy wasn't so great then, let alone Europe's, but his father invested heavily in technology and tried to corner that market for the long term. He was playing a long ball." Hutchens smacked his desk and smiled, a businessman recognizing brilliance in another. Hart dutifully nodded in agreement.

"Come the mid-1990s, the world is moving along again. The French government is investing in agriculture, trying to boost the foundation of their economy. Suddenly, farms bought more equipment, and the government subsidized much of it in hopes the agricultural sector across Europe would blossom. Claude and his father happened to be the only game in town that had been developing new equipment. They were in a rare position to name the price and control the market with a constant demand. Well played, don't you think?"

Hutchens sat forward and tilted his head, as if he were gauging Hart's interest. He slid gold-framed spectacles out from his shirt pocket and picked up a piece of paper sitting on his desk.

Hart was curious but kept a straight face. "I'll venture a guess they had a strong lobbyist to push for more government regulation and spending for farmers."

Hutchens smiled and slurped his coffee from a Yale mug. "Astute of you. Renard played the game from multiple angles and laid the groundwork for the massive company Renard Industries is today."

Hutchens glanced at the paper in his hand. "We'll have a great opportunity with him. Like I said, he's a client but doesn't have more than some idle cash sitting with us. But we want to ramp up his investments, and I think he could be easily persuaded to bring over millions with the proper incentives."

Hart digested the information, unsure of what it all meant for him. "I can get started on some background work, have an associate help compile some holdings and statements, but I'll need to reach out to Renard's people to get most of that. May take a few days to review it all, but we should be able to start outlining a plan soon. I can probably have something by the end of next week."

Hutchens grunted but gave no further acknowledgment. He rested his elbows on his chair and clasped his paw-like hands together.

"Well, there is a tricky part to this. The European Union is actually ahead of the United States' regulators for once." Hutchens shook his head in disbelief. "It is now law to identify the largest majority shareholder—an actual person—of any company, private or public. It's called 'know your client,' or KYC. This is in response to that shitstorm the Panama Papers created. But now Uncle Sam has decided that instead of waiting a few years, US companies should do their due diligence to the full extent of their capabilities right away. We're playing catch-up." He shrugged.

Hart scratched his stubble. "Well, that could be hard if Renard has a complex ownership structure. Holding companies, different countries, regulations, and continents for that matter." Hart questioned whether this was a problem worth having; it would be a lot of work. "What exactly does Renard want in the US?"

Hutchens waved the question off, but Hart could see a hint of a smile. "Well, maybe Renard would be interested in owning an American company through an acquisition. Setting that up could be really profitable for us. I must say, Paul, this client will make or break your career here. Your goal is to have him bring over more assets."

Hart swallowed. Winning business wasn't in his job description. He knew he'd been on thin ice at the firm for a while, but now it seemed he had an ultimatum. He looked about the office and felt a pang of anxiety when his gaze rested on the family photo behind the desk of a smiling blond woman on top of a gray horse. Hutchens caught Hart's gaze and held his hand out, as if commanding Hart's attention. Hart pushed the photo and the flood of memories from his mind.

"I know things have seemed unsettled for you lately at the firm, but this is the best deal you're going to get."

Hart shook his head. "All I ever wanted was a chance to prove myself."

Hutchens stood and adjusted his pants by the belt loops. "That's why I'll give you a fair shot at keeping your career here. I want you to go to Paris and meet with him. Take a look at what he can bring us, and do a bit of digging so we can cover ourselves on these due-diligence matters with this ownership thing."

Hart's confusion showed as he hesitated, searching for his words.

"Yes, I said Paris. Interested?" Hutchens glared.

Hart thought he'd misheard his boss. His mind raced. Why would Hutchens send him? Perhaps Hutchens' sense of urgency revolved around the idea of regulators coming into the office, wearing drab suits and boxy shoes, and requesting documents and customer information, only to find Calhoun Capital had international clients with little to no background information on file. The trip felt like an errand, but Paris and the ultimatum he'd been given made his chest pound.

Hart ran the scenarios. Go to Paris for a few days, collect basic ownership information, and if he connected with the client, he'd make money and save his career. The downside was—worst case—he got a trip to France paid for before needing to start a new career. The trip was a wildly unexpected opportunity, but he also knew he didn't have a choice.

"When would I leave?"

Hutchens smiled and walked back over to the window. "You're booked on the 5:30 p.m. to Charles de Gaulle. I hope you can find your passport."

3

New York City

The town car stopped outside Terminal Two at JFK Airport, and the driver raced around to open the rear passenger door. Hart slid out of the car, grabbed his bags, and threw a, "Thank you," over his shoulder at the driver.

After leaving Hutchens' office, he had rushed to his apartment to hunt down his passport and pack. He'd thrown in his best-fitting suit, two white dress shirts, two navy-blue ties, and his Burberry raincoat. His briefcase held his computer, a tablet, and some reading about Claude Renard for his eight-hour flight.

Hart knew he would have extra security before he boarded. There would be a flag on him in the risk algorithms airlines had been using for the past fifteen years for buying a last-minute international ticket. He strolled to his place in the security line, and sure enough, the agent circled his boarding pass for additional screening. Hart took off his shoes and pulled his computer out of the bag, longing to be in the lounge having a drink before he had to board.

He relaxed after he'd cleared security and headed straight to the lounge. Travel was invigorating for him. It meant accepting you were a passenger and not in control of how fast you got to where you were going or what route you were taking. This was why he always felt so comfortable at airports: he didn't have to make any decisions.

The Centurion Lounge had a queue at the check-in counter, so Hart watched the monitors, to find Flight 617 to Charles de Gaulle was on time. He had an hour before boarding and decided he had enough time to grab a drink. There would also be plenty of options on the flight thanks to Hutchens booking him business class. If one had to travel for work, it was not a bad way to go.

After flashing his passport, boarding pass, and American Express card to the receptionist, he made his way into the lounge. Lime-green chairs, shapely purple sofas, and orange coffee tables sprinkled the lounge as travelers passed the time with a plate of food or a drink.

Hart found a seat at the empty bar. The bartender strode over and smiled. She was tall, with light-blond hair and almond-shaped brown eyes.

"What will it be?"

Hart always enjoyed a flirt, especially while traveling. He smiled and scanned the bar.

"How are you this fine afternoon?" He paused to read her name tag. "Nicole?"

He surprised himself with his bravado. He was in a good mood but immediately regretted sounding like an overeager tourist. But perhaps he could forgive his own enthusiasm; he was traveling to Paris all expenses paid.

"I'm fine. But no one really ever asks me that unless they want to know what time I'm finished here." She laughed to save Hart the awkwardness. "So, what can I get you to drink?"

His advance had been halted, and he retreated by giving his order. "I'd love a Johnnie Blue, neat, and maybe a strong pour for me. I've had quite a day so far." He shrugged and offered a shy smile.

She turned to grab the bottle off the top shelf; his attention was caught by the tight fit of her dress shirt. He looked up to find her smiling back at him, holding the bottle of scotch. He'd been caught and felt his cheeks warm. She poured his drink, filling nearly half the glass, and left the bottle on the bar.

For the next half hour, Hart enjoyed not one but two glasses while consulting his dossier on Renard and learning little. It dawned on him that the trip was going to be more work and more stressful than he had imagined, but it could be worth it to prove to Hutchens he was capable.

Hart sipped his scotch and watched Nicole hurry back and forth across the bar, which was slowly filling up with weekend commuters. His career might be on the line, but he found a sense of relief in the ultimatum given to him. His current role was limited and his future unknown, but his career could flourish if he earned Renard's business. He wondered why Hutchens had chosen him but told himself to just enjoy the ride, and pushed the uncertainty from his mind. There was pressure on him, but who didn't have that in their job? He checked his watch; he needed to be at the gate soon.

"We would like to begin the boarding process for Flight 617 to Paris Charles de Gaulle at Gate 15," the airport PA called out.

Impeccable timing, he thought as he drained the last of his drink and stood.

He made eye contact with the bartender, gave a small wave, and handed her his credit card. She brought him the bill and set it down in front of him.

"Seems like you're heading to Paris. Have you been there before?" she asked.

"Yes, I am. How did you know?"

"Your face lit up when they announced the flight."

Hart laughed. "I've been there once. Never for work, though."

"Oh, and what will you be doing there?"

"Hopefully, proving my worth." He smiled and tucked his card back into his wallet, leaving the receipt on the bar. "How about you? Ever been?"

Nicole's eyes widened. "No, but working at the airport has perks. I can fly free on a few airlines thanks to some friends I've made. Just have to pay taxes on international flights. Maybe I'll go meet a nice Frenchman over there someday, you never know." She threw her head back, laughing, her blond hair bouncing as she walked towards the end of the bar.

Hart grabbed his bags and made his way down to where she was. "You know, you don't have to go all the way to Paris to meet a nice guy." He shrugged playfully and thought, *What the hell?* He was leaving the country anyway.

She shook her head in amusement. She walked back to where he'd sat and left his receipt. Folding it, she handed it to him. "Don't lose this. You can expense your bar bill." She said with a wink, "Tips of the trade. Bon voyage." And before he could do any more than smile and raise his arm to give a quick wave goodbye, she was gone through the double doors into the kitchen.

He silently thanked Nicole for the great idea and stuffed the receipt in the inside pocket of his suit jacket. He would have to swing by the next time he was at the airport and say thank you.

Ten minutes after leaving the lounge, he was sitting on the left side of the Air France Airbus A330 in seat D1, being served by a tall French brunette in a red pantsuit. She smiled courteously and gave Hart his espresso, with a neatly wrapped salted caramel on the side. After looking over the dinner menu, he placed his order, which was to be served forty minutes into the flight. The usual airline-food stereotype did not apply when it came to Air France. The cuisine was a product of collaboration with one of France's most distinguished and respected chefs, Joël Robuchon. The starter was a lobster bisque, the main course was stuffed chicken breast with candied foie-gras crumples, and for dessert, chocolate and raspberry crème brûlée; red Burgundy from Beaune complemented the meal. His career was put on the line, but if push came to shove, at least he'd be going out in style.

Hart relaxed in the plush seat as his fellow business-class passengers got settled before the transatlantic flight; everyone dancing about, putting bags up in the overhead bin, and only a moment later getting back up to take something out. A pompous man in a large pinstriped suit wearing oversized loafers talked loudly on his cell. Hart had a soft chuckle as he imagined the man fitting in to the quiet French café culture.

He took the last sip of his espresso and set it down, and it was whisked away immediately by the flight attendant, who offered a soft smile. Hart gave a deliberate, "*Merci beaucoup,*" and in return received a, "You're welcome." *So much for assimilating.*

As the Airbus A330 taxied from the gate and made its way down to the end of the runway, his mind wandered back over his unexpected day. When he took his usual commute to the office, he didn't expect that later that day he'd be sitting in business class on the way to Paris. While the uncertainty of his objectives gnawed at him, he also felt a sense of opportunity, a strange mixture of enthusiasm and anxiety. He wouldn't let this pass him by.

Hart watched the airport lights slide by as the plane lumbered down the runway, gathering speed; then, as if shot out of a cannon, Hart was pinned to his seat as the Rolls-Royce engines roared to life. New York City fell away to the drone of the engines. He pulled the receipt from his jacket, curious to discover how much two glasses of Johnnie Walker Blue Label had cost, and unfolded it. As the plane pierced the first layer of clouds, Hart found a note on the bottom, *Next time you're in town – Nicole*, with her number and a smiley face.

4

Paris

Fall in Paris. The sky was a piercing bright blue, painted with wispy white clouds that stretched over the Jardin des Tuileries. The trees lining the garden had become victim to the fall and changed color to auburns, yellows, and oranges, their leaves rustling in the breeze that lazily swept across the Seine.

From his room at the Hotel Regina, Hart could see the large Ferris wheel that resided on the edge of Place de la Concorde, past Rue de Rivoli. Behind it, the Eiffel Tower, partially obscured by the slanted rooftops of the Left Bank, stood watch over its city. Straight across the Seine, which separated the First Arrondissement from the Seventh, was the Musée D'Orsay, a converted train station that held one of the world's most prestigious art collections, including works by Monet and Van Gogh. To the left of the garden, the glass pyramid of the Louvre reflected the early-morning sunlight. Hart felt he had gone back in time to when he visited as a wide-eyed teenager. Paris could do that.

Hart's affinity for Paris made it hard not to be romantic about the city. He had traveled to Europe in his freshman year of college, a lifetime ago, but the trip had left an indelible impact on his then-impressionable self. Paris had represented all the world could offer a young man: ambition, culture, and, of course, probably what he remembered the most, the beautiful Parisian women. The city gave him a glimpse of life in the way only a city like her could.

Hart turned from the window and his memories to his ornate hotel room. The room was modest in size, but small rooms were common in Parisian hotels, as he'd learned many years ago. The city was meant to be enjoyed, explored, and lived in, and a hotel room was simply for sleeping, with or without someone—but, as Paris would like it, preferably with.

At the hotel, he'd taken a shower, trimmed his stubble, and dunked his head in cold water to ensure he was fully awake after his flight. It was 6 a.m. in New York and he hadn't slept much on the plane. The jet lag had not hit him yet, but it would in time.

Hart had a meeting with Renard scheduled for 1 p.m. at a restaurant near his hotel. He'd been sent an calendar invitation from a Miss Nouvelle when he landed, with a note telling him the walk would be ten minutes. It was perfect because it gave him just enough time to freshen up and think of what questions to ask Renard so that he sounded prepared.

Hart sipped coffee—the first thing he'd asked for when checking in at the hotel was a pot of coffee—and selected his blue suit and his white dress shirt. They had been freshly steamed, thanks to a scorching hot shower that filled the bathroom, where he'd hung it to smooth it out. It was a trick he'd picked up from his father, who had been an avid traveler.

Hart gave himself a final once-over in the mirror to ensure he was looking respectable. He left through the Hotel Regina's front lobby, its charm created by the thick claret carpet, gold fixtures, dim lighting, and bellmen, who were eager to offer a friendly hello or a curt goodbye.

He made the three-block trip to the square expanse of Palais-Royal in five minutes. A chunky black gate with golden arrows on top guarded the entrance, which led to a wide courtyard, its crimson trees being photographed by a handful of people enjoying the afternoon weather. The courtyard was framed by a covered walkway, flanked by shops housing artists, salons, and antique stores until the north end of the courtyard, where Le Grand Véfour stood. Hart's footsteps clicked off the cobblestone as he approached the restaurant. The front doors had a red carpet rolled out to the valet, with two men in black suits guarding the entrance. Hart smirked. The restaurant would be elegant, pretentious yet somehow remarkably charming, and without question the food would be delicious. Golden letters spelled out its name, contrasting with the glossy black exterior, while sheer white curtains were hung inside the windows, offering discretion to its guests at the cost of the magnificent view.

Hart stopped walking, took a deep breath, buttoned his suit jacket, and made his way inside.

The Peugeot Sprinter van crossed Rue de Longchamp and sped towards La Défense. The van passed the retreating workforce of the Sixteenth Arrondissement on the sunny Friday afternoon. While most people, especially in the wealthy neighborhood of Neuilly, were heading home, or to a weekend getaway at their country estate, or even to an afternoon rendezvous with someone other than their spouse, Claude Renard was heading to the office. He wasn't too troubled by his afternoon schedule, and his mode of transportation for his twenty-minute commute didn't bother him at all. The Peugeot van was outfitted with a table in the back, where four black leather bucket seats sat facing one another. There was a minifridge stocked with demi-bottles of champagne, red wine, and Perrier.

Renard watched the sidewalks for a moment, casting casual glances at the Parisian women, effortlessly fashionable in bright fall colors and confident strides. The men, wearing dark suits, brightly polished shoes, and drab ties, made their way home from their offices on the Champs-Élysées. He didn't envy them; their weekends started early, but their lives could not be as remarkable as his.

He grabbed his cell off the table, dialed the number saved into the encrypted phone—one could never be too careful—and listened to the international ringtone. On the third beep, his call was answered.

"Hello?" a coarse and groggy voice answered. "Who is this?"

Renard could hear the person sit up in bed, the covers ruffling.

"James, this is Claude. Did I catch you on your way into the office?"

He knew that James Hutchens would be sleeping; after all, it was 6 a.m. on a Friday in New York City.

"Yes, just about to head out the door." Hutchens cleared his throat as Renard heard a table lamp click on.

"Wonderful. I am calling to thank you for sending your man here. I trust he is as I requested."

A pause. "Yes. Paul is easy to deal with, as you requested. Make him feel important, and he'll do whatever you ask. He'll be eager to please because he knows how important this trip is to his career."

Renard grinned. "This is beautiful. I hope that my short-notice request was not an inconvenience to your company, but I wanted to have someone in town for potential meetings today."

"Glad to help, and please give Paul anything you feel comfortable sharing with us and he'll look over it to see what we can do for you. Grow this partnership, eh?"

He could hear the desperation in the man's voice, but it was to be expected. The American would want more opportunity, more access, and more money.

"Of course! *Bien sûr*, I will certainly give Paul plenty of information. Trust me when I say he will be of great use to me."

5

Paris

Hart was greeted by a toothy smile and a stiffened back from the maître d'.

"*Bonjour, monsieur. Avez-vous une réservation?*"

"*Oui, avec Monsieur Renard.*" Hart craned his neck to peek into the dining room.

The maître d' stood tall, wearing a black suit and subtle gray tie, which made him appear younger than his white hair would lead one to believe. His face was wrinkled, but when he smiled it became smooth, as if the stress of years of smiling for countless patrons was erased. With a slight bow of the head, he turned and held his hand out: *Please follow me.* Hart fell in line behind his elegant and practiced gait.

Le Grand Véfour was a decadent restaurant, filled with aristocratic blood on a Friday afternoon. The dining room was covered in Victorian-era crimson wallpaper and many mirrors with thick gold frames so the patrons could indulge themselves in their own reflections during their meal. The lunch crowd were busy having discreet meetings of the necessary variety—hushed dealings between old men in fine dark suits, a few younger women with their lovers—and in the back corner, sitting alone at a small table, a beautiful woman peered out the tall windows towards the Palais-Royal.

The restaurant was animated as sparse fits of laughter and the soft clink of fine china filled the space. Hart navigated the treacherous seas of the dining-room floor, following the brisk pace of his leader, whose chin was held high in an assured manner.

Hart was so consumed by the people dining, crafting short storylines about their lives, that he did not realize he was being led to the corner booth, where a lone woman sat on the plush red leather.

"*Monsieur, bon appétit.*" The maître d' turned on his heel and dutifully returned to his post.

"*Excusez-moi.*" Hart tried to grab the attention of the fast-retreating maître d', but to no avail. Hart, defeated for the moment, managed to mumble out, "You must have the wrong table," as he turned back to the woman sitting alone. She stood and held out her hand.

"Monsieur Hart, my name is Clara Nouvelle. I work for Monsieur Renard."

Hart lost himself in her sea-green eyes and slowly took her hand, managing a confused smile. Her hair, a dark-espresso color, was pulled back and pinned up in a tight bun. She had high cheekbones and dark-red lip gloss; her eyes were unassuming, but she looked him over quickly. She wore a long-sleeve, ivory silk blouse modestly cut, revealing a small pearl necklace that matched her knee-length black wool skirt, with a subtle cream polka-dot pattern. She was shorter than him, but not by much, thanks to her glossy black heels.

"I'm Paul Hart. Pleasure to meet you."

She smiled at him. "*Enchanté.*"

Her hand was soft, but she gripped his firmly. He leaned in and offered the traditional French double-cheeked greeting. Her perfume was strong. As his face brushed her cheek, he tried to place the smell—floral, citrusy, with a hint of jasmine. She motioned for him to take a seat as they settled in the booth. He took notice that she was petite, with a supple curve of her hips highlighted by her high-cut skirt.

This was a business lunch, Hart reminded himself, but he was glad he wore his best suit. She was stunning. He stole another look as she placed the white linen napkin in her lap.

There was a certain confidence that many Parisienne women had—the perfect posture, chin up, eyes engaged but uninterested—and Hart could tell she had it since birth. Her hands were folded on the white tablecloth, but he shouldn't be fooled: she was coiled and ready to strike.

"So, how was your flight?" Her English was smooth, with only a hint of an accent.

"Great. Thank you for asking."

"You're not too—what is the expression?—jet-lagged?" Her voice danced over the phrase, unsure of its correctness.

Hart smiled at her. "No, unless I look it."

"You don't." She smirked as if she liked what she saw. "I hope you don't mind, but I am starving. Could we order right away?"

Before he had time to answer, a waiter appeared at their table. "*Oui, mademoiselle?*"

Hart took notice that the waiter had referred to her as *mademoiselle*; as he understood it, it meant she was not married. At the very least, she didn't wear a ring.

She ordered a carafe of water, along with a glass of Burgundy from Nuit-Saint-Georges, duck-liver terrine, and roasted monkfish, forgoing dessert. Hart, who scanned the menu with urgency, followed her lead but ordered a glass of Château la Clotte, from Saint-Émilion, along with the same first two courses, but also ordered cheese for dessert, with a request of extra bread. He wasn't sure how the lunch was going to go, or why he was meeting her in the absence of Renard, but he did know two things: first, dessert in France was always a good decision, and second, it would inevitably prolong their lunch—another good decision, he assured himself.

The intoxicating aroma of seared foie gras and beef wafted through the dining room. However, Hart felt an uncertainty hanging over the table like the morning fog on the Seine. Forgoing the urge to make small talk and perhaps flirt—*Must be professional, Paul*—he opted to dive straight into business.

"I'm sorry, but I thought I was meeting with Mr. Renard. My understanding was this lunch was to discuss his business."

Clara smiled. "I'm sorry that I'm not good enough company for you." Her eyes flickered like a bonfire, warm, mesmerizing, and potentially dangerous. Before Hart could explain himself, she continued. "Yes, you were correct in assuming this meeting was to discuss Mr. Renard and his business. However, you misunderstood who you would be meeting and speaking with. As my email invitation showed, it is just the two of us for lunch. I am Mr. Renard's director of affairs, which is an elegant way of saying his gatekeeper. I let in who I see fit, and when."

She was composed, not offended by his question, but showed a hint of amusement as she watched him work out the logic. There was silence for a moment, and Hart turned to survey the room, ignoring his urge to complain about the sleight of hand. *She is the gatekeeper*, he thought. *I will have to impress her.*

"So, Clara," Hart began, "how long have you worked for Mr. Renard?"

"Well, it has been several years of working for his company, but only the past year working directly with him. I happened to be an administrative assistant for one of his directors in the Bourse office, just off the Paris stock exchange. The Euronext. I'm sure you're familiar. It's located in La Defense."

Hart gave a curt nod. He had no idea where it was but wasn't going to give her the upper hand in geography. Clara seemed to be satisfied.

"You've been to Paris before?"

"Once. In college."

"Same as you remember?" Her voice rose a little with curiosity.

"Better than I remember. But forgive me, I want to hear how you came to work for Mr. Renard—if you don't mind, that is?"

Clara couldn't conceal her pride. Hart could see her eyes twinkling.

"Well, our office is located in the new Arc de Triomphe, near the exchange, as I mentioned, because of the commodities trading that goes on at the Euronext, like wheat, grain, corn, everything that is crucial to our businesses. It is quite simple, but the foundation that the French economy is built upon is the agricultural sector."

Clara paused a moment as the waiter returned with the glasses of generous pours of wine. He set them down and without any hesitation raced back to the kitchen. She took her stemmed wineglass and gave her full attention to the Burgundy. She tilted and rolled the wineglass so that it coated the sides, studying the color, and set the glass down on the table and gave it a spin, making small circles against the white tablecloth.

"*Alors*, the man I worked for, the director of governmental affairs and initiatives, a Monsieur Bichot, worked directly under Monsieur Renard. They would meet regularly in person at least once a week. Well, I was in my position for almost a year, never doing much more than compiling reports, organizing schedules, and covering for my boss' adventures, which meant mainly keeping secrets from his wife." She stopped to make sure she still had his attention.

Hart recognized this, and in fact he hadn't touched his glass of Saint-Émilion but sat attentively until Clara went to take her first sip.

She raised her glass. "To our health."

"To unexpected meetings." They delicately clinked glasses.

Hart hoped he had impressed her by his selection and pronunciation of the French wine he'd chosen. He assumed that many business lunches would have consisted of a scotch or perhaps a gin and tonic for lunch to look strong, not a glass of wine with food to enhance the experience. Maybe some would have ordered a Cabernet, because when in doubt it was the one to choose. But Hart wanted to prove his worldliness, as if one could do such a thing with a wine order, but maybe—just maybe—he was in the one country where one could.

Hart watched her as she closed her eyes after her sip. He imagined the taste of the red wine—berries, plum, and a hint of vanilla—and watched her allow it to linger for a moment longer than necessary before she swallowed.

Hart was lost in his imagination, staring at her until she caught him. *Oh yes, this is a business lunch*, he chided himself. *Try and listen, damnit*. He grabbed his glass to not be caught gawking and sipped his wine.

"How's the wine?" she inquired.

"Delicious. One of several things the French do better than anyone," he added with a wry smile.

"Oh? You know these things through observation or experience?"

He laughed. "I wouldn't want us to get sidetracked. Please continue with your story where we left off. I'm intrigued."

Clara shifted in her chair. "So, I'd been working for Bichot for a year, but the perk of my position was that every important document for Bichot, and eventually Renard, came across my desk first. I had to always summarize them for my boss, who was too busy to read every one. This allowed me to gain an insight into the direction the company was heading. What products would be focused on, what partnerships were on the horizon, and perhaps most importantly in the French agricultural economy, what direction the government was leaning in. Because after all, Monsieur Hart, the French government will do everything in her power to protect and promote her products and farmers."

Clara's story was interrupted as several white-coated waiters hurriedly brought the first course over to their table. The duck terrine was set upon toasted crostini, with a cherry reduction sauce, its sweet aroma wafting into Hart's face. He leaned closer to the plate and looked up at Clara. She met his look with a delighted and a conspiratorial raise of her eyebrows. Frenchwomen and their cuisine—truly a love affair as old as time.

The duck was savory and had a hint of smokiness, which was complemented by a healthy sip of his Merlot. He paused and closed his eyes for a moment, savoring the taste. To his horror, he involuntarily made a sigh of pleasure, and he opened his eyes to find Clara giggling.

"Where was I?" Clara said as she delicately dabbed her white napkin to her lips. "Oh, yes. Well, my career was going fine until about a year ago. Mr. Renard had an important meeting with my boss and government officials. The meeting was to be about the prospect of new subsidies that would be lucrative for the business—farmers basically getting money they either spent on our equipment or lost. I remember this day quite well because of the weather that morning."

Clara held Hart's eyes as she told her story, occasionally glancing at a passing waiter dashing to a nearby table. "It was early spring, and, as Paris is in the spring, there are dreary days. It's a French London," she said with a laugh. "However, this day was the first gorgeous day since the colder winter months, with the sun warm and bright. Everyone was out on the streets enjoying the weather. I remember this because I was to go out and buy croissants and pain au chocolat for the meeting. I had gone out to find a *boulangerie*, but I was happy to be outside on the beautiful day."

Hart listened intently, only using his wine as a cover to break eye contact, and it also kept his hands busy. The way Clara spoke with poise and a certain nostalgia, proud of her story, made Hart uneasy, because he realized how attracted he was to her. He had forgotten that he'd been upset Renard hadn't joined him, but now he wouldn't have it any other way. *The little surprises in life.*

"However, a terrible thing happened that morning. The meeting was starting, but my boss was late. I led the government officials to the conference room, where there were breakfast pastries to keep their attention. But Monsieur Bichot was nowhere to be found. I desperately tried to find him, calling his cell phone, his home—nothing. In fact, I spoke with his wife, who seemed rather uninterested and simply offered that her husband had never come home the night before. Perhaps this was not a rare occurrence. Nonetheless, Monsieur Renard arrived and expected Bichot to lead the meeting. I shared the bad news that Bichot was missing. Monsieur Renard could not consider rescheduling, not wanting to appear untrustworthy. He sat fuming at my desk."

Her eyes lit up as the second course arrived. Two waiters placed the monkfish plates and refilled the wineglasses. With a quick, "*Bon appétit,*" they headed off once again. The plate had steamed carrots, potatoes, and rich butter at the base of the creamy sauce.

"I hope there was a good reason for Monsieur Bichot's lack of attendance." Hart pronounced the name well, dropping the *t* sound at the end.

Clara, appearing appreciative of the effort, gave a slight bow of her head. She delicately cut the fish and took a bite. She hummed with pleasure. Hart tried his fish and had a similar reaction; the buttery white fish melted in his mouth.

"I hope I am not speaking too much. I find this story helpful to understand my role with Monsieur Renard." She glanced at Hart, then back to her monkfish, which she cut with the delicate hands of a surgeon.

Hart dabbed his face with his napkin. "Not at all. I am enjoying this. Might I add your English is perfect—I could listen to you all day?"

Clara seemed to ignore the compliment and the attempt at flattery, turning it back to Hart.

"You speak rather well for an American, or at least can order wine better than most. Did you order Merlot with white fish on purpose, or were you simply following my lead of ordering a red?" She laughed.

"I happen to think anything is great with Merlot."

Clara waved a hand. "Anyway, your French is decent. Not like what they teach in schools. Did you learn when you visited in college?"

"Yes, I was lucky enough to travel quite a bit, fell in love with the culture, and learned some of the language, amongst other things."

He did not fight the urge to smile. Clara offered a bemused face, her eyes searching Hart's.

"Well, I must get to the end of my story before we finish lunch, or you shall need to take me to dinner to hear the rest." She had been speaking for the majority of the lunch and mentioned it several times, but Hart had in fact enjoyed it immensely.

He rubbed his chin playfully. "Unfortunately for you, that may end up being the case regardless. I do have a few more days in Paris. But please continue. I am captivated."

He picked up his wineglass and took a long sip. Contentment swirled inside him. Was he feeling the effects of the wine or the company? He reminded himself to breathe.

"Very well. So, Monsieur Renard had quite the problem because my boss, Bichot, was indisposed. So, for reasons perhaps unknown to even myself, I told Monsieur Renard that I was comfortable with the topic of the meeting. I had actually done all the research and planning in the first place." She shrugged as if she couldn't understand her own thinking. "I still remember the look on Monsieur Renard's face. He blew air out through his lips, a classic French expression for *Why the hell not?* We won the business that day. I think the government officials appreciated my presence more than Monsieur Renard's. But they liked what we were saying even more."

Hart nodded approvingly. "That's extraordinary. You've clearly taken the opportunity and run with it." He raised the remnants of his wine. "To taking advantage of great opportunities."

Clara blushed and they clinked glasses.

"Well, I was fortunate Monsieur Renard found a place for me that is near to him. I know he appreciated me helping him when it was needed."

Hart could relate to good fortune in one's career. Fate had played a similar role in his, but he was envious of how far Clara had taken her opportunity. "Whatever came of your boss, Monsieur Bichot? Did he miss the Metro that morning?"

Clara looked at her lap and shook her head. "Funny you should ask, he actually, uh"—she searched for her words and distractedly looked across the restaurant—"well, he, uh, ran away with his mistress. I tell you this in confidence by the way; after all, we've dined together. She was a beautiful redhead from Normandy, but she wasn't all he ran away with, I'm afraid. We think he embezzled a few euros, too, before he vanished. Haven't heard from him since. Probably off on some secluded island."

Clara flicked her green eyes from him and pursed her lips. Hart recognized it was a subject to steer clear of.

The waiter glided over, as if he could sense a lull in the conversation. He cleaned the tablecloth of crumbs and asked if they were ready for the dessert course and turned to retrieve the cheese. When he returned, he brought a small wooden cutting board adorned with Comté cheese—the salty not fruity type, which, he explained, was a sign of longer aging—cherry jam, honey, a small slice of Brie, and Roquefort.

Clara cut a slice of the Comté. "Paul, you must try Comté first because it is the least strong of these *fromages*. If you have it last, you will not truly taste it. Which would be a shame, because the salty type is my favorite."

The murmur of the restaurant grew softer as their lunch outlasted those of the other diners, who had made for the exit in the early afternoon. Hart was looking for the bill well after dessert but reminded himself that in France the bill was not given but asked for. *Why rush such an art as eating?* Clara had been polite enough and, he assumed, engaged enough that she did not mind the time spent lingering. He certainly didn't.

Clara maneuvered in her seat to get the attention of a passing waiter, for to raise one's arms to summon a server in a Parisian restaurant was akin to treason. Hart had learned this the hard way during his college trip, waving wildly at a server, who ignored him with the grace of a proud dog who'd been scolded, adding another half hour to his lunch as punishment.

The waiter brought the bill, along with two wrapped caramels, to their table. Hart insisted on getting the check, and after a back and forth between the two of them that had no end in sight, he handed his card to the waiter and pleaded for him to take it. The waiter raised his eyebrows and dutifully put Hart out of his misery.

"Clara, I have to say I really enjoyed our lunch. The food was incredible, but your company was even better." Hart smiled as his voice trailed off, suddenly unsure of himself.

Clara folded her napkin and laid it neatly on the table before casting her sea-green eyes at him as she waited patiently for him to finish.

"But will I have an opportunity to meet Monsieur Renard?"

She looked at the door, then at him with a subtle smile. "I will take you to him now."

6

London

Riverbed Capital Bank moved slower towards the end of any Friday. The grind of the job—managing risk and studying international events that affected the markets—was difficult any day of the week, let alone on a busy Friday.

Igor sat at his desk and watched the Nasdaq market in the United States on one monitor while reading the *Guardian* online newspaper on another. The newspaper's main webpage showed a series of articles chronicling the changing lifestyles of Brits who had backed the failed "remain" campaign in the Brexit referendum. There was coverage of a terror attack on the streets of Berlin; a refugee had stolen a taxi and plowed into a group of tourists, injuring a dozen. Igor read the article with interest, coming across the line, "Perhaps the UK has done well to separate herself from the migrant dilemmas sweeping Europe, otherwise that cab could have been in Leicester Square."

Igor felt content for the moment, picturing the further fracturing of the European Union. The attacks would drive hatred and bigotry towards the migrants flooding Europe, and governments would stumble in response, the effects of which you could already begin to seen.

On top of the webpage, a red banner highlighted coverage of European elections that had been the victims of the wave of nationalism scorching the globe, sparked by the Brexit vote. The United States elected a protectionist president, and suddenly Europe was next in line to battle isolationism.

Igor's job required him to have fundamental knowledge of, and insight into, political and economic events shaping the world. He endlessly watched the world's markets. The interconnectedness of the economic system meant there was always something to observe and glean. Whether it was the Nikkei in Japan, or the Dow Jones in the United States, any market where his clients had invested demanded his attention, especially geopolitical events.

While his daily responsibilities could become burdensome, the access to different companies and people was priceless. He was in charge of more money than he could ever dream of, and because of the power that came with money, he could execute his master plan. His career provided perfect cover to lure unsuspecting prey, or clients, into a trap by merely mentioning profit.

There were certainly times when Igor could not believe his good fortune that he worked at Riverbed Capital Bank, located conveniently in London's Canary Wharf. The number of financial services jobs in London was over three hundred and fifty thousand, in more than forty thousand companies. He blended in as just another ambitious blue suit with black oxfords, the unofficial dress uniform of London, but that fit him quite well.

He clicked away at his computer, the Friday suddenly going by too fast. He had a meeting scheduled for 4:30 p.m. with his team of associates about client investments for the upcoming year. He knew it was important that he keep up appearances, regardless of the fact he wouldn't be at the company next year. The thought had crossed his mind years ago of working well into his sixties, retiring, and playing golf when he wasn't at the pub, but he knew this wasn't to be his fate. Neither was becoming too comfortable and confident, ultimately letting his guard down. Igor needed to be sharp. He was the grandmaster of his game, moving players about with well-thought-out moves until the ultimate goal was in sight.

The latest pawn he'd moved into place was an American, whose eyes lit up after Igor mentioned there was a client looking to expand into the US. The man had begged for an introduction, and Igor played on the American lust for profits. *Oh, this client will only want to work with someone who can nearly guarantee exuberant returns. Surely, you wouldn't want them.*

From the comfort of his glass office, Igor smiled as he recalled the con: tell someone what he or she can't have, and it is all they will desire. He had placed Calhoun Capital right where he wanted them, another pawn on the chessboard that would be sacrificed without hesitation.

Igor's email pinged with a note from Mitch Clarkson; the subject line simply "transfer rumor." The email read like one between friends discussing the potential transfer of an expensive football player to West Ham United, a club based in the East End of London, but in reality was far more nefarious than that. Apart from the coverage in the *Guardian* of the World Cup–qualifying match that was to take place in London the next week, which had been built up for months, football didn't interest him.

Igor read the email once more, deleted it, and stood from his desk. He looked out his glass office door that oversaw the "Stables," the name affectionately given to the gray, drab cubicle maze spread across the floor. The company could be excused for the tight working conditions of the offices; after all, it was London, with some of the most expensive square footage in the world. The expensive marketplace and cramped conditions didn't affect Igor in his private office, or the two hundred fifty thousand pounds per year, plus commission, he made; at least, that was the official figure he filed for taxes. The actual amount was considerably higher, thanks to his off-the-books arrangements.

With no one on his floor paying him any attention, Igor slipped down the hallway and down the several flights of stairs to the basement offices, where the company's support staff sat. The Single Euro Payment Area (SEPA) function of the bank was tucked away in a dark corner of the building. Igor wasn't a man who feared much, but the thought of being trapped in a dark, windowless room sent a chill down his spine.

The SEPA function was a system designed so that individuals located in the European Union could conduct transfers across country lines without any additional hassle or fees, a cornerstone of the open market system. Every financial institution that operated in the EU had a department committed solely to monitoring SEPA transactions to ensure that laws were followed and no suspicious activity was conducted.

The man at Riverbed Capital Bank who oversaw the monitoring of such transactions was Mitch Clarkson. Igor found that Mitch happened to be someone in the department who didn't mind cutting corners. He barely took home forty thousand pounds a year managing the SEPA transfers from his windowless basement.

Igor was happy to provide the incentive for the corner cutting, an extra two thousand pounds a month for Mitch, which went far living in London. Igor kept their arrangement simple, offering money and a vague excuse in exchange for Mitch's monitoring and deletion of specific transfers. Igor, for added insurance, gave Mitch a late-night visit at his East End apartment: *I know where you live.*

The payoffs and transfers went smoothly. Mitch happily provided Igor the cover for his client from France who needed to send money to England but simply didn't want any record of it—*You know, taxes are the devil.* Mitch looked the other way because he was well compensated and had grown tired of monitoring the money of richer people. The arrangement for Mitch was low risk; after all, he was the only person in the firm who could catch this type of activity. Transfers would be deposited into an account, and Mitch would simply delete the record of the transfer so that if someone were to look at the account, the money would appear to have always been there.

There was risk, but Mitch felt there were enough SEPA transfers canceled every day by banks or customers that nothing would ever look out of place. The only difference was those canceled transfers would see the money taken out of the account and sent back to its original account, unlike what Mitch did for Igor. After months of success, Mitch had worked up the courage to ask for more than two thousand pounds a month from Igor, who begrudgingly agreed. He'd originally budgeted five thousand a month and expected a change of heart eventually.

While the requests were certainly a bit odd and perhaps mischievous, the amounts were not indicative of some massive scheme to launder money into Great Britain. The amounts over the past months ranged from seven hundred pounds to just over five thousand, totaling several hundred thousand, but they all came from various farming companies, with the memo lines indicating they were proceeds from sales.

What Mitch didn't dare ask was, what happened to the money after it arrived? Igor knew because he would take the bank card associated with the account that the money came into under a fake name and head to the wine shop in Borough Market and pour the money right back in through a phony sale of wine. The sale would be for an exorbitant amount but served the purpose of moving the money to a different bank. It was laundering money, hiding the proverbial bread crumbs through legitimate businesses transactions.

Igor sauntered into Mitch Clarkson's cube, tucked away under a harsh fluorescent light, and surveyed the floor for people nearby.

An exuberant Mitch nearly shouted while taking off his headphones as he saw Igor approach. "Hey, mate!"

Mitch immediately recognized his mistake, as Igor's face turned a darker shade of red and his eyes narrowed, before he composed his somber demeanor.

"Thanks for the email," Igor said.

Mitch, enthralled by the excitement of a momentary departure from his mindless job, tried to control his eagerness with little luck. He leaned back in his chair, folded his arms over his slightly faded T-shirt, a subtle revolt against the Canary Wharf business uniform, and grinned.

"Yeah, glad I can help. I'll always let you know when a good transfer comes through." He leaned forward in his chair and giggled, before rolling it closer to the several computer screens on his desk. He clicked away at the keyboard. Every few keystrokes, he would stop, frozen in place, listening intently to see if anyone was coming.

Igor shifted his weight from foot to foot and leaned slightly against the five-foot-high cubicle wall.

"There," Mitch said with a final click. "As if the transfer never happened."

"Brilliant." Igor lowered his voice. "The amount?"

Mitch wheeled his chair across his cube and plucked a sticky note from under the desk. "Already had it written out and hidden under the desk. I know the drill."

Igor grabbed the sticky note and flashed an insincere smile as he turned to leave. "Cheers."

"Hey, Igor, um..." Mitch said as he jumped to his feet. "Do you think, since this arrangement is going so well, we could reach an amount per transfer? Maybe instead of a flat rate you could give me a percentage of whatever it is you're doing. Because—"

Igor jabbed his hand into Mitch's chest. "I am not a guy you want to negotiate with. Do your job. I'll pay you, or I'll find someone else."

Mitch grabbed his chest, rubbed it for a moment, and looked down. "Yeah, course. I..." But when Mitch looked up, he only saw Igor's back as he slipped away down the dark hallway.

Back in his office, Igor took off his jacket and threw it onto his chair. With a key he kept in his wallet, he unlocked his top desk drawer and grabbed his black leather-bound notebook, which had "The Devil is in the Details" written on it in gold foil. He found the red silk bookmark that marked the page of handwritten notes and numbers. Tracking down the left-hand side of the page, he found an empty space and marked down the amount from the note Mitch had given him. He scanned up and down the page, impressed with the progress that had been made nearly a year on, and realized he had reached the goal he'd aimed for. The notebook contained the dates and amounts of incoming transfers that were deleted to the account he managed for his most important client. Better to manually track the money than have electronic records on his computer.

He closed the book, locked it away once again in his desk drawer, and leaned back in his chair. Igor took a deep breath. He was closer to the chaos he planned for and craved, but first he had an urgent appointment to schedule.

7

Paris

The Mercedes S550 sailed up the gradual climb of the Avenue des Champs-Élysées, past the heavy traffic as Parisians hurried out of town for the weekend. Horns blared and motorbikes weaved in and out of the congestion, their engines whining as they passed the slower traffic.

Halfway up the avenue, and comfortably in the back seat, Hart watched tourists pack the sidewalks, marching up to the Arc de Triomphe. He sat next to Clara, who since leaving the restaurant had only paid attention to her cell. The ride was quite the opposite sensation from the one lunch provided, but Hart figured it was because there wasn't any wine in the car to aid conversation. Perhaps Clara had enjoyed her lunch and, more specifically, his company. He hoped she did. She was engaging, even with a hint of playfulness. She was well spoken, with a sexiness that came with her Parisienne devil-may-care attitude. Her French birthright of being a world-class flirt certainly made her even more desirable.

The car navigated past the Arc de Triomphe roundabout, while Hart stopped himself from fantasizing further. *It's purely business, Paul. She is not interested, you idiot.*

He absentmindedly twirled his cell between his thumb and index finger with a flick of his wrist. Clara was still on her own device, and he felt compelled to work as well, so he sent a quick update to Hutchens.

"We'll be heading to the offices to meet with Monsieur Renard. He only has about twenty minutes to say hello," Clara said as she looked up from her phone. "That will be okay?"

That was not okay. Hart could feel his temples pound. He had flown over the Atlantic on short notice, and while he did get a delicious lunch with an attractive woman, giving him only twenty minutes to win business worth hundreds of millions of dollars was not okay.

"That's great. I can appreciate how busy he is." Hart smiled and looked out the window to mask his disappointment. He saw a café covered by a red awning and full of chic Parisians lounging with books, watching the world go by. What would the café crowd think of his predicament? Certainly there would be no sympathy for him. He watched the rest of the street pass, taking in the wealthy neighborhood of Neuilly-sur-Seine, its buildings sparkling white from steam cleaning.

There was no time to feel sorry, and he was certainly not trying to pout, so he turned back towards Clara.

"You know, my father used to tell me a meeting should take no longer than thirty minutes. And if you need more time than that, you're not ready to have that meeting." He paused while Clara laid her phone down on her lap and studied him with a child's curiosity. "He also said that lunch can never be too long with a beautiful lady." He felt his cheeks warming with the unsubtle and clumsy attempt at flattery.

The car was silent for a brief moment. Hart could have sworn he heard the driver suppress a laugh as the air seemed sucked out of the car. Clara appeared to process the words as her eyes narrowed. She smiled hesitantly, but the smile disappeared as quickly as it showed.

Hart thought the squint of her eyes revealed that she enjoyed the flattery. *Was that a smile?*

"Yes, I think that you and Monsieur Renard will get along very well."

Hart felt a sinking feeling in his stomach, like his terrine and monkfish at lunch had taken the shape of a brick. He silently cursed himself. Had he gone too far? After all, she had ignored the comment, but who didn't appreciate a harmless compliment? *She smiled, though, right?* He thought so.

He tried to change the subject. "So, what can you tell me about Monsieur Renard? What is he like?"

This question produced a huff that said, *Where do I begin?* Clara brushed a strand of her dark hair behind her ear as she searched out the window for her words. "Firstly, he is always curious. He must know everything about everyone and then wants to know more. An example is once we had a visitor from a Formula One team seeking marketing partnerships with agricultural companies. It was a project designed around the potential of using sustainable fuels. Keep in mind this was several years ago—technology has changed—but anyway, the individual meeting with Renard was more scientist than sales-man. The two of them ended up spending the better part of the meeting talking about the differences in fuel consumption between a V12 engine and the theoretical future technology.

"The meeting was mostly staring at charts and hearing chemical formulas spelled out—not exactly Monsieur Renard's forte. Well, needless to say, he was not happy at all, the level of scientific discussion making him feel belittled. He was in a foul mood for the rest of that day, but he asked the man for a follow-up meeting in three months' time.

"Those three months, Monsieur Renard poured resources into identifying alternative engine technology. When the man came back to see if Monsieur Renard was interested in a partnership, he told him no, because Renard had created his own alternative idea. And thus, Formula Electric was born. The new Grand Prix grade fuel was built almost entirely out of spite and curiosity. That is who Monsieur Claude Renard is."

Hart's eyes widened. Renard was ferociously competitive. He took a deep breath and blew it out between his lips, causing them to flap slightly, the French way of expressing bewilderment, drawing a giggle from Clara.

The conversation started to flow again as it had during lunch. They spoke about how long he had been at Calhoun Capital, what he did on a daily basis, and the clients his company kept. Traffic eased as they made their way over the Seine and through the business district of La Défense, with its tall office buildings stretching before them, seeming foreign in the City of Light. It was like entering a different world. Gone were the romantic landscapes and vintage feel of Paris, replaced by corporations and ambition.

The chauffeur stopped the Mercedes and raced out of the car to open Clara's door.

"Thank you, Maxim," she said to the tall driver, who smiled courteously.

Hart appreciated the chivalry, but more so, the driver clearly knew who paid the bills.

Hart and Clara walked towards the modernist design of the new Arc de Triomphe, known as La Grande Arche, an iconic office building built in honor of the original landmark. As they walked, Clara spoke while transfixed by the massive structure.

"This building was finished in 1989 to commemorate the two-hundred-year anniversary of the French Revolution. It mostly houses governmental offices, with a few purposefully chosen companies, real estate agencies, investment banks, and us."

They made their way up the white steps towards the arch that stretched thirty-five stories into the sky. Glass revolving doors led the way into the whitewashed lobby, filled with natural light filtering in through high windows.

Clara and Hart passed through the vacant lobby and made for the elevator bank. Two policemen were on patrol, strolling casually in their blue uniforms with gold belt buckles and white holsters. Their black-soled boots echoed softly off the polished floor. The pair politely nodded and gave a tip of the cap to the beautiful lady escorting the gentleman into the elevator.

There was a chime as they reached the sixteenth floor, and the elevator doors opened to a marble lobby with an acrylic sign that read, "Renard Industries." Hart followed Clara through the maze of offices and conference rooms separated by glass walls until they came to a short hallway with a vast dark-wood door at the end. Clara approached the door and opened it inwards, revealing a smaller room containing a vacant teak assistant's desk in front of an expansive view of the skyline of La Défense. Across the room was another door, on which Clara knocked three times.

A strong and loud, "*Oui*," boomed from behind the door.

As she opened it, Clara swiveled her head slightly towards Hart, her chin over her shoulder, and whispered, "*Bon courage*," giving him a wry smile.

Hart narrowed his eyes playfully at Clara and entered the room. Renard stood up and extended his hand as he walked around the desk, breaking into a broad smile. The office was dark, lit only by dim fluorescent track lighting, but before Hart could take in the rest of his surroundings, Renard firmly shook his hand.

"Paul. Pleasure to meet you, and thank you for coming. Please have a seat. Let us get to know one another."

He looked the same from the photo Hutchens had shown, his beard silver with spots of dark stubble but neatly trimmed, his salt-and-pepper hair slicked back.

Renard gestured to the sitting area, where a tufted leather couch and two matching chairs sat facing each other adjacent to Renard's dark steel-framed desk. Before Hart had managed to say a word, the CEO in Renard had established the control and pace of the meeting.

Clara, who remained by the door, excused herself, discreetly raising her eyebrows at Hart as she closed the door.

The two men sat facing each other, Renard casually dressed in a blue blazer over a baby-blue shirt, light chinos, and brown suede loafers, his right leg crossed over his left knee, hands resting comfortably in his lap.

"So, did you have a nice lunch?" His face was animated and his smile revealed pearl-white teeth.

"I loved it. Not only did the French food live up to its reputation as the best in the world, but my company was tremendous. You're quite lucky to have Clara."

This drew a soft chuckle from Renard. "You're too kind flattering us. True that we have probably the best food in the world, but nonetheless. Also, Clara works with me, not for me. But I am pleased you enjoyed yourself."

Hart nodded. "Like I said, she was great company, and I hope she enjoyed it as much as I did."

Renard took his hands from his lap and ran them through his hair, brushing the sides back. "I must admit, Paul, I have this understanding with Clara. You see, as I'm a successful businessman, many people wish for my time. If I were to be gracious and take any meeting, my days would be filled. But she is my gatekeeper, and anyone who is going to get my attention, or business, needs to impress her first."

Hart's eyes searched the floor before meeting Renard's. "And what was the verdict on me?"

Renard turned his head and smirked. "Well, you are here talking to me now, aren't you?" He uncrossed his legs and jockeyed himself to the edge of the couch. "So, tell me about yourself."

Hart swallowed hard. "Well, we are a wealth management firm. We pride ourselves on being extremely discreet with our clients. We choose clients at our discretion rather than taking on anyone. There's an effort to provide access to every investment vehicle you can think of, everything from traditional equities, fixed income, government bonds, commercial real estate, to investing in local pizza-chain franchises. If there are returns to be made, we will find them. Of course, we also provide consultation on a variety of mergers and acquisitions, should they be of any interest for our clients."

"That's very nice. But I meant about you."

"What would you like to know?"

Renard stood and walked behind his desk to the bar cart in the corner. "Can I offer you a drink, Paul? I have Dalmore scotch, or Perrier, the only two beverages I keep." He stood in front of a panoramic view overlooking the Eiffel Tower.

"I'll have whatever you'll have, please." Hart occupied the silence by taking in the large but dark office. The walls had built-in bookshelves filled with pictures, small die-cast cars, trucks, planes, and books.

"How do you take your scotch?"

"Neat, *s'il vous plaît*."

Renard muffled a laugh as he set the glass bottle back on the tray, making a loud clink. "I am glad to see you have a respect for the way things are. Any man who drinks a scotch this pure on ice dilutes a naturally beautiful thing. It's important to respect tradition." Renard held his glass up for a toast. "*Santé*. To respecting tradition."

The men clinked glasses, the golden-hued scotch swirling in the glasses. They both sat down and were silent for a moment, enjoying the first sip.

"Paul, I must be honest with you. I do not care what your company has to offer me. *Mais oui*, preserving wealth, or acquiring it, is undoubtedly important. However, it's always the same at any company or bank. Holding someone else's money isn't hard. Growing it isn't rocket science. No, the hardest part in the wealth management business is actually getting the money in the first place. Which is why you're here, I take it."

Hart looked into his glass, confused by the shift in tone of the conversation. Renard watched him for a moment before he continued. Hart could feel his heart pound. Was he being let down gently by Renard? Was this it, time for him to head back to NYC to meet with Hutchens with his tail between his legs? He could always get a start on his job search on the flight home.

Renard scratched his beard and drew a deep breath. "No, what I want is to know the man and the people whom I will work with. That is the most critical aspect. Yes, I am a client of Calhoun, but I only have pennies with you. So, when James called to tell me he was sending someone to take a closer look at what businesses I own, I got curious. That is why you had lunch with Clara. Her job is to find out who you are and what you represent. Because after all, every employee of every company is a spokesperson, are they not? So, if you did not impress, I could wash my hands of you." Renard raised his arms to his sides and looked about the dark room. "And the small annoyance of looking closer at our books. But Clara sent me a message after lunch. Said you barely brought up work, which shows you're considerate, gentlemanly, and you respect the age-old tango of business. You listened, answered questions, and did not complain I wasn't there. This tells me something." Renard gestured with his hands as he squinted at Hart. Hart hadn't felt his jaw clenching or the strained look spreading across his face. Did the lunch with Clara actually save his career?

"With all due respect, Monsieur Renard, I am glad I've passed the test. But you were the one that came to us looking for business. So, I apologize if I seem a bit confused by the cat-and-mouse games we're playing." Hart took a long sip from his scotch before continuing, unsure of his train of thought. "I appreciate your thoroughness, but please understand we also have our own vetting process. My firm doesn't like to just take any clients. We choose who we would like to work with, and we want to work more with you. Since you're already a client, we can naturally skip the vetting process, but I will still need some documents on ownership structures and—"

Renard's brown eyes lit up, and his eyebrows rose with delight. "Well, then, let us get started with that."

"Well, first, I'd love to see a breakdown of your holdings. The various holding companies and subsidiaries, which I'm sure are vast. Then I'd like to get an understanding of them before I send things back to New York for review."

As Hart spoke, Renard rose from his chair and went over to his desk. He turned on his computer with a delicate press on the keyboard before looking back at Hart.

"*Oui*, of course, Paul, this is simple!"

"I'm curious, though. Why the United States? Why now? You are largely a French company, with a few other countries sprinkled here and there, but nothing in the US."

Hart felt it necessary to press Renard. There was something about his demeanor he couldn't quite place, but it just felt out of the ordinary.

Renard walked back to his chair and ran his hands through his hair. "When you drove here from lunch, did you happen to go through Place Vendôme? Down to Place de la Concorde just before the Arc de Triomphe?"

"Yes, I think so. It was quite busy."

"Then you drove through the Place de la Concorde, then, just after, the Jardin Tuileries at the foot of the Champs-Élysées. Are you familiar with this famous square?"

"I've crossed it many times." Hart took the final sip from his scotch.

Renard nodded as if agreeing with himself to divulge a secret. "Did you know that the tall pillar in the center of the *place* comes from Egypt? It is more than three thousand years old. Surprising that in Paris there is an Egyptian pillar not in a museum, but hardly anyone notices. The Eiffel Tower gets its picture taken, but for me, a true Parisian, my favorite landmark in the city is this pillar. Place de la Concorde is the center of Paris. It is the point where east meets west, and this was the actual thinking in the 1800s, when the pillar was originally installed."

Renard took a sip of scotch and placed the half-drunk glass on the desk. He looked at Hart with confiding soft eyes.

"You see, this square is the living, beating heart of Paris. It is as much a museum as it is a crucial route to get from one side of Paris to the other. This very place was where guillotines were set up in the French Revolution, where kings' heads fell onto the street. Where commerce passed from Europe to America, where the Germans occupied, marched, and headquartered during the Second World War, right in the Hotel Carillon on the *place*." Renard stood and began to pace. "So how fitting that Paris, the most artful, cultured and first forward-thinking, modern Western city, should have a testament to the past in the form an Egyptian pillar from thousands of years ago. Because you see, Paul, the world is much smaller and more connected than we think. I am French, but my tastes and hobbies are international. I wear Italian clothes, I drive German cars, I love sushi, and my women are mostly Spanish." Renard gave a wink and a proud smile. "But I do not have nearly any connection to the United States other than my love of America's bourbons. That is why I sought your company out, and that is why I want to do business with you. I want my legacy to be international, not just European. There are good and bad things, in my opinion, about globalization, but I wish to take advantage of the good parts. You are to be my Place de la Concorde, and you will become my pillar, out on display for the world to see." He finally sat back down on the sofa, and grinned.

Hart pursed his lips, thinking he was about to save his career. "Well, I know we can be that gateway into the United States. I think first, though, I will need to take a look at your financials."

"I am happy you've asked." Renard sat forward and smacked his knees. "So, this means you are interested in helping?" He began typing vigorously on his cell, and before Hart could answer affirmatively, he hurled a follow-up question. "How long were you planning on staying in Paris before heading back to New York?"

"My flight is Sunday morning."

Renard drew his head back, made a disappointed *tsk-tsk* sound with his tongue, and laughed. "No, the weekend is a time for relaxation and rest, not business travel. I have things for you to do here, in Paris. You're okay spending more time here, into next week? No girlfriend to rush home to? If there's one and she's impatient, we could always fly her out here to spend a few days in the romantic City of Light."

"Ah." Hart smiled sheepishly. "No girlfriend. I've learned to not mix business and my love life, anyway."

Renard scoffed. "Perfect. I'd maybe suggest calling James and telling him things are progressing, but you will need a few more days. In the meantime, you can take some documents back to your hotel to review. But I will make sure you enjoy yourself this weekend, see what Paris has to offer."

Renard placed a phone call, speaking quickly in French. "Clara, please come back into my office. I have a favor to ask of you."

8

Paris

Paris turned to night without anyone noticing, as it usually had a way of doing. People were busy at cafés, walking home from work, stopping at the store, or heading for dinner. The sun vanished across the Seine behind slanted rooftops, and the arched dome of Les Invalides finally rested after another day brightening up the City of Light. Night blanketed the city, but only for a brief moment before the streetlights, restaurants, and apartments flooded light back onto the streets.

The Mercedes navigated back through the Place de la Concorde to Rue de Rivoli as the sidewalks filled. Tourists scurried about, their cameras flashing away, while locals strolled, in no particular hurry, making their way to a rendezvous perhaps at a café, as if happiness could be found amongst friends and a glass of Burgundy.

At the front door of the hotel, Hart stepped out and circled around to the passenger-side window. He laid eyes on the black-silk-covered legs of Clara, who sat cross-legged in the back of the car. The urge to stare at them longer than appropriate was overpowered by the need to know his plans for the evening.

"So, you'll pick me up at eight thirty? Where are we going again?"

Clara gave a coy smile. Renard had evidently told her to entertain Hart before they'd left the offices at La Grande Arche, but she hadn't shared the details of her plans.

Renard had made it understood that Hart would be staying through the weekend into the following week. Hart had called Hutchens to explain the new itinerary from Renard's office. The only feedback from Hutchens was a huff of annoyance before Renard had impatiently taken the phone from Hart. Stern but courteous words were spoken, and Renard hung up the phone with a wink at Hart. He'd felt a pang of admiration for the man who had stood up to Hutchens.

Clara peered out from the back seat of the car and met Hart's lingering eyes.

"*Oui*. Maxim and I will pick you up. Just be in the lobby at eight thirty. *À tout à l'heure*," she said with a polite smile as she closed her window. Maxim, the same driver they'd had all day, drove off.

Hart nodded to himself. "Yeah, that sounds good to me, thanks."

The sedan turned off of Rue de Rivoli and went out of sight.

In his room, there wasn't much to do besides fight the desire to take a nap, the original sin of frequent travelers. Instead, Hart decided on a cold shower to freshen up and changed into a fresh white dress shirt. Though jet leg would have normally set in, his adrenaline from the day and the prospect of the night to come kept him alert.

He had several emails from work, including three from Hutchens requesting exact details of his travel changes. Hutchens could be aloof, and overbearing in his efforts to micromanage. The irony was that while Hart had been picked for his client visit, he was still required to be informative at every turn.

Nevertheless, the trip had been surreal, better than he could have dreamed. He sat in his red suede armchair that overlooked the darkened Jardin. The relief of having an amiable client in Renard had provided him the hope that he could salvage his career. But above all else, the newfound company of a beautiful Frenchwoman, whom he had a sneaking suspicion enjoyed the arrangement just as well. His career had taken many turns, but at the moment it seemed easily to be the best it had ever been. The work at the firm had been mundane and testing, but for the first time in as long as he could remember, he felt utilized.

The opportunities had been few and far between, but through a series of unimpressive and demoralizing tasks—the clichés of getting the coffee and picking up dry-cleaning, and the tedious work of typing up minutes—he found himself progressing by the good graces of his boss for a while. The question that had preyed on his mind, however, was how to determine when it was time to seek another path. The thought kept him up at nights when he was frustrated at the behavior of ruthless coworkers seeking credit, or longing for the social life he didn't have. But the question of when to choose the next path would have never crossed his mind had it not been for a client dinner he'd attended years ago in New York.

The encounter birthed an idea that stayed deep within him. Calhoun Capital had taken their client, Robert Mayfair, out to a steak dinner at Peter Luger's to celebrate the sale of his manufacturing company. The deal had been lucrative, and Wall Street tradition called for a celebration of red meat, red wine, and cigars.

Mayfair was a short man, wide set, who swam in his expensive tailoring, cut for a man much larger and taller. He had a bushy gray mustache and was balding, with gray hair that clung stubbornly to the sides of his head. He had built up a bike manufacturing company that produced less energy waste, thanks to solar panels and the recycled rubber used for the tires and handlebar grips. A stroke of luck saw his company become the sole provider for a start-up bicycle company that aimed to create rideshare programs using bikes built from reusable materials.

Hart had met Mayfair when he was seeking help to sell his company. Mayfair had won a competition for green companies, with the city of San Diego rewarding them with their first big contract. That led to San Francisco, then to Minneapolis and Chicago, and soon the small company couldn't keep up with demand.

The deal had come through for Mayfair to sell his company for nearly two hundred million dollars. Hart had been invited to celebrate out of charity because he happened to be in the room at the time of the sale. Over the course of the celebration dinner, he had enjoyed a few glasses of Brunello, the wine seemingly his only companion at the table. The others from Calhoun Capital were in the mergers and acquisitions area, the kind of people who proudly displayed their master's degrees in the art of being condescending.

The celebration wound down, with everyone deciding to go to a club nearby to have some better-looking company. Hart had quietly made for the exit and was waiting for his taxi when he noticed Robert Mayfair had enjoyed himself a bit too much. He stood swaying as both men waited for their rides.

"Congratulations." Hart had smiled and patted the man's back.

Mayfair turned to him and, with one eye a little more closed than the other, spoke deliberately. "You know, no one ever asked me how I felt about all this. Just it's a good deal, take it." He had pulled his hands from his pockets and waved them about wildly in mock celebration. "But what people don't know is this is never what I wanted. I came from a small town where my goal was to do okay so I could hire friends and my friends' children, and provide for my town and family. We started doing too well, and my whole life fell apart. I worked all the time; my wife never saw me. When I did get away and we'd go on a trip to a fancy place that we could have never afforded staying at before, it was just another reminder of my success."

Hart had listened with confusion to the same man who had just sold his company for hundreds of millions of dollars. "Well, now you can enjoy retirement and have some more family time, man." Hart smacked him on the back once more, anxiously longing for his cab.

"No, son." Mayfair looked down at his feet, then back up to Hart and grabbed him by the shoulder. "Things aren't the way they were. There is no going back. Money changes everyone. My wife hates me for choosing a company over her, and there's no changing that, no matter how many trips. Just remember: never forget why you started whatever it is you do in the first place. Always remember why you started."

Hart slumped in a plush chair, looking at the darkening sky creeping over the Jardin de Tuileries. He was exhausted. The grind of the travel, and the pressure to win Renard's business and please Hutchens was wearing. Hart thought back to Robert Mayfair, and his words echoed in his mind. With what ambitions had he started his career? He couldn't quite remember.

9

Paris

The noise in the lobby grew steadily in volume as Hart sat waiting for Clara and his 8:30 p.m. pick-up. The revolving doors shuffled finely dressed people in and out of the darkened space. Most of the men wore blazers with silk scarves, polished black oxfords, and beautiful ladies on their arm. The women wore sparkling blouses, silk flowing dresses, and high heels. A buzz had developed at the hotel, emanating from the bar and dining room. It was most definitely a Friday night in Paris.

Hart wondered about Clara and their rendezvous. How would she act for a night out with a new colleague? Perhaps, Hart thought, she'd dress and act conservatively, but she was Parisienne, after all, and it was a talent of Frenchwomen to draw desire and attention from men who had no business giving either.

Hart checked his watch and figured he would wait outside under the archways of the Rue de Rivoli. There, he watched scooters and taxis with their red roof lights race by.

Finally, a black Mercedes pulled up alongside the curb and crept to a stop. In the front passenger window, a man with dark features, a beard, and long black wavy hair and severe eyebrows glared at him. A woman stepped out. She uncurled her long legs, clad in black jeans along with black ankle boots, and stepped onto the curb. Hart felt the eyes of the man in the front seat upon him and turned to see him staring with thinly veiled menace. When he turned back to watch the woman exiting the vehicle, he found Clara inside the car, hidden behind the woman who had stolen his attention.

"*Bonsoir*, Paul. *Allez!*" Her smile was framed by dark-red lipstick. Her friend in the leather jacket stood by the car waiting for an introduction.

"Paul, this is Justine," Clara shouted from inside the car.

Hart smiled and returned the traditional French double kiss; her jet-black hair brushed off Hart's shoulders. She had an oval face with full lips, dark-brown eyes, and soft skin.

Not to be deterred by the tight intimacy of the back seat, Justine squeezed between Clara and Paul. Perfume filled the car, floral notes with hints of cinnamon and a squeeze of citrus.

Clara pointed to the front seat. "That is Julien. We will all be going out together in Montorgueil."

From the front seat, Julien offered a, "*Bonsoir*," then went back to his cell phone, barely giving Hart the chance to say hello. Maxim, the driver, gave Hart a smile and curt tip of the cap in the rearview mirror, and the Mercedes sped away from the hotel.

Hart thought it must be nice to have your own chauffeur like Clara as they passed the brightly lit opera house, heading north on Avenue de l'Opéra. They veered right towards the Second Arrondissement and past the silhouette of Galeries Lafayette, the famous department store where one could find anything.

The conversation in the car was casual, French with bits of English mixed in thoughtfully so that Hart could keep up. He wasn't surprised Clara had invited some friends to join them, and the added company was more than welcome. Clara seemed in a good mood, laughing and chatting away with Justine.

Hart laughed along with the jokes as he split his attention between the conversation and the window. He suddenly found they'd entered an area with smaller cobblestoned streets lined with cafés and restaurants, passable only by foot.

Maxim pulled the Mercedes up to the curb. "Welcome to Rue Mont-orgueil." He added a small tip of the hat.

Hart stepped out and held the door open for Justine, who purposefully extended her long legs one at a time getting out of the car. Her thin black top, which clung loosely to her, showed her curves and offered a plunging neckline Hart couldn't help but notice.

"*Merci*, Paul."

Her brown eyes flickered at Hart while she strode toward Julien, who stood brooding with his hands in his coat pockets.

Clara slid across the back seat and took Hart's helping hand with a broad smile as she exited the car. She wore dark-gray jeans, a golden-hued silk shirt with clear crystals around the collar, and a navy-blue peacoat jacket, anchored by a pair of dark-brown suede heeled boots. She had redone her hair from earlier in the day, invigorated it with volume and a certain wavy, playful curliness. She bid a good evening to Maxim, and the Mercedes merged back into the Friday night traffic.

The four of them meandered down a slightly sloping walkway, passing loud restaurants full of friends out on a Friday evening. The air was damp with the promise of rain.

Hart found himself next to Julien, while Clara and Justine led the way.

"So, Julien, do you speak English?" Hart inquired.

"*Oui.*"

"Do you live in Paris?"

Julien gave him a soft glare, and Hart could almost see the Frenchman's internal struggle—should he engage with the American or retreat?—but he seemed resigned to his fate of needing to be social.

"My whole life. But I take my summers in Provence," he said with a smirk of satisfaction.

"Beautiful. What do you do for a living, if you don't mind my asking?" Hart was enjoying getting under the man's skin.

"I'm a writer."

"Oh? What do you write?"

"Novels."

"Interesting. What about?"

Julien scoffed. "Life."

"Ah, I bet it's profound."

"*Oui.*"

Hart stuffed his hands into his pockets and rolled his eyes. He steadied himself for one last attempt at questioning before he would surrender.

"And forgive my curiosity, how is it you know Clara?"

Julien made a puzzled grimace. "I only know Justine. Justine wanted to introduce me to Clara tonight."

Hart realized that Julien's cold nature was perhaps because he viewed him as competition.

Justine and Clara led the way further down the street, leaning against one another to combat the unevenness of the cobblestones, which had become slick with dew. The street grew more secluded. The lively restaurants and cafés gave way to smaller boutiques, closed at the late hour, and quaint narrow bars that stretched away from their small doorways. Hart and Julien lingered several yards behind the women.

"So, you and Justine are good friends, I take it?" Hart said.

"We met a few weeks ago. I've seen her once or twice. She invited me out tonight and I thought, why not? I love this part of the city. Plus"—Julien raised his eyebrows and nodded towards the women—"not too bad. You really can't go wrong. Perhaps I'll take both home."

Julien picked up his pace, threw a playful elbow, and joined the ladies.

Hart cursed himself for agreeing to go out. It seemed it would be a long night. His inner gentleman protested the behavior of Julien. The women weren't a game where a man could win the best prize. Hart realized why he'd become upset. *I've got feelings for Clara*, he thought. Naturally, he enjoyed gorgeous women as much as the next man, but there were values he would not sacrifice, such as being chivalrous, and especially not with Clara.

He figured there was a chance she had an interest in him and wasn't about to dilute that by entering a contest with Julien. He knew he had been burned before when his intuition was wrong, but it was what, he reasoned, made him good at his job. It gave him an edge in almost any interaction because he didn't trust anyone. He could collect information, facts, likes, dislikes, and their quirks, but at the end of it all, in his experience everyone was out for themselves.

With the arrival of Julien by their side, Clara craned her neck, as if she were looking for Hart. He was still a few yards behind and, knowing she was watching him, faked interest in passing shop windows in an effort to appear distracted, before Clara beckoned him with a wave.

"Paul, *allez*. If you don't keep up, you'll lose us and be lost wandering the streets all night by yourself!" She laughed at the idea.

"*La-bas*," Justine said in French as she pointed to a nondescript stone archway that framed two blue doors. A small silver sign on the wall read "Cocktail Lounge." She knocked twice, and the doors were opened from inside, revealing a large man dressed in a black suit, who greeted them with a serious look on his face. He looked the group over, ignoring Hart and Julien but lingering on the women before motioning for them to come inside.

The lounge was dark and obscured from the front doors by thick red velour drapes with gold tassels pooled on the floor. Behind the dimly lit bar were dark-red brick walls with shelves of bottles. Furniture was scattered across the room, creating private corners and nooks for people.

Hart was struck by the fruity musk lingering in the air, mixed with liquors—gin, bourbon, whiskey—which gave a strong but sweet smell. The conversations of the packed bar provided a hushed but constant buzz. A group of women, dressed suggestively in low-cut tops and heavy jewelry, were laughing the night away, sipping pink drinks from goblet-style glasses.

Clara took Justine's hand and led her towards the back of the room, elegantly elbowing people out of their way to find two couches facing each other and a reservation sign. A waiter in a chic uniform—buttoned-up white oxford, leather apron, where he kept a notepad and numerous pens, over dark jeans, rolled up at the ankles, exposing large, clunky brown boots—offered that while there were no menus for cocktails, the barmen would be happy to make any drink.

Justine sat on a leather couch close to Julien. Hart found his place at a professional distance on the leather couch with Clara. Clara gave an, "*Oh là là*," taking the room in, and spoke excitedly to Hart about what to order. A small wooden cutting board was delivered, with nuts, pretzel mix, and what appeared to be Cheetos, and set on the table between them.

"I love this place! What do you think?" Clara beamed with delight as she looked at Hart and Justine.

Justine glanced over her shoulder at the crowded bar. "It has been so busy since it opened. You have to put your name on a list; then they send you directions how to find the entrance. Glad we got in!"

Hart nodded. "This place is great. I just hope they have enough Cheetos." His eyes met Clara's, which lingered on his just a beat too long, before they both broke into laughter.

Once they had ordered and finished their first drinks, the conversation found a natural flow between the four of them. The topics included Justine's current career as a social marketing manager for a Parisian clothing company, where her boss had an odd obsession with not allowing shoes in the office. Then Julien, inspired by Justine's story, told an adventurous one of his own about the time he brought a group of his friends to his yacht in Saint Tropez. As they cruised out to sea, one of his friends, who was wearing boat shoes, walked across the bow, slipped due to his shoes, and found himself hanging on to the railing of the starboard side for five minutes, since no one noticed he was gone. Julien burst into laughter, while everyone supplied him with thinly veiled smiles and grunts of forced amusement.

Julien pulled his phone out to start showing pictures, but exclusively to a stoic- looking Justine, who'd realized she had invited along a terrible drinking partner. Clara leaned close to Hart so as not to be overheard. He could feel her warm breath, smell her perfume—white flowers and orange peel—and almost taste the champagne from the French 75s she'd been sipping.

"I just met him. More Justine's type than mine. I'm sorry he's so *bobo*."

He scrunched his face in playful confusion. "I'm afraid I don't know what *bobo* means."

She slapped Hart playfully on the knee. "French slang. Means he carries himself with his chin up in the air."

Hart squinted and tried to piece together the translation in his mind. "Ah, like he is quite proud of himself."

"Yes, you got it. I hope he doesn't ruin your evening. You're having fun?"

Hart chuckled. "A great time. But I must say, your company is actually a bit boring. I think I prefer Julien and his yachting stories." He gave a wink to make sure his sarcasm was not lost in translation.

Clara leaned into Hart's shoulder to muffle her laugh. "You are funny. I imagine your girlfriend back in New York is missing you and your jokes tonight." Clara's eyebrows rose, letting the question that came in the form of a compliment hang in the air.

He took a sip from his Sazerac cocktail—cognac with an absinthe rinse, mixed with orange liquor, sugar, and lemon—and savored the bite of the drink.

"Well, she probably doesn't miss me very much." He took another sip, enjoying the tension for a moment. "Because I don't have a girlfriend. My career is all I have to keep me company."

"Oh please, no business talk tonight, but—"

Clara was interrupted by Justine asking them about their drinks. She gave Clara a concerned look, nodding towards Julien, who was slamming them down. Clara laughed and paid her no attention. The night seemed light and cheery, strangers getting to know one another better as the drinks did their job.

The lounge became busier, with the crowd becoming at least four people deep at the bar, shouting for service.

Clara moved towards Hart on the couch, grabbing his shoulder, and leaned close to his ear. He was not surprised that she touched him—the liquor and atmosphere lent themselves to it—but it still made his heart race. "Sorry, it is a bit noisy in here for me. I want to make sure I can hear you." She continued on as Hart took another sip of his drink. "Now we can both spy on Justine's conversation and whisper to each other what we find hilarious, although I may have to translate some for you. Julien is discussing his favorite ski runs in Switzerland."

Hart could see Clara's green eyes sparkle at him before she turned to watch her friend continue to flirt. Julien became more interested in getting the waiters' attention than keeping Justine's and ordered several more rounds for the group. Hart noticed Julien begin to sway on the couch, his eyes drooping and glassy. Justine attempted to cut him off, taking the new drink he'd ordered from his hand to a look of rage from Julien that Hart had seen building. Julien let loose a spew of profanities as Justine sat, disbelieving, her lips beginning to tremble.

Julien suddenly stood and towered over Justine, whose only defense against the unhinged man was a look of utter shock. Hart heard Clara gasp as Julien swayed back and forth, cursing. Hart realized that this portion of the evening was over and stood, grabbing him by the shoulders.

Years ago, he had taken a self-defense class in college to impress a girl he wanted to spend more time with. The relationship failed miserably, with the girl falling for the course teacher, but along with four credits, Hart picked up a few tips on how to deal with physical conflict.

Julien turned and shoved Hart. "Don't touch me, you fucking American."

Then came a barrage of angry French from Julien, in which Hart only caught various names he'd been called. Again, he tried to grab the drunken Julien, but he shrugged his shoulders and threw them forward to be free of Hart's grip.

"I think you've had enough fun for one evening. Let's get you a cab. Sound good?" Hart looked at Clara apologetically.

Julien swung around, his eyes menacing and a far departure from the rest of his wobbly appearance. Justine stood and said she would take him home, offering an apology to Clara.

"*Ta gueule, salope.*"

Clara's eyes went wide as she realized what Julien had called her friend. Justine tried to lead him by his arm towards the door, but Julien protested with a shove that caused Justine to lose her balance and fall back onto the couch.

Hart sprung and grabbed him by the scruff of his collar and turned it clockwise, tightening Julien's sweater so his arms were immobilized. "All right, pal, we're done here."

He started Julien on a controlled march towards the door, careful to not attract any more attention than was already earned around the bar. Julien spun and attempted a head-butt, which drew an audible gasp from Clara and Justine, but it was slow and lethargic. Hart grabbed Julien's head where it landed and held it on his shoulder. He gave a fake laugh and patted Julien on the back, as if two drinking buddies were having a great evening. A female bartender had stopped mixing a drink to watch them and motioned to the doormen.

Hart grabbed Julien's sweater and pulled tighter, bunching it further, rendering his arms useless. Julien became a marionette puppet as Hart casually walked him towards the heavy drapes at the exit. Julien's energy had gone, his battle fought for the evening. Hart strained under the deadweight as he trudged towards the door. He got Julien outside with the help of the bouncers, who weren't too pleased with the prospect of a drunk sitting outside their establishment or having to clean up any mess he made, so they called a cab.

Justine had followed them outside, but Hart told her to head back inside with Clara and that he'd be fine. The cab came, and Hart paid the driver as Julien spluttered out the address in the Sixth Arrondissement. Julien kept saying in English to Hart as he plopped him in the back seat, "My apartment's got a fucking beautiful view of the Seine." The cab took off, and with it, Hart's unforeseen problem for the night.

Back at the table, he ordered himself another drink to combat the rush of adrenaline. Clara consoled Justine, caringly rubbing her back. They whispered for a few moments before Justine was back smiling and enjoying herself. *The resolve of Frenchwomen*, Hart thought. *Nothing will stand in the way of a fun Friday night.*

Clara praised Hart's actions, and she teasingly called him the "American badass." The two women pretended to reenact the scene, much to the amusement of Hart. A few minutes later, a tall, dark-haired, well-dressed Parisian, complete with a jet-black leather jacket, came over to make sure Justine was doing all right. He'd seen the scuffle break out but couldn't make his way over in time to help. He offered her a drink at the bar, an invitation she accepted with a conspiratorial wink to Clara.

Both Hart and Clara stared at their drinks, which had done their part earlier in the evening, and now their chaperones had left them alone.

"You doing all right?" Hart asked a tired-looking Clara.

Clara said through the end of a yawn, "I am quite tired. It has been a long day. Pardon me, I am not normally this tired."

Hart chucked softly; it was he who had had a long day. He had barely slept in twenty-four hours. He made eye contact with the server and asked for *l'addition* before turning back to Clara. "Well, I should be the tired one. I had no idea I'd end up in Paris tonight, but hopefully you won't have to deal with me much longer."

"Really, you didn't know? Anyway, I am kind of enjoying your company, actually."

Hart feigned disappointment. "Well, something should be done immediately to stop that. Let's go."

They worked their way through the crowd, finally stumbling across Justine. She was finishing her drink and grabbed Clara's arms as they swept towards the door. Hart heard Justine yell a goodbye to her new friend, who'd bought her a drink.

The heavy velour red curtains parted as they stepped through to the street. Clara momentarily lost her balance. After several drinks, walking and decision-making could be dangerous. Hart offered Clara his hand to help her through the doorway and out into the night, and the three of them made their way onto the darkened streets.

*

Cigarette smoke swirled inside the car parked several blocks away from where he'd watched them. The three figures could barely be seen down the narrow, cobbled street by the naked eye. The man appeared to offer a hand to help the women down the steps onto the street. A perfect gentleman, it seemed, but looks could be deceiving. The group turned left and right, talking amongst themselves, as if deciding which way to go. It was the perfect opportunity to see the two faces that were of interest.

The shutter of the Nikon D810 professional camera, specializing in long-range, low-visibility conditions, fired away, clicking softly. He stubbed out the cigarette in the ashtray because complete focus on the subjects was required. One woman walked off by herself, and the pair went in the opposite direction, she holding on to his arm, his hands deep in his coat pockets. It seemed the night had been a success. Now there was a picture to go with the name of the visiting American banker and his newfound French interest.

10

London

The pub was crowded, as any pub in London would be on a weekend evening.

Presiding over a pint of London Pride, standing alone at The Sussex pub, Igor planned the next steps. He stood amongst the sea of people filling the diamond-shaped bar area. The door funneled the patrons back towards the expanse of the bar, and whoever didn't fit, or chose to smoke, spilled out onto the sidewalk.

He leaned against a pillar, one of many, and watched the door. People came and went, providing the perfect cover for discreet meetings. A musty smell wafted through the pub, spilled beer mixed with smoke from outside finding its way in through the opening of the door. The pub was classically decorated, like most pubs in London, with wooden floors and green wallpaper. A large mirror hung behind the bar, a Fuller's London Pride advertisement sketched across it.

The English were a proud people, Igor thought while sipping his beer. They were quick to point to history to prove their worth. The world was getting faster and the past was being forgotten; those hanging on to tradition soon found themselves overtaken. His need to change the way the world worked, no longer just the allure of his ideals, was his call to action, and he had all the pieces now.

The pub was in Covent Garden, a tourist paradise with narrow redbrick roads lined with shops. Igor took another sip from the same beer he'd been nursing for twenty minutes. He would make it last until he made contact. He didn't mind the wait; in fact, he planned for it. Better to get accustomed to a space, blend in, and be a man with nowhere to be. There was a certain comfort one learned to have in pubs while living in London. But it wasn't always this way for Igor—far from it.

*

Circumstance saw Igor move from Russia to Maidenhead, just outside London, when he was only a young boy. The move was a necessity brought on by his father, who had been a member of the former Soviet Union government. Vladimir Romanski worked on a research and development team that supported the KGB. He was more scientist than spy. Nonetheless, Igor liked to believe his father made a profound impact on the Cold War.

His father's career was put to considerable test when he was coerced by a Western agent and left with a choice to betray his country or face certain death. Vladimir's lack of foresight shaped Igor's childhood and, for that matter, his life. His father had made a choice, even if he never realized it.

In the early 1980s, the Cold War raged on, the grand game fought by recruiting intelligence assets to outmaneuver the other side. Vladimir had been working on upper-atmospheric radar projects, which everyone at that time thought would be the next frontier. Ronald Reagan, the American president in the mid-1980s, had even started the second space race by declaring in 1983 that the "Star Wars" program would be implemented. The program was designed to bring military capabilities to space, swatting Soviet missiles from the sky. This created a massive reaction from the Kremlin; the mere notion, no matter how plausible, of losing their capability to ensure mutual and mass destruction was unacceptable. Resources poured into Soviet space programs and high-atmospheric research. Vladimir, a smart and promising radar technician, was selected to lend his expertise to crafting the Soviet response.

Vladimir joined the program and was befriended by Ivanov Kolosvo, an affable middle-aged man. They often met up at bars after work, and Ivanov would buy Vladimir vodka and they chatted about work in hushed tones. Ivanov decided they should start going out in the evenings more often to let off steam from their stressful jobs, and their friendship blossomed.

They went out often, which meant Vladimir wasn't spending nights at home with his young wife, Karlina, and newborn baby boy, Igor. This routine went on for months and grew from a few drinks at a bar to a few visits to nightclubs and plenty of nights away from home. Moscow's finest young women kept them entertained, with dancing in dark clubs and mischief in smoky backrooms. Ivanov's extravagant spending at the clubs never struck Vladimir as odd, but it should have. The West managed to deceive Vladimir into believing he had a true friend in Ivanov; the classic tactics of befriend, build rapport, trust, and then ask for commitment. Vladimir recognized he had compromised his life, but by the time he understood, it was too late.

Compromising photos from nights that were too rough to remember laid the trap and Vladimir was presented with a choice. Either start working for the West as an agent, passing along information, or face the scenario of the Soviets finding out that he had been colluding with a Western spy. Perhaps worse for the young father, the photos would be shown to his wife, who had been sitting dutifully at home raising their young son while Vladimir committed treason.

Doing what he thought best for his family, Vladimir Romanski played the hand he was dealt. The meetings occurred in a variety of places—park benches, buses, in the back of clothing stores, and at their old bar hangouts. Each time, as Vladimir saw it, he betrayed his country.

The practice continued for nearly two years. Vladimir provided information that by itself did not represent an intelligence treasure trove, but combined with other information, the pieces fit together like a large puzzle. However, towards the end of the Soviet Union, paranoia ruled as the KGB sought out traitorous spies, and Vladimir's luck ran out. As was commonplace in hunting what were called "enemies of the people," the KGB planted false information in his department and watched to see where, if anywhere, it came out. Vladimir unknowingly passed the information on, exposing himself and putting his family's lives at stake.

The key to being a great spy, he was often told by Ivanov, was to be a master at persuasion. Influencing people without them realizing—that was the key. But even more important was finding everyone's weakness and exploiting it. Vladimir was not an anomaly, Igor often told himself, but rather a young father with misplaced trust who became a victim of circumstance and paid the price.

The Western intelligence services washed their hands of him, pulling their asset Ivanov out of the country. Vladimir, to his credit, fought for the survival of his family, begging Ivanov for help. He was passed off to a British agent with little more than a pat on the back. Betraying his country left him friendless and out of options, faced with the certain death of his family if he stayed, until finally he caught a break, but at great cost.

Vladimir was to meet an agent at a park to plan the getaway to a safe house before sneaking the family off to England. He took Igor as cover, a father out for an evening stroll with his son, but their lives would never be the same. The meeting was smooth and a course of action set upon. Vladimir was to return home and tell Karlina they'd be leaving the next day, but he never had a chance to tell her. When Vladimir returned home, they saw KGB agents taking Karlina away. It was Igor's last and most painful memory of his mother.

The West interfered in his father's life, and like a stone tossed into the middle of a glass-surfaced pond, the ripples were vast and carried away Igor's mother to a gruesome end. Igor's father lived his life in sadness and shame, only putting on a brave face for the sake of his child. His only hope was that Igor would be worth the sacrifices and mistakes he had made, but Igor had been seeing to that for many years. The West had ruined his family, and worse, his own country had murdered his mother. He was filled with hate, vowing to strike back for his mother and to erase the sins of his father. Her only sin was being too kind; his father's was that he was too foolish; those were both mistakes he wouldn't make. He needed help, though, and there were only so many enemies of both the West and his former homeland in the world.

The door to the pub opened, and with it a flood of light filled the dark room. Igor strained to see over the people crowding near the door to catch who entered the bar, until he felt the presence of someone beside him. He turned slowly and faced a young man—skinny, with dark skin, black eyes, wearing a red Nike hat—leaning against the counter.

A loud cheer echoed from the corner of the pub as a goal was scored, the London derby between Arsenal and Spurs on the televisions. The Arsenal supporters clinked glasses as the pub grew louder with replays of the goal.

"Are you a Gunners fan?" the man said in severely broken English.

"Only when they're wearing red. You?" Igor paused for a moment, listening out for the code that there was something amiss, but the man, who Igor came to know as Nasir, only nodded and stayed quiet.

Igor finished his beer. He set it back on the wooden countertop next to the coaster he was using and slid a stack of banknotes he'd procured from the bottle he picked up at the market. He pushed the coaster over to the young man, who was still next to him. The young man stood there, thumbing through the newsfeed on his mobile phone, and grabbed the coaster and cash, slipping them smoothly into his pocket without looking up.

"It's to happen next week. Prepare yourself," Igor whispered in a soft growl.

He could tell Nasir was about to speak, but he turned before anything could be said. Without another word, Igor made for the side exit, working his way through the crowd in the pub out onto the street and into the night.

11

Paris

A soft streak of golden sunlight crept into the room, breaking through the edges of the drapes, bringing forth a new day. But the sounds of scooters zipping by and lorries rumbling past woke Hart from his deep, dreamless sleep long before the sun did. The room was still as he lay in bed, staring at the ceiling. He rolled across the bed and found his watch: 9:37 a.m. He'd slept in, alone.

After walking Clara to her apartment near the Place des Vosges, in Le Marais, he acted the perfect gentleman. He said goodbye with a soft kiss on the cheek—just one so it was not to be confused with the customary goodbye. Clara had rewarded him with knowing eyes before she slipped behind the vast red doors that protected the courtyard of her building.

What was he thinking, foolishly mixing business with pleasure? How the hell had he developed feelings for this woman? He scolded himself; it was juvenile and bound to be a mistake. It had not even been twenty-four hours, but she reigned supreme in his mind. Hart could almost feel the soft kiss on her cheek from the night before. Of course, she was smart and gorgeous, but what did he really know about her? Against his better judgment, he realized, he intended to find out.

The last trip into these turbulent waters did not work out well. A lesson he would do well to remember was that a river, like a relationship, no matter how beautiful or inviting, could turn into rapids, where you live or die at the mercy of what lies under the surface. But he knew the heart is not rational; he'd learned that lesson before, painfully.

Veronica was gorgeous and ambitious. She had invigorated his life from the moment they'd met a few years after college at a bar in Manhattan. Hart, with a few associates from work, was blowing off steam from another week of dealing with narcissistic clients and myopic bosses. Veronica was at the Stanton Social as well, just off Houston Street,, in the frenzied bar on the second floor with several friends.

He'd been at the bar ordering a fourth round of Yuenglings when he turned too quickly and smacked into her, spilling the beers. She happened to be wearing a white cashmere sweater, dark-gray jeans, and caramel suede knee-high boots, which did not mix well with beer. Before he could even apologize, she slapped him hard. The sting stayed with him that whole night. She had glared at him and then stormed away. The bar was captivated and went silent.

Hart held up both hands as if to accept his guilt and punishment. He asked the barman for another round and apologized profusely for the mess before leaving a generous tip. He set off into the crowded, dark bar to find the woman. Perhaps he was a glutton for punishment, but he did eventually find her, surrounded by friends who were blotting the stains and trying to dry her off. Sheepishly, he approached them, receiving dumbfounded glares, and perhaps there was a bit of fear in the eyes of the woman who had slapped him.

"I'm sorry I slapped you. This was my favorite sweater," she said before he could open his mouth.

"Well, I think it was perfectly deserved," Hart said, barely able to look at her, like a reprimanded puppy that just soiled an expensive carpet. "Can I buy you all a round to make up for it?"

While he hadn't had the chance to really look at her before, he realized she was exquisite. She had long dirty-blond hair, a small birthmark on the lower left part of her chin, porcelain skin, and golden-brown eyes, which grew softer with his apology. The days of chivalry were over as far as Veronica had been concerned, but Hart seemed different.

After he'd paid for the drinks, Hart left her group but stopped to apologize again on his way out of the bar.

He said with confiding eyes, "I hope you'll find solace in the fact my friends will never let me forget this. So, in a way you'll stay with me forever." He smiled and turned to leave.

She replied, as Hart started for the door, "Hey, you. It is a good thing you're cute, because otherwise this would have been a big problem."

"Would you do me a favor, actually?" he said while throwing on his winter coat.

Veronica raised an eyebrow in confusion. Do *him* a favor?

"You see, I will still feel sick to my stomach if I don't ensure that I've set things right with you. Let me take you out to dinner. Just to make sure there's no lingering hard feelings?"

Once he got her number, he'd realized they hadn't been introduced and with humor shook her hand, introducing himself as "the dumbass Paul that spilled drinks on you."

She introduced herself as Veronica Hutchens, smiled, and waved goodbye.

They had been dating for several months, but Hart felt as if she was hiding something. He began putting the pieces together. She was well informed and savvy about financials whenever he'd bring his work up, but wasn't in the industry. She knew Hart worked on Wall Street for a small wealth management firm that only had one big client, in the form of a pension fund for the Wisconsin teachers' union, but always implored him to see the benefits of ambition.

The pieces to the puzzle didn't fit together until they had a dinner with her parents at a quaint sushi joint on East Side, in Murray Hill, with radiantly colored walls and fluorescent lights, so she could introduce the man she'd been with for over six months.

The four of them were tucked away at a corner table. Veronica's mother was named Beatrice. She was beautiful and looked just like her daughter. Her father, James Hutchens, had a handshake like a bear trap and a politician's smile. The dinner provided Hart with ample opportunity to show off his ability to pivot and deflect the barrage of questions. What was his upbringing like? Family? Career plans? How did he plan on managing a career and relationship? After a bombardment of what felt like Senate investigation panel–style questions and an embarrassed Veronica, it appeared he had won them over.

A few weeks after the dinner, Hart received a curious invitation for a lunch. James Hutchens had requested a meeting and had his assistant set it up with all of the formality one would expect of a business rendezvous—Outlook invite, finite amount of time scheduled, and the address of the restaurant. It was to be at a French café tucked away in the Brookfield Place shops near World Trade.

The conversation was all business, with a clear set of objectives to reach before their time was over. The discussion's crescendo was that Hart needed tremendous ambition if he was to keep Veronica. This advice was given more as coming from a father who knew his daughter than a man trying to scold another for a lack of success. The message seemed genuine, but had felt uneasy. Was he even ready to become this committed? Once the family was involved, things could become precarious.

As they had left the restaurant, Hutchens turned to Hart. "I have an interview for you lined up next week. I don't want an answer now, but give it some thought and think of what you want for yourself. If you want this opportunity, that's great, and if not..." His voice had trailed off, and he had taken Hart's shoulder and held it firmly for a moment, then smacked him on the back and walked off.

The decision was easy: leave the small firm he was at and trade up for an opportunity it would have otherwise taken him years to earn. The complications that lay ahead were evident, but it was an easy choice nonetheless. Hutchens seemed kind to him, and he would try to work tirelessly to prove himself worthy.

But the fact that he never really had a choice hurt him. He could either take the job for the girl or say no and give the parents the excuse he wasn't the man for their daughter. Forced into a decision, he'd chosen the path that offered him more, not less.

A cloud of doubt hung over him for months after taking the promotion, and in the end Veronica despised him for it. The crossroads came when she found an upgrade in the form of a client of her father's. The young, rich kind of guy that wore impossibly well-cut suits, trendy Italian loafers, and copious amounts of hair gel. He carried himself with a certain disdain for everyone and had little time for small talk. Travis Curtis. Educated at Yale, he owned a venture capital firm that sparkled with angel investor dust.

Hart had first noticed the flirtation at the annual Christmas party, where he spotted the two being introduced and jovially chatting until he came over. The end was in sight for them, even if neither of them believed it. The adventure they had once shared slowly morphed into reality, culminating in a life they didn't recognize or ever think they would have.

In the weeks following the party, Veronica's poorly veiled attempts to learn more about Travis came in the form of questions related to Hart's work. He felt abandoned in the passenger seat of a car spinning out of control towards a cliff, with no choice but to close his eyes. He was in an indefensible position, surrounded by mistakes. Be the first to cause the messy breakup, and he'd risk alienating the man who had gifted him a chance, or he could say nothing, play the fool, and wait for her to put him out of his misery.

In the end, she was swift about it. They both knew the game and what was to be won and lost. Hart had gotten a great career and plenty of fun along the way. In the end, he realized her spontaneous and adventurous nature meant she could never be in one place; what had brought them together eventually tore them apart.

Hutchens, for his part, was professional. He'd seen Hart work for the better part of a year and did not make a big deal of the news but rather had an impromptu discussion with him in his office, away from prying eyes.

"Listen," Hutchens had said as he clamped his paw on Hart's shoulder. "This could be an awkward place for you now, but know you're on solid footing with me. As far as I'm concerned, your life is separate from your career. I won't speak a word of it. Deal?"

Hart responded with an appreciative head bob and a simple "Thank you, sir."

True to his word, Hutchens never seemed to hold it against Hart, but he'd been given the ultimatum to go to Paris. Hart thought maybe he did hold a grudge after all.

Hart shook his head from the memories, rose from bed, and walked to the window to view the Parisian morning. It wouldn't rain today, he thought, because when life is good the weather stays sunny. He'd always found it curious how when one is melancholy, the weather seems gloomy and gray, with a constant chance of rain. But perhaps it came down to perspective; the mind saw what it wanted to see. He felt his stomach growl in anxiousness for his day, or perhaps he was just hungry.

He brushed his hand through his wild morning hair, his head throbbing slightly. Hart had figured that the drinks would have worn off, just like the connection he had with Clara, except neither had. The feelings still loitered somewhere deep in his mind, and he couldn't resist exploring them. The smell of her perfume clung to him from when she'd leaned in close to whisper jokes; the kiss that lingered a moment too long on his cheek before she left him for the night. The long walk back to his hotel, wandering through Le Marais as locals spilled onto the sidewalks, drinks in one hand, lovers in the other, was a slow, torturous journey that part of him enjoyed. Having hope was invigorating, yet dangerous.

Come now, Paul, he steadied himself. *Don't go down a road where you can't turn back.* She was a client, a colleague, and business was meant to be separate from personal life. *Where it should stay this time.* He'd crossed the line once before, but he was the lucky one, the exception to the rule. He tried to shake the thought from his head. *But maybe lightning can strike twice.*

He looked back over to the bed, his dirty clothes scattered across the comforter. He looked at the desk, where his computer sat. One could spend a glamorous time in Paris, but instead he was stuck in a hotel room. But work could wait. As Renard had told him, weekends were for pleasure. He showered, changed into a fresh suit, and headed outside.

12

Paris

A few blocks from the hotel, off the Rue Saint-Honoré, Hart found an open table at a small café. Instead of immediately checking his phone or attempting to look busy, he sat and watched the morning pass by, the official pastime of Paris. He sipped an espresso and felt awakened by hope, a dangerous drug.

The café was lively, filled by people taking breaks from sightseeing. The First was a tourist arrondissement, after all, and the locals would be somewhere else. A few tables over to his left, he watched a middle-aged couple poring over a map of the city, large Nikon camera set on the table. They were arguing with each other—well, it seemed like they were arguing, Hart thought. It could be tough to tell with the thick British accents and dry humor.

Amongst his favorite hobbies, people watching usually gave way to inspiration. The idea that came to him this time, however, was more necessary than brilliant. He needed to do some shopping, since he was going to stay a few more days. Perhaps more importantly, he wanted to be looking his best the next time he saw Clara. Even a well-dressed American could feel helplessly unfashionable in Paris, never mind one without a change of clothes.

Hart recognized he was going shopping to impress her, but he conceded there was nothing wrong with a little bit of effort. He strained to gain the waiter's attention, because he needed change, and once he caught the passing waiter, he apologized for only having a large bill. The waiter counted out the change and threw it onto the table before turning on his heel and vanishing off once again.

As Hart counted out the coins, he felt the presence of someone near his table. He expected the waiter returning for the bill but was surprised to see the British woman who had been sitting a few tables over.

"Excuse me, sir. I'm sorry to interrupt, but we overheard your English when you ordered."

She had a square, frumpy haircut framing her pinkish face. Her husband sat looking down, staring at the map.

"What can I do for you?" Hart said with impatience.

"Well, you see, my husband hates the coins here, and well, it's difficult to ask anyone in French to exchange coins for notes, so I was hoping actually that you may have a spare five-euro note that you could give us. We have eight euros' worth of coins in exchange. Would that be all right with you?"

Her head turned like a dog's would as it begged an owner for a table scrap. Hart was anxious to be done with this interaction, and there was a profit to be swung. He pulled his wallet out and thumbed through his bills, confused but indifferent.

"Here's a five."

"Oh, bless you!" Her face had become a shade of red with excitement. "Bless you, dear. Here's the eight. Thank you!"

She wiggled her way through the minefield of chairs on the terrace back to her husband, and before Hart had risen from the table, the two of them were long gone around the corner.

Hart walked north along the same route he took only the day before, down a street parallel to the Jardin du Palais-Royal, Rue de Richelieu. The necessity for new clothes had brought him out for the most part, but he also needed fresh air and to explore the city.

The street was narrow, and Hart hugged the wall to let strangers by. He paused as he found a boutique with chic mannequins in the windows. A quick look inside revealed stylish employees in the exuberant showroom, with the colors orange, red, and blue cascading off the walls. Since it couldn't hurt to have a different look than a suit, the store seemed a smart choice.

Hart received a warm, "*Bonjour*," from the shop-floor attendants as he entered; he smiled and began browsing as the old wooden floors creaked under him. Fine cotton dress shirts, colorful sweaters, leather jackets, and drawstring suit trousers were hung, stacked, and folded artistically around the store. He picked out a shirt, asked to try it on, and was politely shown the way to one of two curtained-off areas by a tall, smiling associate.

He took his suit jacket off, hung it on a hook, and unwrapped the blue dress shirt from its tissue paper. The shirt fit perfectly—soft material, and trim cut. The shirt would do, but there was still a bit more shopping left, and perhaps he'd head up towards Galeries Lafayette. Hart took the shirt off and fumbled around in the small room. He was reaching for his suit coat when it fell off the hook and clunked onto the floor. He paused momentarily out of frustration; he did not need a dirty jacket. Hart picked his crumpled jacket off the floor and gave it two good shakes to rid it of dust and dirt.

Hart's vision caught a small object, perhaps a button flying from the jacket. He heard a soft click of something that fell to the floor. Curious, he looked around for what had danced across his vision. Hart moved around slowly, searching the spotless wooden floors. What exactly had come out from his jacket? Maybe his mind played a trick on him; maybe it was just a bit of lint or a button.

He checked his coat pockets, found his hotel key, wallet, and phone, and turned to leave the curtained-off stall. He pulled back the curtain slightly and found a gold coin on the wooden floor. He bent down to pick it up. It was one-euro coin, one of the new ones in his possession since his exchange with the British couple. Holding the runaway coin in his hand, he noticed that it appeared cracked across the top, and he immediately felt duped. Evidently, they had traded him fake currency. *Quite the theft for five euros.*

He studied the small coin. He was baffled. How would a coin crack? The weight didn't feel odd, but the top appeared to be coming away from the bottom. Hart grabbed both sides as best he could with his lack of fingernails and pulled the two sides apart like splitting open an Oreo.

"Are you alright?" the saleswoman asked. "Can I get you another size?"

"*Ça va, merci,*" Hart said absentmindedly. He was focused on the fake coin.

The coin had fractured when it hit the floor, but he pried it apart, revealing a tiny cylindrical green part about a fourth the size of his thumbnail. The inside of the coin appeared to be a microchip. He flipped the coin over. A small green device fell out into his palm, and Hart held it up close to his eye. It took him a moment to place it, but it was similar to something he'd seen when he had a dog during his childhood. The veterinarian had showed Hart the small microchip he would surgically implant in his dog, a wheaten terrier, so that if it ever ran away from the yard, they could find the dog via GPS.

What the hell was this doing in a coin? He stood still. Everything slowed. He could feel his blood pumping to his head, and his mind began to race. His ears became hot and his throat tightened. Maybe the coin was a security device to track the movements of currency. Maybe it was a forgery. Whatever it was, the coin had broken apart to reveal its secret.

He reasoned he couldn't ask the store workers, because they may confiscate it or question his ability to pay. It couldn't be what he assumed, a GPS tracking chip. Who would want to track him? Did the British couple know what the coin was when they asked for change? Was someone tracking them? Or him? Why not just leave the coin somewhere? He didn't believe in coincidences. He forced himself to breathe.

Hart went ahead and bought the shirt, all the while reassuring himself there was nothing to worry about. His mind was playing tricks. He set off on the easy walk to Galeries Lafayette and tossed the coin and its hidden contents in a garbage bin. But he still felt vulnerable with every step he took. Every look cast his way caused him anxiety. He pushed the thoughts from his mind and finally decided that jet lag had set in, hitting him hard.

He'd been successful shopping at Galeries Lafayette and walked back to his hotel, down Avenue de l'Opéra, in the afternoon. The sun was warm on his face, and an early-evening breeze began to make its way into the city from off the Seine. He now could go back to the hotel, relax, and order room service. Clara had told him the night before that the croque madame and house salad were a specialty. It never occurred to him to ask how she would know. Had she stayed there? She lived so close to the hotel, maybe she had a rendezvous there with a lover once. Hart caught himself before he spiraled into anxious thoughts about Clara. He knew the hotel bar would be a welcome sight.

As he walked along the busy avenue, Hart had the strong urge to keep checking over his shoulder. He carried on, willing the thought from his mind. *It's the jet lag*, he told himself. *That's all.*

13

Paris

Hart sat at his desk, having finished his omelet, reading the online version of the *Wall Street Journal*, when his phone buzzed. It was before 9 a.m. on a Sunday—2 a.m. in New York. He shuffled across the room, wearing his hotel embroidered terry-cloth bathrobe and room slippers, baffled about who would be texting him.

It was Clara.

Meet me at the Museum D'Orsay at 1pm?

He smiled and waited a few moments, enjoying the euphoria, his jet-lagged mind reenergized. Of course, he would go.

Hart spent the morning relaxing and watching the French news, where he only caught every fifth word, before changing into his new blue mélange sweater, a white T-shirt, and dark-gray chinos he'd picked up from Officine Générale, at Galeries Lafayette.

The walk to the museum was fifteen minutes at the leisurely pace of a Sunday afternoon in Paris. The thick plane trees lining the rues and avenues of Saint-Germain were shedding their leaves, and as Hart made his way down the sidewalk, he crunched them under his feet.

Hart waited by the ticket booth, until he caught sight of Clara across the courtyard, nearly skipping towards him. She wore dark-brown ankle boots and dark-colored jeans, with a gray cashmere shawl that hung at her sides. Her hair was relaxed and bounced along happily as she approached.

"*Bonjour*, Paul!" she said as they kissed cheeks. "I am happy to see you." She smiled, her lips soft with glossy, rose-colored lipstick.

Hart took in the old façade of the museum that had once been a train station. "This will be fun. I can't remember the last time I was here."

"I hope my invitation was appreciated." Her eyes danced around the courtyard, swelling with tourists. "I assumed, since you were in Paris on short notice, you wouldn't have any plans. And any excuse to go to a museum is fine by me."

Hart laughed. "Well, I am happy to be your excuse."

They wandered both floors of the main hall, dipping into the adjacent hallways to view the galleries of different time periods. Hart lingered the longest in the hall of Van Gogh, where a simple painting of the artist's room captured his attention. Cheerful colors—yellows, oranges, and greens—characterized the painter's *Bedroom in Arles*. It was a small bedroom that Van Gogh had stayed in during his time in France.

Hart knew Clara had been watching him intently, with her head tilted slightly as she studied him. Perhaps she felt there was something contrived about Hart being captivated by the painting, but he hoped she would be impressed. The truth was the painting affected him. It was a masterpiece, turning the routine into something extraordinary.

Clara appeared by his side, looking back and forth between the painter's work and Hart's mesmerized stare. She lingered for a moment as tourists buzzed in and out of the room, the old wooden floors creaking as if whispering soft hellos and goodbyes.

"Did you know Van Gogh drew three of those?" she asked, her eyes not leaving the painting.

"Why three?"

"He liked the original quite a bit, but it got damaged. So, he made copies. Amsterdam and Chicago have the other two."

"Well, you can never have too much of a good thing, I suppose."

Clara scoffed. "Says the banker."

Hart didn't look at her directly, but he would have sworn he saw her lift the corner of her mouth in a smirk.

They walked down marble steps and across the steel walkway that connected the right and left sides of the old train terminal, suspended above the main hall's marbled and bronzed statues.

"I'm sure you've been looking forward to this trip for quite a while," Clara said.

Hart laughed softly. He turned to face her, recognizing a mixture of intrigue and concern, her eyes narrowed as if she were gazing at the sun. He shrugged and put his hands deep into his pockets.

"I don't think you'd believe me if I told you. But like I mentioned the other night, I didn't know I was coming. I was told about five hours before my flight."

"Really?" Clara paused and angled away from Hart. She muttered to herself in disbelief before turning back to him. "I don't understand. Why send you without being notified in advance? What was the point of the trip being so urgent?"

Hart nodded in agreement. "I've been confused about that as well. Almost embarrassed, to be candid." Hart stared at his shoes for a moment before he had the courage to meet her now seemingly hesitant green eyes. "I was reluctant to tell you but..." Hart trailed off and rubbed his stubble. "Honestly, I don't know why I was sent here, but I'm trying to use the opportunity as best I can, because it's all new to me."

Clara pondered the revelation, chewing her rosy lip in confusion. She took a few steps and peered over the edge to the main hall below. Hart cursed himself for being truthful. Clara would think of him as some unprepared moron who didn't ask questions but rather just did what he was told. So much for the confident man who ordered well at restaurants, dealt with unruly drunks, and acted a perfect gentleman, even after a bit too much to drink. That façade was gone, and his true feelings were now known.

Clara spun back to him on her toes, suddenly lit with energy. "Renard likes you, and I gave him my support for you, which of course didn't hurt, because I am his gatekeeper."

Hart nodded. "Yeah, you did mention that." He felt guilty, as if he had deceived her, but Clara appeared to be optimistic about his usefulness.

"Now you're here. Your company sent you for a reason. Plus, Renard isn't difficult to work with. In fact, half the battle is won—getting in the door. He likes you, and you're American, which means opportunity and more money for him. But I must say it's curious that you were sent without advance notice, don't you think?" Hart could see her mind racing, thousands of thoughts forming. "Maybe your company doesn't value us much and didn't put thought into this."

Danger! a voice in Hart's head screamed and a small trickle of sweat rolled down his side. He didn't think that revealing his travel plans to Clara would result in her taking offense. Her voice was different, almost accusatory.

Hart, fighting off panic, smiled to reassure her. "We value our relationship with Renard, there is no doubting that. I have made it seem worse than it really is. I am sure my boss trusts me, so please don't think too much about this." He turned to face her, but her arms were crossed as she stood sideways to him, staring over her shoulder.

After a moment's pause, she seemed to dismiss a thought and motioned for them to walk. They entered a desolate, high-ceilinged room. A painting hung on the far wall depicting Romans sprawled across a courtyard in a drunken slumber. Hart read the title, *Romans During the Decadence*, and studied it.

"So, I am curious." Clara turned, ignoring the painting. "What are your thoughts on Monsieur Renard's dealings with Calhoun Capital? Do you think they make sense?"

She stood with her head at an angle, ready to study his reaction and not his words.

"Monsieur Renard's holdings with us are minimal, deposits only as of now, with no real investments. In fact, we haven't invested anything since the money came to us about a year ago." He shrugged and studied the painting, hoping the conversation would end.

Clara pressed on. "Do you find that"—she pursued her lips to search for her next word—"odd?"

Hart shook his head. "No." Clara gave him a skeptical look. "I guess I could see the appeal of being able to say you have business in the United States, but maybe it is a little odd."

Clara picked lint off her shawl for a moment before continuing. "I'm sorry about talking so much business on a Sunday, but my curiosity will not go away. Do you have any specific suggestions for Renard to conduct business with your company?"

Hart turned to study the painting of Romans stretched out, envious of their carefree postures. He certainly was more stressed than they were at the moment. He attempted to stall for as much time as he could to come up with an idea, but he found no such brilliance before responding, "There's a few more things I'd like to learn more about first. Then I'm sure we'll come up with a great plan."

Clara seemed to sense she'd pressed her line of questioning too far but pushed onwards anyway, with a slight frown as if to say, *Why not?*

She stepped closer to him, and he could see small freckles on her nose. "I've been giving it some thought, you see, and well, I think there's a way in which we could both benefit here. Forget this notion you don't know what you are doing here. What if we came up with an idea that would be beneficial for the both of us? You can get credit and look good and earn some business for your company, while I get even further into Renard's good graces. I think that would certainly help us both out, no?" She raised her eyebrows but narrowed her eyes the way women could when they were looking for a certain answer, daring you to get it wrong.

He studied her for a moment. Her face was soft and unassuming—trustworthy. Moments ago, he figured she would have moved on from whatever it was he thought they shared. "I'm intrigued. What do you have in mind?"

She brushed a strand of her hair back. "A penny saved is a penny earned. Taxes these days can be quite burdensome. Does your company have any business in London?"

Hart shook his head. *Why is she asking about London?* he thought. It had never been brought up before.

Clara drew a deep breath and exhaled. "Well, that is enough business talk for today." She turned and pointed down the hallway.

"There's an exhibit titled 'Renoir's Women,' with a wonderful collection. Shall we go?"

"With pleasure," Hart replied absentmindedly, still thinking about Clara's offer and subsequent mention of London.

Clara had started to walk towards the exhibit, her gray shawl fluttering as she went. Hart watched the long shawl float and reveal her derriere. She glanced over her shoulder, catching him in the act: *Were you watching me?* Her dark hair danced across her face, and she swept it back behind her ear. Her green eyes flashed as they caught the light coming from the high windows in the hall.

Hart felt a surge of electricity in his chest. His mind focused completely on Clara's company for the afternoon, void of responsibility or fear, thinking only of her green eyes and soft smile. *What am I getting myself into?*

14

London

Igor stepped out of the afternoon drizzle and ducked inside The Ivy. The late-afternoon meeting had made for an awkward crowd—too late for lunch, yet too early for dinner. Instead, the patrons all seemed to have the same idea: grab a strong drink before heading out, or home, for the evening.

Igor shed his raincoat and tossed it to the overdressed maître d'. The inside of the famous restaurant was not unlike others he'd done business in: refined and elegant, with a certain air of superiority one felt when visiting. The dining room was set with white tablecloths, rose-colored chairs, and green velour booths. The most unusual feature of the restaurant, Igor noticed, was the lack of windows. Instead, stained glass blocked the view of the street, with colored rhombus designs. It reminded Igor of a church, and he hated it. But he didn't pick the venue; that was chosen by the client he was meeting, whom he saw seated at the end of the bar.

Igor snuck up behind the man, who appeared to be enjoying at least his second Martini.

"Josh, have you started without me?"

Josh Cornwall spun, his silk suit, which hung off his lanky frame, remaining glued to the velour chair. He freed himself and stood to give Igor a hug. The men exchanged quick pleasantries, and then Igor, once he found out there weren't any chilled bottles waiting for him, ordered vodka on the rocks.

"We'll have to order something a bit more celebratory perhaps the next time we get together if your deal comes through," Josh said.

Igor forced a smile. Josh's personal portfolio had been with Igor for several years, before he'd finally broken into the business side of things. Josh was the CEO of an English construction company that specialized in housing. The company could build houses in a matter of days. Recently, there had been rumors that Josh was either about to land a major contract or be bought out. The company was publicly traded, and the stock price had been rising on speculation that a move was imminent.

"Yes, well, you better get me that celebratory drink. After all, I am the one who made the introduction!" Igor playfully smacked Josh on the back.

It was true, Igor thought: he did owe Josh plenty. He, after all, was set to become the pawn that Igor would sacrifice, having set the move up perfectly. Several months prior, Igor had arranged a meeting between Josh and a venture capital firm that specialized in investing in humanitarian causes. It wasn't important that the deal would never actually go through—Igor wouldn't allow it—but rather that Josh hit it off with them, detailing the efficient nature of his structural design, which could be used to create mobile hospitals, housing, or even forward military bases. Igor had leaked the news to several friends in the business, and within no time, Josh's company had quite the reputation on the streets.

"Well, we've seen our stock go up fifteen percent in the last few weeks. Just wait until we announce the merger."

Igor downed his vodka. His DNA wouldn't allow him to sip it, because it was to be taken as a shot. "When will you announce?"

"We are figuring in the next week or so. I still need to present it to my board for approval, but it's just a formality at this point. In the meantime, our stock will continue to go up." Josh ate the two olives from his Martini.

Igor felt his heart pound. There wasn't a lot of time to waste. He flagged the bartender down for another vodka and peered around at the clientele, indulging in their afternoon gossip. The type of warfare he waged, Igor thought, was so different to that of Nasir, the young man he'd met at the pub. Igor's weapons of choice were polished oxfords, a quick wit, business intelligence, and plush, carpeted restaurants. Nasir operated on a different level, with weapons more straightforward in nature, but Igor considered himself to be just as effective. They were like cats and dogs: they went about the kill in contrary manners. Igor was a cat—slow, methodical, and when primed to strike, like lightning. Nasir, he hoped, was more brutal force and thunder.

The second vodka came, and Igor appeased Josh with more gossip about the markets, current political trends, and football. Igor wanted nothing more than to get back to his flat and begin further preparations, but appearances were to be kept. He politely laughed at Josh's jokes and patiently listened to outrageous stories. After he'd heard all he could about a recent cruise the Cornwalls took off the coast of Spain, Igor dropped some pound coins on the bar and stood.

"This has been a pleasure, but I am afraid I have urgent business to attend to."

Josh frowned. "I was just getting started. Seems like I'll have to keep myself entertained for the rest of the evening. Wife took the kid to the movies."

Igor saw the perfect opening. "Speaking of your wife, I hope she's looking forward to the Riverbed Charity Gala this week."

"Oh yes." Josh slurped the last of his Martini. "She loves getting dressed up."

"Well, you can now afford to spend some of your extra earnings on the auction, you know."

Josh snorted. "I would if I didn't have a sneaking suspicion you kept all the profits." Josh smacked the bar and laughed at his joke.

For how stupid the guy was, Igor thought, he wasn't far from the truth. Another reason he'd have to kill the man—one amongst the many.

"Well, I hope to see you at the party." Igor stood.

"Of course. We wouldn't miss it for the world."

Igor smirked and threw on his raincoat. "I'm counting on it."

15

Paris

The early-morning Parisian sunlight crept into the vacant dining room thanks to the tall windows overlooking the street. Hart drank as much coffee—steaming and strong—as he could. He knew he'd need it for the day ahead. He'd gone without much sleep at the weekend and needed to be functional at Renard's offices.

Hart wore his navy suit and a white shirt with a blue silk tie. His black oxfords were freshly polished, and he was seated in the middle of the room. Hart's company was a copy of *Le Monde* that sat on the table. Below the fold, a photo captured the chaos of a small refugee boat washing ashore in Italy. At least fifteen people were crammed together in the boat, mostly women and children. The headline read "*Le residus du guerre, le bateau de refugies* —The residue of war, a refugee boat." Next to the article was further coverage of the migrant who stole a taxi in Berlin and mowed down a group of tourists. Hart found it miraculous that no one died. The newspaper quoted EU politicians calling for migration restrictions and questioned the Germans' perhaps misplaced hospitality.

Hart shook his head. In the US, these events might be talked about briefly on some news-flash update, then forgotten. He thought of the people misplaced and without a home, striving for some semblance of a life, but the reality was it made him uncomfortable. Oftentimes Hart found it best not to think of uncomfortable things, so he flipped the newspaper over.

The hotel café was starting to fill up with men in expensive suits—gray tweeds and blue pinstripes—and women in stockings and silk blouses. A breakfast meeting in Manhattan meant be at the table no later than 7:30 a.m. and was conducted before office hours, not taking up the morning.

Hart considered the difference in culture and toyed with the idea that maybe the French got a bad rap but didn't defend themselves because they knew the secret. Long, tranquil mornings made life worth living. Why wake up at 6 a.m. to climb the corporate ladder when one could sleep in until 8 a.m. and take a business meeting over croissants and poached eggs? Perhaps in a different life, Hart thought, he had been Parisian.

His morning, however, consisted of black coffee, scrambled eggs with diced peppers and tomatoes, and twenty-seven emails from work. Hutchens had been working while flying back to New York after a weekend golfing in West Palm Beach. The emails were his way of keeping tabs and contained several paragraphs of Hutchens' usual stream of consciousness. Hutchens requested that Charles Roberts, a financial analyst, compile the original onboarding documentation from Renard. The dreary paperwork consisted of identification and articles-of-incorporation, documents which were stored deep behind the Calhoun Capitals security wall. Hutchens had also requested that Roberts connect with Hart.

Hutchens asked for profiles of the agricultural equipment competitors in the EU. Hart felt for Roberts. He was sure the better part of the young analyst's evening would be spent at the office compiling a mountain of information. Lastly, Hutchens had requested that Hart spend his day solely focused on expanding Renard's interests, thus solidifying connections to Calhoun. His boss could be unrealistic with expectations, but Hart learned long ago it was better simply to ignore the scatterbrained thoughts. They would eventually fade away from Hutchens' memory and were rarely acted upon. Plus, Hart was not one to question orders.

The plan was to head to Renard's offices and spend the day reading documents. Maybe there would be an opportunity to speak with the man himself, to better grasp how they could make money off each other. But beyond business, Hart was anxious to see Clara, and he wore his best suit for the occasion.

Hart left his table and the gloomy newspaper and headed through the lobby, buzzing with guests. Before he reached the door, a familiar man dressed in a black suit with a matching driving cap jumped in front of him.

"Monsieur Hart?" Maxim beamed. "Monsieur Renard said you would be leaving the hotel to go to the offices, and I am to take you."

His thick French accent came through a broad smile. Hart realized he hadn't been formally introduced to the man who drove him around with Clara. He was darker skinned than Hart remembered, and short black hair that peeked out from under his driver's cap.

Maxim opened the rear door and helped Hart into the back of the Mercedes. Maxim merged with the traffic scurrying about on Rue de Rivoli. Hart observed out of the rear passenger-side widow that the area was filled with chauffeured sedans ferrying guests to and from their nearby luxury hotels. Hart caught Maxim looking at him in the rearview mirror, and his driver seized the opportunity to talk as they rolled along with the traffic.

"The traffic to La Défense will not be bad this morning. Most of the people going there already live on that side of Paris. The arrondissement where you are staying is either hotel guests going shopping at Place Vendôme or the locals that live in Le Marais. But they are all painters or artists and don't find themselves heading west too often."

Hart nodded politely, intent on gathering his thoughts for the day. What was he going to ask for at the offices? It made sense to make it appear as though he at least had a plan, which he knew he didn't.

Maxim was undeterred by the silence and pressed on.

"So, what do you think of Paris, Monsieur Hart?" Maxim's thick French accent hit the *th* syllable like a *z*.

Not wanting to be rude, Hart, against his own desires for a quiet ride, gave more than a one-word answer. "I love the city. I've been before, but it is beautiful, and there's no other city quite like it." He'd emphasized *beautiful* to drive home the compliment for Maxim, who appeared to appreciate the notion, giving a toothless smile in the rearview mirror. Hart knew the true way to the heart of a Frenchman was to compliment his country, because while the French didn't need to hear it, they would never tire of it, especially from an American.

Maxim made several clicking sounds with his tongue and his jaw set firmly before he spoke again.

"You are quite right, *monsieur*. It is one of a kind. Just like our women, eh? *Oh,* là là, nothing like a Frenchwoman." Maxim's eyes narrowed as he strained to look again in the rearview mirror for Hart's reaction.

Hart chuckled. "That's the truth, my friend." He looked out the window as the car veered left through the Place de la Concorde. Hart could make out the top of the United States Embassy, the American flag flapping in the breeze. There were armed French police patrolling the sidewalks, steel fencing in the road, and a large green tent with metal detectors in front of the gated entryway to the embassy. A line of people holding folders, bags, and umbrellas stood across the street.

Again, Maxim caught his eye. "Your embassy. The people across the road aren't employees but waiting to get through security for their visa appointments. Everyone loves to give America a hard time, but everyone wants to go!"

Maxim laughed, which Hart politely tried to join in with.

Deciding to partake in the conversation, Hart did what he knew worked in any setting: ask someone a question about themselves, and they could carry the entire conversation. There usually wasn't anything more interesting to someone than speaking about their life.

"So, Maxim, how long have you lived in Paris?"

Maxim's lips flapped as he simultaneously shrugged his shoulders and slapped the steering wheel, the French equivalent of an indeterminate answer.

"*J'sais pas*, I've lived in Paris for, I guess, the last ten years. I am from Marseille, but my aunt moved up here for a rich man many years ago, and when he died I needed to care for her. I moved to Paris to help her, *et voilà*." Maxim smiled and craned his neck so that he could see Hart in the rearview mirror.

"Well, it's not a bad place to go." Hart had a sense of déjà vu looking out his window as the car climbed up the gradient of the Champs-Élysées.

Maxim navigated the pedestrians crowding around the arch and weaved his way into the oncoming roundabout traffic. Once the Mercedes straightened out, the tall buildings of La Défense could be seen stretching into the sky before them.

"So, Maxim, do you only drive for Clara?" Hart asked.

"Oh yes, sir, I am busy but happy with this!"

Hart allowed his question to linger, hoping that tying in work wouldn't make his motive for the line of questioning too obvious. All men knew the game, and each played it their own way.

A knowing and suddenly darkening glare danced across Maxim's eyes in the rearview mirror as he did a double take at Hart.

"*Oui, bien sûr*. She is a very beautiful woman."

Hart ignored the comment, feeling foolish for asking such an obvious question as a silence fell over the car. Maxim let it remain for a moment, the only sounds heard were the high-pitched whines of scooters weaving in and out of the stop-and-go traffic.

"But if I may, sir." Maxim cleared his throat and spoke, his eyes softer. "Clara is a special woman, quite close to Renard. Nearly untouchable, if you understand…" His voice trailed off. Maxim turned the radio on for a moment, and France Info came to life, then turned the volume down and raised his index finger. "But I happen to know that she is fond of exceptional food. Being that she is from the southwest of France, she must have great food. Should you ever find yourself out to eat with her, where you go and what you order will have an impact on her. This is silly but true. She appreciates men with fine taste, what they wear, what they talk about, what they like. That is merely an observation, but one I've learned over the years driving her, and maybe, perhaps, between you and I, overhearing conversations. I do not say this is all she cares about— because she is a woman, we will never know it all—but I think this will help."

Hart was appreciative of the man's endearing effort. "*Merci, mon ami.* Any other helpful ideas for someone, let's say, to understand Clara?"

Maxim tapped the steering while with his index finger, as if debating how much he should divulge. The car rolled to a stop at a stoplight.

Maxim turned quickly to the back seat and gave Hart a confiding stare. "With women, one never knows." His finger had stopped tapping. "But Clara is not difficult to understand. She works hard, lives alone in an artsy part of town where businesspeople don't usually stay. They live in the Sixteenth or Fifth Arrondissements, but I guess she likes it. Monsieur Renard trusts her with his life. But like I said before, the way to this woman's heart is culture, appreciation, not always speaking of business. It will—how do you say?—go a long way."

Hart spent the rest of the ride pondering his next move. How many days did he actually have left in Paris? He couldn't be sure. This idea of a fling with Clara was madness, he told himself. He should remove it from his mind. Whatever possible dreams he had of their future together would be lost to the circumstances of place and time. They were two different people from two different worlds.

But as the large sedan took the sweeping boulevard left towards Renard's offices, the anticipation of seeing Clara made Hart's stomach tighten. This had the feeling, he conceded, of being much more than a fling. *Just take it one step at a time and see where it goes.*

Maxim pulled the car up to the front door and jumped out, racing to the rear door before Hart had his seat belt off. A tip of the cap and a, "*Merci, monsieur,*" and Maxim was back in the driver's seat and speeding off before Hart was through the revolving glass doors.

16

Paris

Hart spent the morning in a glass-walled conference room, with his laptop and papers littering the table. He had been utterly alone for the better part of the day, besides an assistant who stopped by every hour to see if Hart needed water or *du café*. Office types in power suits and sleek dresses meandered by between meetings, peering with curiosity into the fishbowl where he sat. Hart, in turn, appeared to look busy, typing copious notes on his laptop with papers strewn about, but the truth was he wasn't accomplishing anything.

Hart's head pounded. He couldn't shake a feeling of helplessness from being stuck in the conference room. His job was to learn all about Renard's company so that Calhoun Capital could say it did its due diligence on its foreign client, but he needed assurances in some form that Renard would move more money over. When Renard spoke to him in grandiose terms of the West and the Place de la Concorde, he wasn't going to stop the conversation; he was ready to take credit for the expanded business. It was Hart's chance to prove to Hutchens and, for that matter, to his former lover that he belonged.

He found solace in the work, boiling it down in his own mind, so that if Renard were akin to a chef, his business interests would be equivalent to having a role in every aspect of the restaurant business. He was the server, bartender, and busboy, but also the supply chain that provided the food and brought it from the farm to the table.

Renard started in the business of manufacturing and supplying agricultural equipment and over the years expanded Renard Enterprises LLC, which grew exponentially in market share, while expanding into different sectors. In order to cut down on production costs, they'd bought out several manufacturing companies and then a small steel company, then branched out into the agricultural field. He purchased several wine estates in Bordeaux, and although the vineyards used old-fashioned manual labor, the small ventures turned into a solid distribution chain when Renard purchased a freight company, allowing his estates to distribute wine across all of Europe.

It was clear to Hart that Renard had bigger dreams than simply selling farming equipment. There was some unquenchable thirst that drove him, evidenced by the man's diversified holdings.

Letting out a deep breath, Hart rubbed his temples and dropped his head. There was an echoing clank as the glass door was thrust opened, the glass walls vibrating and starling Hart.

"I hope I am not interrupting."

The accent was thick, and Hart knew who it was before he even looked up.

"Monsieur Renard, nice to see you."

Hart stood and forced a smile as he shook hands. He cursed his luck; he was ill-prepared for their next conversation.

Renard glanced at the messy table and back to Hart. "No need for formalities. I just wanted to stop by to see the sausage being made, as they say." Renard smirked with pleasure in getting the English expression right.

Hart stood awkwardly, with his hands suddenly hidden in his pockets, desperate for Renard to leave and not ask any questions. If the truth be told, he was overwhelmed.

Renard found a swivel chair and took a seat. "Please sit down. I have a few minutes before my potentially vigorous lunch appointment." Renard again glanced at the smattering of papers across the table. He undid the top button of his shiny navy suit jacket, showing a purple silk inner lining. He wore no tie but a white pocket square.

"A potential client meeting?" Hart inquired, looking to redirect the attention.

"*Non*, not a client, a beautiful woman who has the fiercest blue eyes you have ever seen. Some men choose to drive expensive cars, gamble, golf, or have a yacht, but I find solace in beautiful women." He leaned back in his chair and shrugged, frowning. "That doesn't mean I don't have expensive cars or yachts, but I prefer exquisite women."

Hart let out a nervous laugh and shook his head. A thought crossed his mind for a moment: *Did that include Clara?*

Renard sat forward, placing his forearms on the table, and folded his hands, revealing a polished silver Cartier wristwatch with a blue-jeweled crown. "You know, when Clara messaged me after your lunch and said I should meet with you, I was curious, because while I've been a client of your company, we have never really engaged before. Then out of the blue you appear. Did your boss share with you the specific purpose of the trip?" Renard squinted at Hart as if he were holding the last remaining hand in a high-stakes poker game, waiting for the cards to drop.

"James asked me to go for some due-diligence work and get to know you better."

Renard scratched his stubble. "That is all? *Bon*, the good news for you is that I like you—or should I say Clara likes you? And I trust her. So, I like you. And I know that it takes time to build relationships." Renard studied Hart, who nodded in agreement.

"But once I form a bond, this is not easily broken. For example, I have been going for the same massage at the Mandarin Oriental on the last Friday of every month for the past twelve years. The masseuse is named Yvette, and she knows my body like the back of her hand." Renard drifted from the conversation for a moment, as if he were recalling her in his mind. "When I think of her, a story comes to mind. I had gone on a hunting trip to Scotland. I'd never been hunting, but a friend of a friend had this castle with dogs and invited people for a hunt on his property. I had to carry this heavy hundred-year-old shotgun all week. Of course, you need to carry it a certain way, and by the time I was back in Paris a few days later, my back was absolutely killing me. So painful, I could barely walk or breathe. So, I had an appointment with Yvette and told her my left side hurt, but she simply said lie down. She took maybe two, three minutes just going over my back muscles, and next thing you know, she is massaging my right side!" He held his hands up in the air, palms to the sky, dramatic confusion spread across his face.

"So, I say, Yvette, *non*, it's my left side that hurts! She stops, leans in close to my ear, and in her soft voice tells me she knows best. Oh, *mon ami*, I didn't exactly care about my back at that point, you know? But after she was done, no pain. Absolutely none. I felt brand-new. She told me that my left side hurt because I had compensated for my right side. It made sense. I didn't even know my own body. So, Yvette tells me, because she can see in my face I am stunned, that it is her job to know me better than I know myself. She has an ability to get to know my muscles, the weak spots, the parts needing extra attention, and those that need minor maintenance. She says that this is her mission, to leave me in better shape than when she found me every time. She does not even need to be told where to go looking for issues. She just finds them and fixes them, because that is her job. And you know what this reminded me of?"

Hart was startled by the question, because he was busy fantasizing about having his own masseuse. "No."

"Well, it is quite simple—"

Renard was interrupted by knocking on the glass door as a woman wearing a dark-cherry-red safari dress with black high heels peeked her head in to let Renard know his car was downstairs waiting.

"*D'accord. Merci*, Iris." He spun back around and looked at his watch for a moment before shrugging and continuing. "As I was saying, it's simple. I thought that Yvette was profoundly insightful in that in every relationship there needs to be an intimate understanding of each other, especially in business. Paul, this is what I see you as." Leaning forward once again, with his elbows on the table, Renard made direct eye contact with Hart as if he were willing an understanding between the two men. "I know that going to clients and pretending to be interested can be tedious. But you are to be like the masseuse I spoke of, only your client is my company, my future, our ventures together. Study everything you'd like to. You'll have access to anything, everywhere, anyone, at any time. I want you to be able to find my weaknesses and take care of them without me even having to point to them."

Renard stood slowly and buttoned his suit jacket. Hart continue to sit, as he felt the discussion was not yet over.

"I know Hutchens is eager for more capital. So, I've arranged for a two-million-euro transfer to my account at Calhoun Capital. It's a little thank-you for being so accommodating. Because I know how the game is played—you want to take care of me, and in return look good yourself—so I'd like you to also short a specific company for me at half their current price. It's based out of England and is somewhat of a competitor. I have the cash resources to take a short position in them; put a million on it. Think of it as icing on the cake."

Hart scratched his stubble. "You want me to short a company that is a competitor of yours because you think you'll put them out of business soon?"

"Yes, well, something like that. I have strong convictions the position will have booming returns."

Hart nodded. There was nothing illegal about taking a position in a competitor— most companies couldn't do it because they didn't have the capital—but he was beginning to understand Renard was unlike anyone he'd worked with.

"Just give me the name of the company and I'll look into it."

Renard smiled. "Good. I am glad, Paul. Because the best relationships are where things do not need to be spoken but are simply understood intuitively. I'm also happy that you don't need to run back to the United States, because now that I have you here, I have your boss' attention, and I quite like that." Turning for the door to leave, Renard dug a slip of paper from his coat pocket and threw it on the table. "This is the company name. You have my permission to do as we discussed."

Hart glanced down at the neatly folded, cream-colored paper that lay on the glass table. It seemed Renard was offering a goodwill gesture, a deal that would make everyone happy.

"Oh, and one more thing." Renard held his hand up. "Clara is out of the office today on business, but tomorrow I think it would be nice for you two to catch up."

With a wink and a smile, Renard walked down the glass hallway and playfully tapped on the window as he strolled away.

17

Paris

Hart confined himself to the conference room as the day dragged on. He anticipated hearing from his office, so he'd decided to skip lunch, opting instead for a bottle of Badoit sparkling water and some sea salt cookies that had been kindly brought in.

An email notification finally pinged at half past one, from Charles Roberts, with a smartass subject line: "*Thanks for ruining my weekend.*" Attached was a report on the agriculture sector in the EU by country, and the second file was the original client application and documentation from Renard's account opening.

Diving into the first report, Hart read about the EU's strong agricultural economy but determined it best to call Roberts, who, as he'd politely reminded Hart, spent the weekend writing the report.

Roberts answered on the first ring, with the soundtrack of New York City—honking, sirens, and general pandemonium—in the background.

Roberts scoffed. "Hey, man, thank you for ruining my weekend. I hope Hutchens will pick up this international call bill too." Roberts sounded his usual gruff self.

Hart pinched the bridge of his nose in an effort stay patient. "I read it over, but I am curious to know your thoughts on everything."

The line was silent for a moment, other than NYC in the background.

"You want my opinion?" Roberts' voice rose in confusion.

"Yes, related to our client. I'm sure you formed some opinions while preparing your research." Hart paused for a moment. He knew he could trust Roberts, and honesty was a currency in which Hart liked to deal. He was looking for feedback or any ideas he could craft into his own.

Hart knew Roberts was an analyst and only accustomed to research, but he never gave an unvarnished opinion. His career was constricted, and he toed the line so that if something broke one way or the other, his analysis would seem fair.

Roberts huffed. "Paul, I'm assuming this stays between us."

"Of course," Hart replied.

"Well, I am confused as to why Renard wants to work with us. There are plenty of other firms that could manage him, but maybe it's lucky for you. Hutchens sends you on a compliance field trip, and Renard sees his chance to get more attention from us. But as far as his holdings in Europe go, the guy's company does pretty well. He has the market nearly cornered in France, from manufacturing, distributing, and to selling his agriculture equipment. If anything, maybe there should be stronger diversifications into other spaces, but why expand into the United States?" Roberts paused. "That confuses me."

Hart nodded to himself. He'd felt the same, and when he heard Roberts echo the sentiment, it was as if a loose thread had been pulled in his mind.

Roberts carried on. "I think he should start investing more while business is good. Their organic growth will stay capped unless Renard Industries invests further."

Hart jumped in. "You are thinking Renard has to spend more money in order to earn more?"

"Exactly. You know, it's what Hutchens is always talking about. At a certain point, you're not going to earn any more unless you get better at what you do, or there's a significant event that changes the outlook—something like Brexit or disruptive technology for that matter. But if you don't have a large catalyst like that, the only real option left is investment."

Hart was glad he asked for Roberts' opinion. He had good ideas, some that Hart might even make his own. "Spend more money—original idea. But what about shorting a competitor? If you're convinced your outlook is superior, don't you think it's an interesting play?"

Roberts laughed. "Where did you get that crazy idea? If there is cash to burn, you're better off investing in the markets. That to me makes more sense than earning pennies shorting a stock of a competitor."

Hart was flustered and chose to ignore the answer. "I appreciate the hard work on this, Roberts. Try and leave the office early tonight, huh?"

"Anything for you, boss."

Roberts' reply dripped with disdain, but Hart heard a chuckle before the call ended.

Hart leaned back in his chair and rubbed his stubble absentmindedly. Roberts had been cynical about Renard's requested trade, although Hart left that part out, offering the idea as his own. He considered his options. Defy

Renard and suggest something different, or continue with the request and have Calhoun second-guess his own value. He played out the two options in his mind, finding little conviction. He had an obligation to appease his client, and more importantly, the trade could further bolster his standing with Hutchens. The downside, Hart thought, was minimal, and after all, he'd set out to win Renard's business, and it certainly appeared he had.

Suddenly, Hart felt anxious to get out of the conference room he'd been in all day. He had a visitor pass but was reluctant to venture further than the bathroom for fear of getting lost. The glass table was littered with papers, but Hart knew he had only gained a general understanding of Renard's company structure and personal holdings. But even a team of auditors would have a difficult time deciphering it all with only a few days. Hart glossed over the hundreds of accounts and various holdings companies and legal entities operating all across Europe. The enormity of the research slowly eroded his patience and soon his ambition to finish looking over every document. Hart reasoned he'd done the job as best he could, making copies of documents to ensure that Calhoun Capital could say it had done its KYC work. The prospect of reviewing more documentation was too daunting, and it was late in the day. Hart had seen fewer people making their way back and forth, peering into his fishbowl, and decided it was time to leave.

He thought of Clara and was disheartened he didn't see her. He still felt foolish for having confided in her at the museum about his uncertainty. She'd been more confused than concerned, but he felt the shining amour of his American banker façade had been stripped.

Renard had reassured him with his trust, and a seemingly lucrative trans-action request, and he wanted to make him happy. Hart recognized the only person who didn't seem stressed or worried about that plan was Renard. The irony was not lost on Hart that Renard seemingly had the most to lose: his money.

Hart's phone buzzed, upsetting some papers, and he scrambled to find it. He saw the caller ID, and his stomach tightened.

"This is Hart."

"So, how's it going out there? Had enough croissants yet?"

Hutchens' booming laugh caused Hart to hold the phone away from his ear. Hart solemnly dropped his head, resigned to having to play along.

"Yeah, thanks for the vacation. Almost feel bad expensing things."

Hutchens sneered, and Hart could hear the ruffling of papers on the other end of the line.

"How is Mr. Renard? Are you two getting along? Bringing over more money?"

"He's ambitious, that's for sure. I know he's eager to expand into the States and sees us as the key to that doorway."

Hutchens grunted in approval. "We've been in casual talks for months, but things seem to be coming together now. I saw he sent over a few million. Good work, Hart. I should have known he'd want to talk shop. Looks like there's still a place for you in our firm, after all." Hutchens drew out the last phrase, daring Hart to tell him the truth that he felt overwhelmed.

"I'm glad I got to help."

Hart heard Hutchens smack his desk. "Good. Remember I have eight associates, but I chose you. I didn't realize this would turn into an extended trip, but as long as he brings us cash, I don't care. Keep me informed. Use my cell."

"I will, thanks." Hart debated whether to ask something that had been lingering in the back of his mind. He decided to go for it. "Just curious, but how did we end up with Renard as a client?"

Hutchens cleared his throat, seemingly pleased by the question. "Well, a few months back I took a trip to London to finalize a deal. I worked with a banker from some firm for almost a week before it was finalized, but once the week was over, this banker, a guy with a funny name—Igor, I think—recommended I get in touch with Renard. He said he was a client who was looking for an American firm to work with. Said we would be perfect together. So, Renard is with us, but I still want more capital from him. Like I always say, you have to spend money to make money."

The call ended abruptly, with Hutchens telling Hart to charge everything on his company card and hanging up without saying goodbye.

While Hart cleaned up the conference room, he longed to be back at the hotel, but there was one bit of business to do first. Logging into the client portal for Renard, he found that indeed the two million euros had been transferred, like the man said. Hart pulled the piece of paper from his pocket and placed a short position, on Cornwall Public Limited Company, the million-dollar position Renard had requested. Hart snapped the laptop shut without a second thought.

Just past the front desk, Hart caught Iris, the assistant who had taken care of him all day, as she entered the elevator. Hart followed her inside.

"Ah, Monsieur Hart. Heading out for the evening?" she said.

Her demeanor was slightly less warm after the official working hours had ended.

"Yes. I think I'll grab a taxi or the Metro. Any ideas how to get back to the Louvre area? Or where to go for dinner?"

He put his briefcase down on the floor and buttoned his raincoat as the elevator descended. He was intrigued by what fate had to offer, and he expected a detailed suggestion or an entirely different idea from Iris.

Her eyes narrowed, and he thought the corners of her full lips turned into a smile briefly before she spoke. "There's a car outside for you—same driver, Maxim, as this morning. Good night."

The elevator reached the first floor, and Iris slid out sideways before the doors were fully open. *So much for what fate had to offer*, Hart thought.

Maxim hurried over to Hart in the lobby and peppered him with questions about anticipated plans, and offered suggestions. Hart simply asked to be taken back to his hotel.

It wasn't until just past the Arc de Triomphe that Hart realized he hadn't heard from Clara about their plans for Tuesday, as Renard had mentioned. It was after 6:30 p.m., but since she'd texted him on a Sunday morning, he figured that professional protocols were abandoned and sent her a text.

Hope you had a nice day. I understand we are scheduled for a dinner tomorrow?

She responded well after Maxim had dropped him off. Clara said she'd meet him for breakfast at the hotel at 8 a.m. Hart grinned and thought, *I am eager to see you too.*

18

London

The ring pierced the silence of the apartment. Igor scowled with disgust. He glared at his phone, as if daring it to continue ringing. It was unbelievable to him that the phone actually was ringing, because it meant there was an emergency. On the sixth ring, he reluctantly answered, pinching the bridge of his nose and silently cursing this luck.

On the other end of the line, there was only a faint white noise. Straining for a moment to focus on the background, Igor could just about make out labored breathing. He told himself to be calm, but his temples pounded like an angry war drum.

"I would like to place an order for delivery," a meek voice mumbled in a thick guttural accent—Middle Eastern.

Igor took a deep breath and exhaled slowly. He lit a cigarette before responding; the hiss of the butane cigar lighter filled the empty silence. He snapped the lighter case shut and threw it on the table with a clank.

"We are closed," he said, spitting the words out.

The caller sounded worried, not desperate. The call was a waste of time. The burner phone was meant for emergencies, the type where the police were about to break down the door, not simply for cold feet.

"I was really hoping to—I mean I need..." The voice trailed off. "I need to eat."

Taking a long pull from his cigarette, Igor let the smoke settle deep in his lungs to steady his nerves before blowing it from his nostrils. This was not the type of emergency he wanted, but duty called.

"Try the shop on the south side of Covent Garden. Tourists keep things open all night. Goodbye."

He snapped the flip phone shut, then, in a rage, tore the device in half.

Holding the phone pieces in both hands, he began to shake. Why did things have to be so difficult? Why were people so weak? There wasn't time for this. That phone call could jeopardize years of work.

The paradox of his life demanded he work hard to get where he was, but it was just a means to an end, because eventually he needed to destroy the career he built. Without the ambitious life he pretended to live, his secret life would be impossible. All he wanted to do was come home after work and have a strong drink, relax in front of a dirty movie, and go to bed, but it was not his fate this evening.

He grabbed his dark-blue Burberry raincoat and left his flat. The night air was damp, and it felt like it would rain the next day, like it seemed to do every day in London. He drew a sharp breath and cursed out loud. The last thing he wanted to do was travel halfway across London. He took pity on himself for a moment, cursing the hand dealt him for the evening once more. It would be a long night, doing standard surveillance direction routes, or SDRs, across London. It seemed that anyone could execute them, because of Jason Bourne movies. But Igor was not like anyone else; it was in his blood, and he was a savant at being two steps ahead.

He was devoted to his cause, and the role of ambitious banker was perfect. He took on the role so effortlessly that he himself believed it was the truth from time to time, although he would never allow himself to admit it out loud. A lucrative new client signed, the perfectly executed trade, the large quarterly bonuses, and the business trips entertaining clients all over Europe brought their own moments of bliss. But it was all a means to an end. The irony was his career gave him the access to the money and people he would use to destroy them. He was a villain shielded by the greed he preyed upon.

He took a stairway-shaped SDR to South Kensington Underground station and caught a Tube to Piccadilly Circus. Igor was not surprised there were people still milling about late on a Sunday evening. Most of the shops had closed, but a city like London was never truly still; there was always something to do. Walking on the west side of Regent Street heading north, Igor did his best to glance across the street into shop windows, where he could see his reflection. While Regent Street was quite wide, the shop windows were large enough that one could use the opposite side like a mirror. Satisfied no one was following him, Igor crossed the street, heading east past the Nike store, with flashes of light from enormous screens inside showing Premier League highlights.

Continuing east, Igor finally entered Covent Garden from its north side, the streets busy with foot traffic from the nearby bars. Patrons stood outside having a smoke and a pint, clogging the sidewalks, but it was what made

Covent Garden the perfect meeting ground. The storefronts provided continuous reflections, and the urban maze of streets and hidden alleys made it easy to disappear.

Doubling back through several streets, pretending to window-shop on the left side and returning the way he came down the right side of a tight, dimly lit cobbled road, Igor felt confident he hadn't been tailed. He knew he was paranoid, but that was how one stayed alive in a game of cat and mouse.

In the office at Riverbed Capital, where he was a portfolio manager, Igor could relax and be the consummate professional. He attended meetings with clients, managed their money—or, as his company's marketing material said, "Increased one's legacy"—by investing in stocks, real estate, and bonds. His firm's mission statement: "To provide timely, sound, and dynamic advice so that our clients, and future generations, are secured." But the actual company motto was "Make money at all costs."

The more money under management, the larger the expectations were. Igor had labored away at Riverbed for years before realizing his parents' dream of living in the Soviet Union under communism was preferable. He'd felt firsthand the deterioration of people's morals and their corrupt actions, which caused harm and broke a country. Every day, he watched Europe become weaker, chasing profits, leaving behind countless people and third-world countries. Thanks to the greed of others, opportunities formed from the ashes of forgotten peoples in need of help. For Igor the victims were the migrants who struggled to make a life for their families, as Western culture stripped their desolate countries bare of resources and infrastructure. Igor knew he would make the West pay, with help from those forgotten. They were innocent like his mother, killed by his father's ignorance and the greed of the Western allies to win their so-called Cold War. His revenge was calculated; he would further inflame tensions across Europe by funding terrorist attacks by migrants, turning a profit on their specific actions.

Igor knew his course of action wasn't easy, but he believed that the foundation for his offensive was already laid, but more importantly to him, worthwhile. While there were strict laws pertaining to high finance, he had found ways around them. His company was perfect cover: small enough that he knew everything that went on, but big enough that things could be hidden in plain sight. He could manage money, create returns, and meet the wealthy upper-class citizens of Europe while operating with a great deal of freedom. It also meant he had time to meet with his other, secretive, resources. Like the evening encounter he was waiting on.

*

Igor gazed at the large market, its slanted roof housing boutiques, such as Ladurée chocolatiers, Shake Shack, and a plethora of other small shops. The expansive paved walkway leading up to large doors doubled as a delivery dock afterhours for the Covent Garden boutique houses. He watched as late-night drinkers came and went, couples holding hands, a few well-dressed Londoners hurriedly walking in overcoats and scarves scattered about. The area still smelled of cooking oil from fish-and-chip carts that had been there earlier in the day.

He watched the passersby with interest. He'd always found it imperative to understand people—who they were and what they did. It was intuitive, a gift he liked to believe he got from his mother; certainly, his father didn't have it. Igor could read anyone, and he was rarely wrong. Understanding someone, what they were driven by, what made them happy, what their weaknesses were, was like a sixth sense to him. It was how he found and approved Nasir for the job in his operation.

Wearing bright-white Nikes, dark skinny jeans, a camel parka, and his red Nike hat, Nasir looked like any other trendy urban Londoner. He made his way under the overhang of the building and leaned against the brick wall. From a distance, Igor watched the surrounding area for several minutes. No one seemed interested in Nasir or loitered conspicuously. When Nasir looked at his phone, the screen lit his face, and Igor could make out the young man's thin beard. After ten minutes of waiting, Nasir shook his head and headed south towards the River Thames.

Igor let Nasir slip ahead of him as he took a small alley towards The Strand. The alley gently sloped downhill, and Igor walked carefully on his heels to make sure he didn't alert Nasir. Having waited for ten minutes, Nasir would think that Igor stood him up and would go back to wherever it was he came from, but Igor didn't know where, as planned, due to the operational security they'd both agreed to.

Once Nasir reached The Strand, he turned east, heading towards Trafalgar Square. Igor quickened his pace and closed the distance and, in front of Charing Cross station, pulled alongside Nasir. Igor felt the young man tense as they fell into step.

Igor spoke first without looking at him.

"This meeting protocol is for emergencies only. This better be something that's an emergency," he spat out through clenched teeth. He'd been irritated since the moment his phone rang. Not even the hours in between or the long evening walk did anything to calm his rage.

"It is. I mean, I think it is—an emergency. For you. I mean, us too." Nasir spoke softly like a scolded child.

"Well, let's have it."

"I'm not sure that I'm ready. I don't feel ready, and I think it's best if we delay this a few more weeks. To prepare more."

Igor cut him off with an annoyed grunt somewhere between a growl and a bark. They were silent as they walked into Trafalgar Square under the cover of darkness. Swiveling his head around in both directions to ensure no one was close enough to overhear their conversation, Igor spoke firmly.

"You knew the game would play out this way when you agreed to this arrangement. You're doing this in the name of Allah, for the security of your family, for future generations of your family, so that they know you not only served Allah but also struck at the core of the West."

Nasir dropped his head, letting his chin bounce softly against his chest as he walked, pouting like a teenager. "Maybe I don't even know what you want. Where your loyalties lie, or even if you believe in Allah or our cause," he quipped as they continued to walk along, crossing the square and continuing west towards Hyde Park and Mayfair.

Igor closed his eyes momentarily; the frustration of dealing with Nasir would soon be over. He reminded himself just what he needed to get from him, the crucial role he'd play.

"Listen to me," Igor started as he pulled out a cigarette and took his time lighting it. "I am supporting you and the cause. Who gives a damn whether I bow my head five times a day? What you need to know is your enemy is my enemy, and that makes us allies. Together we'll bring them to their knees. The people I work for chose me because they knew I could deliver."

Nasir was getting cold feet, or maybe attempting to make a better deal for his family, but Igor didn't care. He took two long pulls from his cigarette, flicked the butt onto the wet pavement, and watched the dying glow of the tobacco for a moment. Littering a cigarette butt was now against the law in England and punishable by a fine of up to eighty pounds. It was just another reminder of how weak the West had become.

Igor was fed up with Nasir and wanted to go home.

"I am not speaking of this anymore. You've been chosen, your family will be well taken care of, and you agreed to this." Igor stopped, his anger getting the better of his composure, and turned to glare at Nasir. The Ritz Hotel sign behind them lit up the street. "However, you, of course, have two options left."

Nasir met Igor's dark eyes. "And those are?"

"You can continue as planned and fight in this war and strike, as has been asked of you, or you can decide this isn't what you wanted, after all, and you can walk away."

Igor pulled out another cigarette and put it in his mouth unlit. "But if you choose the second option, you should know it will not be pleasant for you." He lit his cigarette. "No, let me rephrase that: considerably unpleasant. Because we have found your mother and little sister in a refugee camp in Stockholm." Igor turned to see Nasir's eyes flicker with fear. "So, if you should decide your services are no longer available, we won't make any effort to protect your family anymore. We will move them out of the apartment we've gotten for them. Your beautiful little sister—what could become of her? Maybe she gets left in the rough part of the refugee camp—the one we rescued them from; the part with the men who have grown tired of not having women around. Maybe your mother will be there, too, and they'll make her watch. When they beg for mercy and cry out, 'Why us?' The last thing they will know before they die is that their pain and ill fortune are because of your cowardice. They were part of the deal, and if you don't fulfill your end of the deal, well..." Igor let the words linger in the air.

Nasir was silent except for heavy breathing. Igor knew firsthand that no matter how deranged, manipulated, or evil someone could be, their family was everything, and it could cripple them.

"They are safe and out of the camp? Praise Allah. I have not known this. You only said they were protected."

Igor scoffed. "We're done here. Carry out your mission, and only communicate to me if it is an emergency. If you call me again for a bullshit stunt like this, I will not be kind to your family. That is a promise. We will make contact in a few days' time."

They reached the corner of The Strand, with Hyde Park to their right, a wide roundabout directing traffic. There were signs pointing the way down to the underground walkway below the busy roundabout. Nasir turned to ask Igor more about his family, but when he looked left, he saw Igor calmly crossing the road as cabs and a double-decker bus went by, and when they had passed, Igor was gone.

19

Paris

The morning of Tuesday, October 11 was accompanied by waves of dark and relentless clouds slowly passing over northern France. The storm, picking up cold water from the English Channel and unexpectedly warm air from the day before, grew angry as it unleashed its fury on Paris. The skies remained dark well into the morning, long after the sun was supposed to rise; instead sheets of rain, fierce winds, and bellowing thunder blanketed the day.

The windows of Hart's room shook, causing him to wake well before his alarm. He lay still, his body heavy, sinking deeper into the mattress as he fought to keep from falling back asleep. The jet lag had finally caught up with him, albeit a few days late. Once the adrenaline from his whirlwind travels left him, he felt exhausted and sore, like he'd been hit by a truck.

He rolled out of bed and trudged to the bathroom, showered, trimmed his beard, and put on khaki chinos from Officine Générale and a gray cashmere sweater from Maison Kitsuné with a tasteful little French flag embroidered on the front in the shape of a fox. The woman at the shop had told him that *kitsune* was Japanese for "fox," and *maison* was French—a brand of different nationalities. He figured playing upon French nationalism could only help his chances of seducing Clara.

Combing his unruly hair, he couldn't help but think of her. Why did she want to meet at the hotel? Perhaps she wanted a change of scenery from the office to an informal setting, but what for? There was only one way of finding out. He couldn't prepare for a meeting, Hart thought, where he didn't know the topic.

The dining room was busy, since no guests were brave enough to face the morning weather. The clinking of coffee cups being set back on their porcelain saucers, soft murmuring, and the smell of freshly baked pastries put

Hart at ease. It was certainly a better setting than the conference room he'd been confined in. He was sat at the table nearest the window and immediately requested black coffee.

The waiter returned with a large French press, the steam slowly rising out of the spout. Hart was informed that he should wait several minutes before serving himself. Not wanting to appear rude when Clara arrived, he requested a double espresso for her, but only to be brought out once she was seated.

The waiter bowed his head. "Of course, *monsieur.*"

Hart was patient enough to wait for several minutes to float by before pouring the coffee. He pondered the last week of his career—and life, for that matter—hard-pressed to find another time when things had been so spontaneous. The irony was he hadn't made any of the decisions. It was Hutchens who sent him to Paris, Renard who asked him to stay. It was as if he were on a rudderless ship, tossed about on a tumultuous sea, the direction not up to him, but rather at the mercy of the seas and tides, being taken in whatever direction he was pulled.

Hart, over the rim of his coffee cup, caught sight of Clara making her way through the dining room. She wore a khaki Burberry raincoat, its collar turned up against the morning rain. She handed it to the maître d', who had kindly offered to relieve her of her jacket. Hart rose and watched her saunter across the room. Her espresso hair was in a tight bun, with a gold clip holding it in place. She wore a clementine-colored dress that draped across her shoulders that flowed down to her knees, complemented by a gold necklace and patent nude-colored high heels. She made her leisurely way to Hart, who like most of the men in the restaurant, happened to be admiring Clara as well.

"Bonjour, *mademoiselle.*"

"Good morning, Paul. I see you've started without me." Her lipstick, the color of grapefruit, framed her sideways smile.

Hart pulled out her chair while the waiter brought out Clara's double espresso and gave Hart a quick wink before walking away.

"That was quite sweet of you, thank you," she said to Hart as she grabbed the menu from the white tablecloth and studied it closely.

Hart was quiet for a moment before his curiosity got the better of him. "So, to what do I owe the pleasure of breakfast with you this morning? Or maybe it's the delicious pastries here."

She didn't stop looking at the menu, but her eyes darted up conspiratorially at Hart: *Be patient.* He folded his hands. Clara sipped her espresso, finished browsing the menu, and found the waiter, who was eager to reappear.

"We have a busy day ahead, I'm afraid." She spoke in English for Hart's benefit and ordered the small fresh pastry basket, along with a breakfast smoothie with mango, orange, strawberry, and kiwi. Hart requested an omelet with red pepper, potato, and Gruyère, along with a side of toast.

"So, what were you planning on doing today?" inquired Clara as she sipped her espresso.

"I don't really have any plans." Hart drummed the side of his coffee mug while he spoke, a nervous tic he didn't realize he had until Clara gave his fidgeting hand a quick glance.

"I was hoping that you'll be flexible with your scheduling. You see, I have to be in London tonight." She playfully bit her lip.

Hart hid his disappointment by grabbing another sip of coffee. "Probably off to some beautiful hotel for an extravagant dinner." He smiled but was sure Clara could see the truth in his eyes.

"Actually"—her face softened—"it is exactly that. Nice hotel, extravagant dinner, but there is one thing you're missing."

"Oh? Please do tell."

Clara smirked. "The event is a black-tie charity auction with lots of big spenders. There will also be copious amounts of champagne. So, you're correct, but the problem is I happen to need someone to accompany me. Monsieur Renard canceled on me yesterday."

"I see." Hart could feel his pulse quicken. *She's going to ask you. No, don't be a fool. It's too good to be true.*

Clara paused as her smoothie arrived, a deep-claret color with an arrangement of sliced strawberry and banana decorating the glass. She grabbed the straw slowly with her fingers and moved it up and down to test the consistency. She then bent down to the straw and took a sip, looking up at Hart, who needed to clear his tightening throat. She stopped and seemed to nod in approval of the drink before turning her attention back to Hart.

"I'd like you to come with me. It's a chance to meet more people in Renard's circle. There will be a few colleagues from London I'll introduce you to." She stirred her smoothie and watched Hart's reaction.

Hart was thrilled and gave a fist pump under the table. "It's too bad I left my tuxedo in New York." He laughed, mostly because he didn't actually own a tuxedo.

"*Bon.* The good news is you're in Paris, and maybe going to London." She narrowed her eyes confidingly. "The two best cities in the world for shopping. If you can't find a tuxedo that fits without tailoring here or there, you wouldn't be able to find it anywhere in the world."

Hart nodded. "How long do you plan on staying there?"

"We," she clarified, "would plan on being there for just the evening tonight and return to Paris tomorrow afternoon. If all goes to plan." A mischievous smile crossed her face.

Hart carefully started into his omelet while his mind raced. Clara grabbed a croissant from the basket, tore it in half, and dunked it several times into her espresso.

"*Bon appétit.* You're going to have a busy day ahead of you. We leave in a few hours. I already booked our train tickets. Eurostar from Gare du Nord to St. Pancras, which will get us to London midafternoon."

"Already booked my seat?" Hart laughed. "But I haven't said yes."

Clara smirked. "Well, you're not going to say no. It would be considerably disappointing to Renard and, might I add, myself."

"You were confident in your abilities to persuade me," he said with a wry smile, but somewhere he felt uneasy about his predictability. He'd realized that he kept being asked to do things without much choice, and no one seemed to bother ever asking his opinion, although with this particular request he didn't mind.

"Well, I guess I should check out of the hotel for the evening."

Clara held a freshly dipped croissant in her hand as she spoke. "I don't think that will be necessary. Monsieur Renard is a part owner of this hotel. *Pas de problème.*"

Hart was packing his leather duffel bag when his mobile started vibrating across his desk. The number started with a +33 country code: France.

"Paul, it's Claude. I understand you're going on a trip today."

It had been only about ten minutes since he'd finished breakfast with Clara and had quickly made plans to rendezvous again before their train. Either Renard knew the plan ahead of time, or Clara had told him immediately after leaving breakfast. For a spontaneous trip, Clara and Renard had communicated well.

"Yes, I'm looking forward to it. We leave—"

"At one o'clock, yes. Your train leaves soon, but you'll have plenty of time to get ready before the gala tonight."

"I appreciate that I've been chosen to go on your company's behalf with Clara. I'm humbled." Hart could hear someone enter Renard's office and hushed voices. Hart zipped up his duffel while he waited for Renard to talk.

"Paul, sorry for that. Urgent meeting. Must run."

"I understand. Thanks for the call. Speak with you soon."

"Oh, Paul, one more thing. I'm going to have Maxim drop off an envelope at the hotel for you. I need you to take this to London and give it to my banker there. His name is Igor; you'll meet him tonight. Good man. It's something he needs immediately."

Hart, accustomed to delivery-boy duties, didn't know why he was being asked instead of Clara, but he didn't give it any further thought.

"I'd be happy to."

"Wonderful. *Merci et au revoir.*"

"Thanks, have a great—"

But Renard had hung up before Hart could finish.

He decided to let the office know his change of plans and drafted an email to Hutchens but realized he didn't even know what hotel he was staying at. Hart decided to forgo the heads-up to his boss; it made no difference to him, Hart reasoned, what country he was in as long as business was getting done.

Hart sat on the edge of his bed and stared out the window at the unrelenting rain. The weather had pounded people into submission; only a few brave souls with large umbrellas and unsteady walks, thanks to the strong wind, could be seen scurrying to and from work, home, breakfast, or a presumably quiet museum.

He was exhausted and thought of a time in his life when a rainy day meant lying in bed all day with someone, waiting for the day to be over. He allowed himself to drift, closing his eyes, and imagined his life the way the far corner of his mind saw it. On dark, stormy, rainy days, the time only measured by the number of strokes his hand could make against her soft skin, which glowed with every flash of lightning. Holding him tighter with every crack of thunder as he brushed her hair gently behind her ear and lifted his chin so their lips could meet. Clara—it had to be her; she was the only one his mind could picture.

Hart flopped on the bed, pushed the dream from his mind. It would be a busy day, and it may be one of the last quiet moments he'd have for a while. The rain made him tired, as did his full stomach, and his jet lag was in full swing. He checked his watch. 10:38 a.m. He was to meet Clara in about an hour. Plenty of time for a quick nap. He grabbed his phone to set an alarm for twenty minutes. Before passing out, he checked the weather in London; it was to rain for the next two days. Perhaps, after all, his daydream would come true.

He felt himself drift off and stay somewhere between sleep and alertness, until the ring of his phone jolted him from his stupor. He fumbled over to the nightstand and grabbed it on the third ring.

"*Bonjour.*"

"Good morning, Monsieur Hart. Your taxi is here, and we have an envelope for you at the front desk."

"I'll come down for it shortly, thank you."

"*Avec plaisir.*"

20

Paris to London

The Eurostar from Paris Gare du Nord to London St. Pancras would take two hours and fifteen minutes. The train reaches 186 miles per hour on the way to London or Paris, traveling under the English Channel by way of the longest underwater tunnel in the world.

Hart watched Paris fade away. His seat faced the direction they traveled. Clara sat across from him with her back to London. The chairs were spacious in the premier cabin, with a dark-gray seat cover, and dark-purple pillow headrest, the colors hiding the wear from numerous travelers—over ten million per year. After they'd cleared the suburbs of Paris, the conductor came over the intercom to give their approximate arrival time, which was 4:15 p.m. Greenwich Mean Time, gaining an hour back in London. Hart planned on using every minute of the train ride to talk with Clara, and certainly not about business. Hart was pleased that he and Clara were in a more private arrangement than the four-person table across the aisle from them.

The train hurtled along, with the constant thumping of the tracks and the groan of the metal carriages as it picked up speed. The passing countryside was a grayish green on account of the stormy day. The tinted windows made the dark-gray clouds that hung above northern France even more ominous.

Between them on the table lay a small gray Sony laptop, next to Clara's black-pebbled leather Smythson notebook and several sheets of printed paper. Clara grabbed the papers and rifled through them. She'd put on a navy-blue cardigan to combat the chill of travel.

"So, I think it would be wise to go over the itinerary for this evening's event. The details of where it is, who will be there." She showed Hart the printed calendar. "I want you to know what to expect."

He felt her eyes studying him as he read. Clara pointed to the hotel's address. "The event is at the Shangri-La Hotel by London Bridge, the Ren room. You'll recognize the hotel. It's in the Shard tower, more famous than the bridge itself."

Hart was already feeling overwhelmed. A black-tie dinner at the Shard, the five-star hotel, in a massive glass building that looked like a giant tower of ice breaching the earth's crust in the middle of the London skyline.

"I'm sure it will give us a beautiful view of the city."

Clara smiled. "Exactly. This event draws out some extraordinarily wealthy people. It's a charity gala, with cocktails and a dinner, which goes quickly because everyone wants to get to the auction that follows. These people mean business, and there will be some impressive things up for sale. It's oftentimes a contest to see who can give the most money away. Last year, there was a thirty-yard yacht donated, fully refurbished and equipped with a three-person crew for the first year of ownership. The bid went for, if I recall, ten million pounds." Clara's face showed her incomprehension of the amount of money spent, and she shrugged. "While the Shangri-La has plenty of space for us to stay, I've booked us instead at my favorite hotel in London. The Savoy. It was also a favorite of Sir Winston Churchill. Do you know it?"

Hart was busy trying to think of a joke. *Did you get us a king-size or two twin beds?* crossed his mind, but he thought better of it.

"Savoy. Can't say I have. Passed through London once or twice over the years but never a proper visit. Suppose we'll be too busy working to see all the sights."

Hart feigned disappointment while glancing out the window as the train passed quiet fields, devoid of machinery or people due to the pelting rain. He saw the dark circle of a tunnel approaching. The pitch changed once it was in the tunnel, the noise constant and loud.

Hart couldn't see Clara's face, as she buried herself in her leather notebook, reviewing her notes. A stewardess came by, asking what they'd like to drink, and announced that a small snack would be served briefly. Clara ordered for them both, two black coffees, giving Hart a look out of the corner of her eye asking for reassurance it was okay by him. It certainly was, so he gave a small nod. There was something sexy and relaxing to him about having his order taken care of by her, a woman who knew what she wanted for both of them.

Clara stood once the stewardess had poured their coffees and said she was going to the ladies' room. She sauntered off in her high heels down the aisle.

Hart looked back down at the table, making sure his side was clear before the food arrived, but found Clara's notebook spread open in the middle of it. He glanced down the aisle and felt it safe to glimpse at her calendar.

Between the hours marked 8 a.m. and 10 a.m. *petit dejeuner avec*

Paul—trip/logistics was written, and *TGV* between 10 a.m. and 4 p.m. He looked further down the page and saw *Riverbed Charity Gala* at 7 p.m. in Clara's slanted handwriting. Hart was about to flip the book back over when he saw *Igor* penciled in after the gala in much smaller print than the other entries. What this a late-night rendezvous? The name was familiar. He leaned in further to inspect the notebook when he felt a hand on his shoulder. He spun in his seat, his heart pounding. He been caught with his hand deep in the cookie jar.

"*Pardon, monsieur*," the tall stewardess in a gray Eurostar cap said as she leaned over and placed the trays in front of him and Clara's empty seat.

"Ah, *merci*." Hart watched her turn back to serving the other passengers and breathed a sigh of relief.

He was placing the book, which was now closed thanks to his startled reaction, back on the table when Clara arrived. She took her seat in front of the tray with *jambon iberico*, two types of cheese—one soft, and one hard—a small dinner roll, some fresh fruit, and a small salad. She was busy eyeing the *jambon* when Hart spoke up.

"I must confess," he said as he watched her delicately rip apart the ham with her fingertips, "when the food came, I moved your book. I didn't want it to get dirty."

A look of indifference came across Clara's face as if she was searching for the reason why Hart felt it necessary to mention such a thing. She smiled politely before returning to her meal.

Since Hart had read "*Igor*", he felt a profound sense of guilt at having invaded her privacy. Or perhaps, he thought, it was remorse for the foolishness that now caused his mind to panic. He didn't know Igor, but the name had been coming up lately. Renard had said he was the man the envelope was for, and Hutchens had even said a name that was similar, the mutual friend of Renard's.

Igor was possibly Clara's lover and based in London, and her calendar note was of a late-night rendezvous. Hart was resigned to the fact he wouldn't find out who he was until the time came later that evening.

"The taxi ride will be short. Once at the hotel, we can go to our"—she paused to take a fork to her salad—"rooms." Emphasizing the *s*. She smirked, aware that she was teasing him. "Then we will head to Regent Street to find a tuxedo. If not there, we can try Jermyn Street. Savile Row is famous, but for custom tailoring only. There are a few shops that sell off the rack, but they will insist on a tailoring before selling you anything. Nothing worse for a clothier than to sell ill-fitting formal wear." She giggled and continued on. "Won't be cheap, but hopefully work will pick the tab up for you. After all, this is a business trip."

Hart saw an opening and attempted to capitalize. It seemed like the chance to get to know her better.

"Well, I'm glad I'll have you as company to help me shop. I mean, you always look stunning. I actually thought you moonlighted for Chanel or Saint Laurent."

Clara's reaction was not what Hart had envisioned, but rather she wore a look of confusion.

"Moonlighted? I don't know what this means."

Her blank stare left him feeling foolish. *So much for the compliment.*

"It's a word for having another job. I was making a joke that you were also a model." He shrugged and offered an embarrassed smile: *I find you quite attractive, but you already knew that, didn't you?*

"Ah, I see." Her words were in contrast to her face, which had lit up at the compliment. Clara looked out the window to the wet English countryside, as if thinking how to respond. "So, you think I am a model now." Her eyebrows danced up and down as she pouted out her lips and dramatically squinted her eyes, shifting her shoulders, as if posing for a magazine cover.

They both laughed away any awkwardness. The elderly English couple across the aisle, both with thick white hair and worn wool sweaters, gave a glance of contempt for the laughter Clara and Hart shared. The stuffy premier-class cabin was a space usually reserved for hushed business conversations and the quiet musings of lovers, not for blossoming love.

Clara had decided to check her laptop for any emails after lunch. After they emerged from the tunnel Hart watched the fire-orange sunlight flittering through the thick rolling clouds of the countryside in the distance. The sun had burned a small opening in the clouds, revealing an icy-blue sky that flooded the compartment with bright light.

He was relaxed about London and the evening ahead, until he remembered the envelope he was carrying for Renard. Maxim had apparently dropped it at the hotel with no address on the outside, but Hart knew he was to deliver it to Igor. Why had Renard asked him to bring the envelope when he knew well enough that Clara was going too? Furthermore, why did she have Igor's name on her calendar? The rest of the train ride, Hart couldn't help but notice he had tightness in his stomach. The arrangements didn't feel right, but perhaps the feeling was just born of jealousy, or maybe it was something else.

21

London

They arrived at the Savoy barely thirty minutes after their train had pulled into St. Pancras. Their taxi drove down the narrow entrance and stopped between a lime-green Lamborghini Aventador and a black Rolls-Royce Phantom. Hart made a comment to Clara about her evidently good taste and was blown off by a huff of air and a devilish grin. They made their way into the hotel.

Revolving wooden doors led into the lobby, checkered black-and-white tile running the length of the floor. The walls were dark, rich mahogany; several portraits hung of Victorian ladies sitting idly. Through the main foyer and down a wide set of teal-carpeted stairs was a great room, where a massive wrought-iron chamber, the shape of a birdcage, towered thirty feet into the air. The small wooden tables hosted afternoon tea, with towers of edibles—sponge cakes, macaroons, toffee puddings, and cucumber sandwiches—spread about as guests chatted away. Hart and Clara were escorted to their separate rooms, which were on the same floor and shared the same view overlooking the Thames.

They had agreed to meet in the lobby at four, and took a taxi the short distance to Regent Street to find Hart a tuxedo. Their shopping proved to be exceptionally easy. Hart found a black narrow-lapel tuxedo and slim silk black tie at the first store they tried. The massive, three-story Burberry flagship had several options for Hart to try off the rack. Hart asked Clara to stay by him to give her opinion. She'd sat on a plush green velour sofa and watched him model the options. Nathaniel, the salesperson helping Hart, couldn't get over the fact that a size 40 regular jacket needed no alterations. Clara snickered and blushed as Hart spun around, modeling, fiddling with his French cuffs.

Nathaniel tugged and prodded at the jacket, sharing his opinion that the tuxedo fit perfectly and that they were an adorable couple. "A French and American together in London is the perfect combination," he'd said as Clara continued giggling at Hart. The tuxedo would be pressed and sent over to the hotel before 6 p.m.

Clara and Hart wound their way back towards the hotel afterwards, the busy evening commute in full swing around them. The air was heavy with a cold dampness as night settled in on the city and the rain stopped.

Clara inched closer to Hart on the crowded sidewalk, making way for the more anxious commuters to get home. "Do you like what you do for work?"

Hart wasn't sure if Clara was asking about his career or just his trip to London.

"Ah well, I do enjoy traveling." He realized the conversation would stall, so he continued on. "But as for my career, if that's what you meant." He looked at Clara for encouragement to carry on; she nodded and then looked back straight ahead, navigating the steady stream of hurried strangers. "I do sometimes. The job I have now came about by strange circumstances. I've had my share of challenges, and some maneuvering has been needed. If you know the term." He looked at Clara to make sure she understood him. Her English was phenomenal, but he found she was giggling slightly.

"'Maneuvering,' *c'est manoeuvre*. It is the same word! English came from French. Remember that."

Hart laughed. "And here I thought the French had only contributed democracy, croissants, galette, and the French kiss. All fantastic things, I might add."

Clara let out an exasperated breath before laughing.

"So why this, *manoeuvre*? Was it a happy move?"

He was pleased by her questions and the fact she seemed to care to get to know him.

"Well, I was put in a compromising position and ultimately paid the price. But I think things have turned around."

"So, I'm curious. What was it about?" Clara asked.

"I don't want you to have any misconceptions about me or my professionalism." He looked off to his right, at a Pizza Hut that looked more like an American diner, complete with ketchup and mustard bottles atop the tables. For a brief moment, he longed to just be sitting at a restaurant, Coke in hand, not worrying about careers, clients, or money, but it was a daydream, not his reality.

"*Alors*, Paul? What happened?" Her voice became more serious, even in tone.

Hart winced. "I had a girlfriend, and her father got me this job, and she ended up leaving me for a client. Her father is still my boss, actually."

Clara was quiet for a moment. "I see. You're still working there?"

"Like I said, it was a compromising position, but I don't want you to think I didn't earn or deserve it. It's a job I never could have gotten so soon otherwise—and *voilà*, as you'd say." Hart risked a glance at her walking next to him. Her face revealed more confusion than anger. Hart continued on. "I think my boss likes me. This whole thing was over a year ago, but since then I've been mainly relegated to grunt work, except for this trip. I just do as I'm told." He paused a beat and took notice of her silence. What if now Clara would view him as damaged goods? It wasn't the first time he'd confessed to something that left him looking foolish.

Clara scoffed as she looked at him. "Sometimes things happen for reasons we can't understand until it's passed. I suppose the true importance is that things will reveal themselves with time. And you were sent here. He wouldn't send you on a trip unless he liked you."

Hart welcomed her words, and his anxiety melted away. "That is nice of you to say. But you don't know me that well yet." He was hoping his sarcasm would find its way through the awkward conversation to elicit a laugh, but Clara only gave him a crooked-mouth smile. But the thought nagged at him: Hutchens did like him, *right*?

They made plans to meet in the lobby at seven before taking a car over to the Shard. As they passed through the revolving doors and through the lobby, Clara arched an eyebrow and grabbed his arm.

"Maybe I actually know you better than you think I do. Because I think you always mean well and want to please people. Clearly bad at packing for business trips, but a good man."

Hart took a long shower, letting the hot water run over his face as he imagined the night to come. He was anxious to meet Igor, to put a face to the name he'd heard several times, from Renard, Clara, and even Hutchens.

He shaved and then answered the soft knock on the door to find his pressed tuxedo delivered by a bellhop. He threw it on, tucking Renard's envelope into the inside pocket, and made his way down to the lobby, where he parked himself on a plush chair. It was, however, difficult to sit, because the envelope inside his jacket was digging into his ribs. He guessed there was thick-stacked paper inside, but it was sealed, and he wasn't about to open it. He hoped the awkward delivery that he had been recruited for would soon be over. Finding Igor and giving him whatever Renard so casually asked of him was the evening's first priority.

He was about to check his watch when he sensed the hush that had fallen over the lobby. He glanced across the expansive space and felt his heart skip a beat. Her hourglass silhouette glided across the tiled floor, the click of her heels echoing across the lobby as time stood still and hotel guests watched with intrigue. She wore a silk emerald-green dress with a V-neckline that elegantly plunged to display a silver necklace with a lone diamond heart. The floor-length dress had a slit that ran midway up her left thigh, showing off her smooth skin. Hart's eyes followed the slit down her legs to her black patent leather shoes. She was wrapped in a black cashmere shawl that fell across her shoulders, and she held a silver clutch, with her dark hair held back by a silver brooch with a green jewel that matched her dress.

Hart stood as a cloud of silence remained over the lobby, all attention given to his company for the evening, who stared at him as she made her way.

"*Bonsoir.*" Hart buttoned his tuxedo, momentarily at a loss for words as he met her eyes, shaded a dark green. "You look.. *Tu es très belle.*" The words were all he could muster, spoken slowly and deliberately in her native tongue.

Clara had a temptress' smile. Her perfume was sweet, the smell of vanilla, peach, and a hint of cinnamon. She was everything he wished for at that moment. Everything he desired. He had no idea which way the evening would go, but he knew he would have difficulty taking his eyes off her.

"May I say that your perfume is absolutely fantastic?"

Hart saw a hint of color in her face, hidden beneath her smooth and glowing olive skin.

"*Merci,*" she said. "It's called Bouquet de la Reine."

He offered his arm. "Certainly, fit for a queen."

They made their way outside, where Clara requested the doorman hail a taxi. Hart and Clara exchanged looks.

"We are going to a charity event where they want to raise as much money as they can. If we show up in a limousine or Mercedes, the vultures will be out, knowing we have money to spend, but if we arrive in a taxi, then we are much more discreet. Trust me, this is a necessity. Otherwise, people will try and get money out of us all night —and not only for charity." She winked at Hart.

The taxi cruised to London Bridge, heading across the Thames, watched by the towering presence of the Shard. Night had descended on London, a darkness that was short-lived, its streets made bright by light flooding from restaurants, hotels, apartments, and streetlights, giving the city an eternal glow.

At Clara's request, the taxi pulled to a stop a block short of the hotel.

"Why show up in a taxi if you can show up walking?" she said in a conspiratorial tone as Hart paid the driver.

They entered the expansive lobby of the Shard, a smattering of tuxedos and long dresses breezing up a small set of stairs towards the elevators. Clara and Hart trekked up the maroon-carpeted stairs, Clara's high heels and tight dress impeding their quick progress. Hart offered his hand, but Clara ignored it, instead insisting on navigating the stairs alone. He was about to comment on her stubbornness when he felt a thick hand clamp onto his shoulder. The large, meaty hand firmly moved him away, and a man made his way past, reaching his hand out in front of Clara.

The man was stocky and square-faced, with jet-black hair brushed straight back, shining as much as his patent leather dress shoes.

"Miss, could I lend you a hand?" He wore a black, double-breasted tuxedo with a silver bow tie, a thick watch, and a big grin.

Clara looked up, startled for a moment, and looked at Hart, before turning her attention to the man.

"Oh, Igor. *Bonsoir.*" Clara grabbed his hand as he helped her up the steps. "*Merci.* Such a gentleman."

Hart stood rigid. This was Igor. The man in Clara's planner; the man whom the envelope was for; the man who'd introduced Renard to Hutchens.

Hart looked him over. He was wearing a dapper suit, had a broad smile, and friendly hands on Clara as he said hello. Hart's fight-or-flight instinct kicked in, and immediately he didn't like him. *He is a threat, so treat him as such.*

"Igor, this is Paul. I've brought him along for the evening," Clara said, registering Hart's apprehension. "Igor manages some of our assets here in London." She smiled awkwardly as she saw both men facing off. Hart had not finished climbing the stairs and stood well below Igor.

Hart thought about taking the last two stairs, but Igor held out his hand.

"Paul. Pleasure to meet you," he said as he bent down slightly and gave Hart three firm pumps of his handshake, nearly pulling him up the last stairs.

"Pleasure." Hart attempted to equal the brute strength of the grip, his jaw grinding with effort as he strained to stand his ground.

"Paul is in Europe for a few days and he—"

"I'm familiar," Igor interrupted. "He's American. And I do believe that he has something for me."

Igor calmly clasped his hands in front of his body, waiting like a teacher for an unruly classroom to quiet down.

Hart stole a glance at Clara. Her eyes darted at him with a mix of anger and betrayal. Hart shifted his weight from one foot to the other as he reached into his coat pocket. He pulled the letter-sized envelope from his tuxedo and handed it over. Igor approvingly nodded with a grin and stuck it inside his coat pocket without opening it. Clara's eyes were still transfixed by Hart, as if she was waiting for an explanation.

Igor clapped his hands. "Thank you, Paul. It was nice of you to bring that all this way. Shall we go upstairs? There are plenty of cocktails, and then after dinner the real fun starts with the auction."

Igor once again held out his hand for Clara, an invitation to escort her the short distance to the elevator. Clara and Igor discussed the weather in Paris, Renard, and the train ride, while Hart felt his stomach tighten, realizing he'd have this man to contend with. Was it a task he was up for? He started thinking of possible ways to get out of the evening. After dinner, a bit tired, he could call a cab and return to the hotel—after all, they were in different rooms—or he could say he had to make an important phone call. He thought of several more reasons to leave on the thirty-second elevator ride up to the Shangri-La ballroom, but he'd made his mind up.

Damn it, Hart thought. He certainly had his work cut out, but he'd stay.

22

London

The elevator doors opened to the thirty-fourth floor. A golden carpet with blue textile patterns stretched down the hallway, and the walls were lined with colorful abstract paintings. The thirty-fourth floor was actually two stories combined, taking up the thirty-fifth level of the building as well. The two-storied windows stretched from floor to ceiling, framing the buildings of Canary Wharf, its lights sparkling from across the river. The grand room was populated with more than a hundred attendees. Men were dressed in black tuxedos, a few bold enough to wear white jackets, while the women wore dresses that flirtatiously revealed a bit of skin and expensive taste.

Hart found the view across the Thames of London mesmerizing as the beautiful people mingled. Every shade of red evening dress was being worn— crimsons, clarets, cinnamons, and scarlets sprinkled the room. There were yellows, midnight blues, and timeless black dresses. The guests were all nursing a flute of champagne or whiskey tumblers—necessary social lubricants in Hart's experience.

Igor pointed to bartenders in vests and bow ties mixing drinks with vigor. "There is a bar located on that wall. If you could excuse me, I must leave for a moment, but grab a drink and I will come find you. Thank you again for coming."

And with that, Igor bowed his head and blended into the sea of tuxedos and loud conversation.

Hart watched him leave. The man's stride was assured as he squeezed through the crowd towards the other side of the room. Clara, not wasting any time, gave Hart a look to explain himself. Out of anything to say, he merely avoided her eyes.

"*Alors*, what was in the envelope?" she demanded, turning to face him squarely.

Hart shrugged. "Renard asked me to give it to Igor. I thought he might have told you."

He offered a weak defense, but it was simply the unexciting truth. Clara appeared satisfied by his answer for the moment, and they started navigating their way through the partygoers towards the bar. Hart offered his elbow to Clara, who seemed not to notice, while swiveling her hips to avoid bumping anyone in the crowded room.

Clara ordered a freshly poured glass of Veuve Clicquot Yellow Label champagne, pointing to an unopened bottle sitting in an ice bucket. This was to the bemusement of the barman, who passive-aggressively eyed the several glasses sitting on the bar for the guests to take.

Hart surveyed the bar as Clara watched the barman open the fresh bottle. Drinking at social business events was a tightrope: have too many drinks, and something embarrassing was bound to happen. Don't have enough to drink, and you appeared too conservative and not nearly as fun to your companions for the evening. Hart knew he had the rest of the night and next day to think about as well. The dinner was to be served with wine, and of course champagne would come later. The problem wasn't the amount he'd drink but rather that he would be drinking several types of alcohol on an empty stomach. He hadn't eaten since the train ride. Seemingly lost in a daze, the barman attempted to ask him what he'd like a second time and moved directly into Hart's vision.

"Johnnie Platinum, please."

"On the rocks, sir?" The tone of English condescension from the barman was delivered with the smoothness of a compliment.

"Neat. Of course."

Hart smiled politely, victorious in his second small battle of the evening. His first one, the handshake with Igor, did not go so well. Something about him—the charm, the touching of Clara, the bravado he showed leading them into the party and taking off to attend to others—left him feeling uneasy. Perhaps even jealous.

Clara sipped her champagne and surveyed the room, the air filled with a mixture of strong perfume and chatter.

Hart leaned against the bar and turned to Clara. "So, I never asked. How did we get invited to this?"

He felt Clara watching the guests as well; they were like two wolves eyeing their prey from a safe distance.

"I thought by now you would have surely known. He is your good friend, after all." Her voice was dry with disdain.

Hart scoffed. "Igor? This was the first time I met him."

"But Renard gave you the envelope to deliver."

Her eyebrow raised, and she stared contemptuously before taking a sip from her flute. Hart was taken aback by her sudden directness and consulted his glass of scotch for a moment to play out the forthcoming conversation in his mind. He had always found it necessary to have something in a conversation to offer as a distraction. Whether it was a water bottle or pen and paper, it usually came in handy. He was glad this time it was something as strong as scotch.

"I am sorry. I was just doing what Renard asked. I didn't think anything of it." Hart took a swig. "I hope I haven't upset you, because trust me, that wasn't my intention." He delivered his apology as genuinely as he could, anticipating that would be the end of it.

Clara had become cold since his interaction with Igor. Was she upset that Renard hadn't asked her to deliver the envelope? Or was it simply that she was upset with Hart for not telling her? Regardless of what he was missing, he thought it best to apologize.

Her face was pensive for a moment. "Did you know what was in the envelope? Asked Renard perhaps?" Her voice was calm once again, with the tone of casual cocktail conversation, while her eyes were trying to read an answer from his.

"I didn't. He just called me before we left and requested I take it. I didn't stop to think about it." His stomach tightened at the prospect of upsetting Clara more than she already was.

"I need to go to the ladies' room. I will be back in a few minutes." Hart watched her weave through the crowd and out of sight. He pushed from against the bar, looking for a private spot to drink his scotch in peace until Clara returned. The prospect of networking with the other guests wasn't appealing. He made to hide by the far window. He wasn't sure how he messed up but was certain he'd done something to upset her. He swayed away his nerves and gazed across the river at the view of London, notably St. Paul's Cathedral.

Sipping his scotch, Hart meant to plan out his next steps. Soon he'd be leaving Europe, heading back to New York City, away from Clara and the privileged career he never thought he'd have—the travel, the elegance, the high stakes. He felt optimistic for the first time in a long while; the trip could turn it all around with the right partnership between Calhoun and Renard, but at the same time he wasn't motivated by them; rather, it was her.

"Beautiful view, isn't it?" The voice came from over Hart's shoulder. He turned around to face Igor.

"Certainly is." Hart took another sip to add a touch of frost and turned back towards the window.

"The view is so good, the hotel can charge whatever they'd like for the space, and no one in London would blink."

"It's fortuitous we're both in banking, isn't it?" Hart remarked, and took another sip.

Igor raised his glass of champagne to toast. After a sip, Igor grunted with pleasure, then marveled at the glass in his hand as both men stared at the London skyline.

"You know, when my firm booked this hotel for tonight's gala, I was put in charge of budgeting. But if you have to ask the price at a place like this, you definitely can't afford it." Igor waved his hands around and continued. "But I don't think like that. I'm a banker. I know the importance of the real cost of things. After all, only a few hundred dollars can change the world!"

Igor stopped to take another sip, and so did Hart, anxious not to continue the small talk. What if Clara was watching him? Hart searched around, but her dark hair and emerald dress were nowhere to be seen.

"So, I set up a meeting at this hotel to pick out the champagne, wine, all of it. Help my company ensure this it is a great event, because we are raising money for charity, right? So, the beverage price list gets to me, and I see how much they are charging for these drinks! It is outrageous; I'm talking eight times the normal price. So, I ask them why there is such a huge difference between prices. I even compare them to fine restaurants that don't cost half as much. Do you know what they told me?" Igor's face lifted up, his square chin pointing at Hart, the cold gray eyes watching him closely.

"I don't know. What did they tell you?" Hart volleyed back to Igor.

Igor grunted again, took a quick sip from his glass, and found the passing tray of a waiter, placing his empty glass upon it without grabbing a new one.

"They said, 'Sir, how is the view of London and the River Thames at your local grocery? The prices of the drinks are marked up due to the experience and ambience.' Can you believe that? You have to love capitalism. We can screw anyone we want as long as there is cash to be made." He took a step closer to Hart and placed a meaty hand on his shoulder and leaned in so that only the two of them could hear. "We do enough evil every day in our jobs, eh? Tonight, let's do some good and raise some money. Never forget, those that have the money are the ones in control." Igor gave Hart a pat on the shoulder and a wink, turned, and drifted into the sea of people.

Hart watched him walk away, still contemplating the strangeness of the conversation, when he saw Clara on the staircase, staring in his direction. She had been watching him, but for how long? She made her way down after their lingering eye contact.

Hart held up his empty scotch glass. "I need a refill. Care to join me?"

"*Oui*. Seems like you needed it, judging by the look on your face." Her tone was flat, but she wore a look of consternation. "What were you both talking about?"

"He was explaining to me the price of capitalism," Hart deadpanned.

He studied Clara's face. Her smooth cheeks had a new glow from her rose-colored blush, presumably from the recent ladies'-room visit. Her eyes were greener, accentuated by her dress. He was lost in her eyes, which regarded him with a certain apprehension.

Clara led the way back to the bar. She seemed distressed by his talking to Igor and subsequent lack of detail about their conversation. Maybe she had something to hide with Igor. Hart pondered this but pushed it aside. His attention was now solely on enjoying her company. He would pay Igor further attention later.

Hart began to feel at ease as the party wore on. The warm scotch in his empty stomach certainly played a role, but he felt confident, as one should in a two-thousand-dollar Burberry tuxedo. They stayed near the bar after finishing their drinks and ordered a third round, still champagne for her and scotch for him.

People came and went ordering a variety of drinks—white wine, champagne, scotch, bourbon, and even a few apple Martinis. Clara kept a close eye on the guests as they came up to order, nodding politely to a few acquaintances.

The buzz of conversation in the room and the background noise of soft piano music could not drown out the silence between them. Clara bid her time by sipping from her flute, while Hart found her difficult to engage. He could only assume it had to do with Igor.

"Is there something wrong? Did I do something? Because if you're upset that I spoke with Igor, he approached me and—"

Clara held her hand out palm down, like she was reaching for a pair of cards on a table. "Paul, please. Everything's fine. I think sometimes these types of parties overwhelm me." Her face was crestfallen. She peered down at her dress, then back up towards him, a pleading look in her eyes begging him to leave the conversation where it was.

Hart was quiet for a moment, but his compulsion to know what was wrong overruled his better judgment. "What do you mean? Overwhelmed by the people or...?" He let the words linger in the air.

She let out a deep, exasperated breath, her eyes drifting off somewhere else, seemingly lost deep in the far corners of her mind. She opened her mouth as if she was about to speak but closed it. She took another sip of champagne and started again.

"Have you ever felt that by your environment, your luck, you've somehow lost who you thought you would be? That you've become a victim of your own circumstances? Doing things for others, beliefs you didn't share but now you do because you have to live them?" She stopped herself. "It's deep conversation for a cocktail party, but it's on my mind."

Hart hadn't seen this coming. Why was she so melancholy? Clara did her best to put on a brave face, smiling as her lips twitched in revolt at their betrayal of her true feelings.

"Finish your drink. Dinner is going to start soon," she said while looking off in another direction.

Hart nodded, slammed the rest of his scotch back, feeling sorry to waste such a thing, and set the glass on the bar. *You're going to need it,* he thought, following Clara into the adjacent dining room and licking his wounds.

23

London

The length of the evening was measured by glasses of champagne, which came steadily, one after another. Dinner was served as conversations grew into lighthearted debates, helped along by the gaiety of charitable feelings and wine. The cocktail reception had ended when the guests shuffled into the large rectangular dining room, its walls a clementine color, with gold crown molding and a striking glass chandelier that ran nearly the length of the room. The chandelier's crystals hung like icicles, capturing the light, reflecting it onto the walls, giving off a burst of orange glow. White chairs were arranged, along with a lectern and a projection screen, at the far end of the room, where the auction would take place. Photos of items scrolled on the projection screen while the guests ate flaky beef wellingtons and buttery Dover soles, deboned at the tableside by waiters in white tuxedo jackets.

Hart was seated next to Clara, with two other couples at their six-person table. The couple on Hart's left was older, and Scottish, Hart surmised by their accents when introduced. The MacMahons both had long silver hair and fierce appetites. Hart never did see the bread basket return once it'd been passed.

On Clara's right sat a younger-looking couple, the Cornwalls. Clara had politely incorporated Hart, introducing Josh and his wife, Anna, by way of telling Hart that Josh was in the construction business. The four of them chatted about the evening, London, and the challenge of managing Josh's booming business, which he glowingly said he was on the verge of selling. The Cornwalls' first child was starting elementary school, and they seemed intent on enjoying a rare evening out, having secured a hotel room after the auction.

The bidding was to begin after dessert, which included the English classic strawberries and cream, or traditional French patisserie from L'Eclair de Genie, in Paris. Bids began not long after the spoons had stopped clinking. The first item was a private safari in Botswana. Hart was particularly impressed by the winning bid of a cool million dollars for a Lake Como twelve-bedroom house for a week, including use of a Bombardier private jet for transportation. Numbered paddles, spread out through the dining room, fought gallantly against one another, as the coy bidders never made eye contact with each another.

Clara's mood gradually improved—thanks to the good food and easy conversation at the table, Hart suspected. She would comment about a bid and snicker to the Cornwalls and Hart, drawing a few disapproving glares from other guests, which Clara met with casual indifference. The drinks had done their job, Hart thought. The night began to flow as smoothly as the champagne.

The auctioneer banged his gavel for the room's attention as the final items came up. The man was older, lanky, with thin, side-swept white hair, long earlobes and a tuxedo that once fit him when he was younger and fuller. He had a whimsical English accent that demanded a quiet room. The projection screen flashed to a picture of a white château with blue windowsills surrounded by green vineyards. The slide changed to a wooden crate labeled "Château Angélus" and flanked by two double magnum bottles of Château Latour.

Hart felt Clara shift upright in her chair, straining to see the projection. She grabbed the numbered paddle that lay on top of her clutch on the table. As if she sensed Hart's eyes on her, she glanced sideways at him.

"Renard gave me instructions to win this item at any price. He's a wine connoisseur," Clara said to Hart. It seemed more like a set of instructions to remind herself.

The auctioneer cleared his throat and dabbed his forehead with a white handkerchief. "This auction is of exceptional wine from Bordeaux, including a case of Château Latour, 1961 vintage from the beautiful Pauillac region. The second is a case of 1982 Château Angélus from the formidable Saint-Émilion terroir, and finally, two 1998 magnums from Château Palmer, of Margaux. The bidding will begin at sixty thousand pounds and progress in five-thousand-pound increments."

At the bang of the gavel, several numbered paddles went up.

Clara sat with her hands across her lap. Her numbered paddle was held so tight that Hart could see her knuckles turn white. When the price reached a hundred thousand pounds, only three paddles were rising. Clara raised hers to call at one hundred and five thousand pounds, entering the contest against a Chinese man wearing a gleaming white tuxedo jacket and Prada sunglasses, who was continuously on his cell phone, and a mysterious paddle towards the front that Hart could not see from his vantage point.

"Do I have one hundred fifteen thousand? Remember, folks, this is for charity and a tax write-off." The auctioneer's wide mouth smiled in glee at the laughing room.

He eyed his audience and announced the asking price several times over. The phone conversation between the Chinese man and, presumably, his wine consultant or disapproving spouse grew more contentious. His face turned red and he tossed his phone on his table and raised his paddle.

Hart heard Clara breathing heavily as she raised her paddle. The other bidder, whose paddle was out of Hart's view, would raise whenever the bidding slowed. The amount gradually crawled upwards, with each number soliciting a shocked murmuring reaction from the room.

"Can I have one hundred and sixty thousand pounds bid? This is for charity and a wonderful investment in wine."

The auctioneer began dabbing at the perspiration on his forehead with a white handkerchief. The Chinese man had dropped out. Clara raised her paddle against the paddle in the front row, a constant volleying. The murmuring grew to audible gasps as the bidding climbed just short of two hundred thousand pounds. Hart watched Clara as her chest rose and fell with every labored breath. The bids continued until they finally reached two hundred thousand pounds.

A final effort to squeeze out more money was made for two hundred and two thousand pounds, and the auctioneer banged the gavel with great enthusiasm.

"Sold! To the beautiful woman towards the back! Thank you. That concludes the live auction."

The crowd gave a gracious round of applause and looked inquisitively for Clara. Hart sat stone-faced in a state of shock at how much money Renard had spent. *Win it no matter what.* He placed a hand on Clara's shoulder and whispered that she did great. She smiled, but he caught her lip gently twitching.

Guests rose and began mingling as soon as the gavel had declared the auction over. Clara was swarmed with questions, but Hart didn't mind losing her to conversations. Out of a burning curiosity, he wanted to find the loser, the paddle from the front row. Guests filtered through the tables towards the doors and the awaiting open bar, the highlight of the evening apparently past. Clara was saying her goodbyes to the Cornwalls at their table, but Hart couldn't resist the urge to see who had bid against her so aggressively.

He made towards the front, but only five steps before someone grabbed him by the shoulder. Hart felt a tug to encourage him to stop. He turned and found himself face-to-face with Igor.

"Wild auction, wasn't it? I'm thrilled we raised so much for charity." Igor's gray eyes were sharp, in contrast to his jovial words and forced smile.

"Great event. If you'll excuse me, I'm quite curious to see who was bidding against Clara. I'd like to see the face of the competition." Hart gave a curt nod. He was happy to have an excuse to leave and turned towards the front of the room.

Igor put his hand out and grabbed Hart's upper arm. Hart glared back over his shoulder at Igor. He wasn't fond of being manhandled and it was becoming a habit. Their eyes met, a flash of anger and recognition from both. Igor's eyes narrowed, then relaxed, before he let go of Hart's arm. Igor attempted to play off the awkward encounter with a smile as he smacked Hart's back.

"I was the bidder! I love wine and might as well make Renard pay much more than market price for charity."

He looked around to see if anyone was overhearing them, then winked at Hart.

Hart felt his pulse race. It only made him feel more justified in his animosity towards Igor. He had no doubt that Igor made plenty of money, but enough to spend two hundred thousand pounds on wine? Unlikely. And if he was doing it to raise more money or simply cost Renard more, it seemed superficial. He couldn't say what, but something about Igor wasn't right: the way he carried himself with his politician's smile and constant arm grabbing. Hart decided to play along. Clara seemed to be finishing up her conversations, and Hart caught her staring at him.

"So, how long have you known Clara?" Hart asked, shifting his attention back towards his newfound adversary.

Igor's eyes drifted across the room towards Clara. He pursed his lips and hummed while he thought. "A few years. I worked with her former boss quite a bit, Monsieur Bichot. But Clara is a wonderful woman." His gaze lingered on her. "Truly remarkable. I've enjoyed getting to know her. She can be quite"—he raised his eyebrows—"pleasurable company."

Igor stood still, his barrel chest stuck out like a proud stallion. Hart's face hardened. Igor wasn't dull—Hart had to give him that. He seemed like a man who knew how to inflict pain and doubt, even in the simplest of ways.

Clara started towards the two men, locked in a standoff between predator and their knowing prey. They both felt Clara's presence and relaxed to feign enjoyment of each other's company. Igor gave her a kiss on the check to congratulate her on winning. He seemed about to leave but caught Clara and Hart's table guests, the Cornwalls, passing on their way out of the room.

Igor put out an arm to stop them. "Josh, nice to see you! I thought I told you to spend your money!"

They smiled and exchanged pleasantries. Igor drew from his coat pocket the envelope Hart had given him earlier. He tore it open, revealing a thick stack of tickets in a rubber band. Igor thumbed out two and held them out to Josh Cornwall.

"Here, compliments of Mr. Hart: two tickets for Thursday's World Cup qualifier match at Wembley. Josh, I think your young boy would love a game with his dad. It's a nice way to celebrate your new deal." Igor smiled, then winked at Hart.

Clara gazed disbelievingly at Hart and swiveled to watch Josh take the tickets from Igor with a big smile. He then shook Hart's hand. "Cheers, mate, that's very kind of you. We can talk more at the game. Have to run. Our room awaits!"

And the couple took off.

Before anyone could muster up a question, Igor gave a wave goodbye and made for the door.

"What the hell was that? You brought tickets for Igor?" Clara's faced was strewn with confusion.

Hart shook his head in disbelief. "No, that envelope was what Renard wanted me to give him. I don't understand. I didn't have any clue what was in it."

Clara opened her mouth but closed it, as if having thought better of speaking. Hart blew the situation off as a mere slight by Igor. He couldn't have denied the tickets were his, seeming foolish. But why did Igor lie about it? Probably to create the exact discomfort that currently reigned between him and Clara.

He decided to change the topic.

"Feeling good about your win for Renard?" Hart asked.

"Relieved. He was rude about it. Told me if I didn't win I shouldn't bother returning to work," Clara retorted, clearly upset.

Sensing the conclusion to the evening approaching, Hart suggested they head to the bar for a drink.

"It has been a long day. I'd rather go back to the hotel," Clara replied, her face sullen, and looking lost in her thoughts. "It has been a night of surprises, and now I need to think."

24

London

The taxi ride back was quiet, other than Clara occasionally drumming her fingers on her clutch, spread across her lap, as she stared out the window.

At the hotel, the two of them had made their way in silence towards the elevators, then to their separate rooms. Clara's face was soft with a melancholy indifference that she hid with a good-night smile.

Deciding to end the struggle that had become their evening, Hart was swift.

"Thank you for the invitation tonight. You looked absolutely beautiful." He thought about moving in for the traditional good-night *bise* but felt it was out of place. Even more so was his foolish idea of trying to kiss her. The evening for them had its moments, but it seemed their fleeting chance at romance had left, along with her real smile. She stood holding her clutch against her shimmering emerald dress, in stark contrast to her demeanor since the end of the auction.

"*Merci*. Good night, Paul."

She made her way down the hall at a sober pace, the carpet quieting her escape from him and whatever had consumed her. Hart couldn't help but feel that the last chance of hope, of her being his reason to stay in Europe, had vanished before him. He entered his room, glanced at the minibar, but thought better of it.

He sat at his desk. The room was dark, since he hadn't bothered turning the lights on. Hart's laptop flickered to life and illuminated his corner of the room in a white glow. He began opening up emails. The first was Hutchens' standard inquisitive type.

There was a knock on his door. He sat still, not sure who it could be. The knock came again, with more urgency this time. Hart rose and, disregarding the peephole, opened the door.

A tall bellhop held out a large envelope. The man wore a black suit, gray vest, and black top hat, complete with a silver Savoy Hotel name tag that read "David."

"Package for you, Mr. Hart. Dropped off several minutes after you arrived back."

"Cheers," Hart said, immediately regretting trying to use the British phrase.

Hart dug into his pocket and pulled out a pound, and with a tip of the cap the bellhop left.

Hart closed the door. The realization set in that he was disappointed. Who had he expected? Did he believe Clara would come running to him like a damsel in distress? *Grow up, Paul,* he told himself.

He returned to the desk, opened the envelope, and found a smaller one inside with his name written on the front and a Post-it note attached that read "Please enjoy." The envelope contained two tickets for the football match at Wembley on Thursday afternoon. The tickets were box seats under the name of Hart's firm, Calhoun Capital. He tossed the tickets on the desk. Utterly confused, he felt betrayed by Renard. Had he misled him on purpose, or was this some misunderstanding? Igor had said the tickets were from Hart, but it made no sense. He didn't buy them, nor did Hutchens. Something wasn't right, and while he had played along with everyone's requests, the fact that Igor was involved soured his willingness to consent to everything. In fact, Hart decided that something must be done. He fired off an email to his associate Charles Roberts asking for background on Igor's firm and, in addition, if any of Roberts' contacts in European banking could share any intelligence on the man. It might be foolish, but Hart wanted to justify his dislike for the man.

The phone in his room rang, one loud shrill that caused Hart to flinch. He sat still in silence and darkness as he stared at it, wondering if maybe the front desk was trying to reach him. The phone didn't ring again, and he gave it no further thought.

He buried his head in his hands and tried to control the building resentment he had for Igor. It didn't help, he realized, that his feelings for Clara were clouding his harsh judgment of the man, but there seemed more to it. He knew something wasn't right.

There were two firm knocks on the door. Hart figured the phone ringing must have foreshadowed another delivery. He headed towards the door and swung it open, his eyes down, hoping the second delivery wouldn't cost him another tip.

He saw bare feet and looked up. Clara stood with her hands on her hips, the same emerald-green dress pooling on the carpet in the absence of her high heels. Her eyes glistened, soft and wet, as if she had been on the verge of tears but none had fallen. She lifted her chin, which had been resting on her chest.

She started to speak, a small sound, barely audible. She shifted her weight from one foot to the other before starting again.

"Invite me in?"

Hart stood in the doorway, bewildered, before he managed, "Please," and moved aside.

She walked in apprehensively, as if wading into a cool sea. He softly closed the door, as if her visit was a secret. Clara looked at the bed on her left, appeared to change her mind, and headed to the window and the padded bench under it. She took a seat and tucked her knees to the side.

Hart flipped on the small entryway light, allowing a sliver of light into the bedroom. He walked to the desk and closed his laptop.

Clara smiled and spoke, in contrast to her mood earlier in the evening. "How about a drink?"

"What sounds good?"

"Champagne."

"What are we celebrating?" Hart inquired with curiosity.

"Then a vodka, but mix it with something sweet."

Hart rummaged through the well-stocked and expensive minibar, finding a half bottle of Grey Goose and Schweppes orange soda. He grabbed two glasses, placed a few ice cubes in each, and mixed the drinks.

They sat and talked, Clara fiddling with her hair, pulling strands that had become loose and curling them around her finger. She unceremoniously asked him why he hadn't told her about the tickets for Igor. He shrugged and said he truly didn't know. She nodded, which appeared to end her line of questioning.

They began chatting about London, the conversation naturally veering towards how easy it was to travel about Europe—you could simply hop on a quick flight or a train to get nearly anywhere—which led to discussing which other places they'd each like to visit. They seemed to share wanderlust.

Hart didn't know why she'd come to see him but thought maybe she wanted to take her mind off something—and that was fine by him. He was living on borrowed time, not knowing how many more conversations they'd have. As their conversation carried on, every word to him was a bonus, a chance to steal another memory. They swapped stories of their younger days, what she was like, and where they thought they'd be.

"I always wanted to be a schoolteacher, teaching children new things every day. Children can be good at whatever they'd like almost, and that fascinates me. But not older children; only age twelve or younger. They seem less worn from the ways of the world." Clara focused on the ceiling, as if stuck in a daydream, living the life she thought she'd have. Her arm rested on the bench as she propped her head up, absentmindedly shaking her now-empty glass, the ice clinking softly.

"I think you'd make a fabulous teacher. You seem to do very well with children. See how well you've taken care of me." Hart grinned, and Clara laughed, the first time she had since dinner.

"And what about you, Monsieur Hart? Do you really enjoy what you do? You always wanted to be a banker? Traveling the globe, making money, impressing vain men, and convincing them you can make them even more money." She held out her glass.

He laughed. "You make it sound quite mischievous." He poured her another drink, unscientifically mixing the vodka and soda. "There are moments when I enjoy my job, but not for the reasons you've said. I like the traveling much more than any deals, but this really is my first business trip." He took a sip from the vodka, its bite cut by the sweetness of the orange soda, which was too sweet for him, but he drank it anyway. "My parents were tax attorneys. A fine profession, but I think they always wanted more. They could never break out from their own path; just year after year of the same."

He paused and studied the light dancing on the walls from the streetlamps while he took several pulls on his drink, and he felt Clara's eyes heavy on him. He shook his head. "I don't really know, honestly. Some days I just don't know what happened. I kind of fell into this job, never asked for it, and it was given to me, so I feel obligated to prove my worth. It's fine, but I don't have what it takes to be successful. I guess it's the vodka talking, but I always wanted freedom, something bigger than myself. I don't know what career that would ever be, but I love the feeling of waking up in a new city with the smell of espresso in the morning. That feeling I get in my chest when I know deep down I need quiet time in my life. The kind of quiet you can only get from a shady terrace with a great view, or a cool wind on a hot day at a lonely beach. Those things to me are truly living. That's what I'd love to do every day." He smiled and shrugged.

Clara made a clicking sound with her tongue. "*Oh,* là là, a capitalist with a conscience." She raised herself up so she was sitting on the bench. "*Entre chien et loup.*" Her voice grew soft.

Hart heard the French but couldn't place the translation. "What was that?"

Clara brushed a strand of hair behind her ear. "It's a French idiom. We love using them. It means between dog and wolf. It's used for the time before the sun is fully set, when it isn't day or night. But what it really means is something that can't be described. That is kind of how I think about you."

He finished his drink and set it on the desk. "Maybe that's a fair assessment."

Her eyes were soft and sympathetic. "But we shouldn't let the regret of not being who we thought we would be stop us from becoming who we are." She finished her drink and rose. "I should be going."

Hart stood as she passed by him close enough that he could smell her perfume. She stopped and turned, her eyes searching the room as if her words were written on the walls. She was just within reach, and their eyes met. She gave him a knowing look and then closed her eyes. He reached for her waist and pulled her close, her arms around his waist. Her body was smooth, warm underneath the silk dress.

Hart gently lifted her chin. They kissed, her lips fuller and softer than he imagined. His hands worked from her sides up her back as he pulled her tighter, and she responded in kind. Their pace was cautious at first, hands gently exploring. Hers found their way up his chest and around his back. She paused as Hart placed his hand lightly on her cheek, their foreheads resting together. Their breathing was shallow and fast. Hart gasped for air as he felt her heart pound against his chest. He held her still for a moment.

"I haven't been able to stop thinking about you since I met you. You are everything." It was as much an admission to himself as it was a thought to be shared with her.

"Don't say that," she whispered.

"I only tell the truth."

She moved her mouth up to meet his once more, at a more fevered pace. He could feel her pulling him as they shuffled towards the bed. His hands found the zipper on the back of her dress. They fell onto the bed, her dress slipping upwards as he lay on top of her. Their kissing didn't cease as he worked his hand gently from her back, across her full breasts and tight stomach, past her thigh. His hand slid down to the bottom of her silk dress until he felt her warm and smooth skin. He felt her shudder as he worked his way up underneath her dress and back the way it came. She ran her fingers through his hair, pulling him in closer.

25

London

Early-morning fog hung in the air and blanketed the small wharf. It encompassed everything, the cold air fighting the moist ground, old enemies sworn to battles since the dawn of time. The morning fog held a grayish light, fitting for the mundane work that lay ahead.

Igor pulled his jacket collar tighter to combat the damp cold. The ground was frosted, and the grass crunched under his boots as he made his way towards the river. The docks were quiet early in the morning, mostly because fishermen didn't use this small bay, but rather a small number of boating aficionados—and on this particular morning, like some mornings past, Igor.

The sun was an hour from fully rising, but a soft orange glow came from the east over the river, lighting up the thick clouds that hung in the sky. In the distance to his left, much further down and across the river, Igor could see the high-rises and bustle of Canary Wharf.

He made his way from the flat parking lot where his car sat, separated from the water by only some thirty yards of grass. The wharf was surrounded by weathered brick apartment buildings, battered by time and the spray of the water, a certain yellow tinge clinging to them.

When Igor reached the river, he noticed it ran smooth. Only small splashes could be heard when a ripple hit the cement sidewalls of the yacht basin. Igor surveyed the river and at first could hardly see the yellow running lights of the boat as it silently idled towards Igor. The boat cut its motor, swung around in a wide, lazy about-to, and pulled up next to the cement wall where Igor stood watching.

"Morning," said the man Igor had come to know only as Charlie.

He slid the silent, twenty-three-foot Century Center Console boat closer to the wall. He tossed a rope, and Igor secured it to a light post, strong enough, with its steel welding and stubborn age, to stop the boat from drifting away. This was their third time working together. The first two times were tests to see how far the courier would go and for what price.

"Easy sailing?" Igor feigned interest, blankly staring at his expensive courier.

"Water was smooth all the way from Corringham. Got these three boxes today from the port, eh? The usual one just isn't cutting it anymore. Needed three this time?" Charlie asked, and grinned, revealing crooked teeth that were dark and yellow with age and too much booze. His skin was a weathered brown thanks to years spent on the river—over sixty, he'd once told Igor. The sun peeked from behind the horizon, shining off the water onto Charlie's gray beard.

Igor wanted their transaction over with quickly and ignored the inquiry.

"You can just unload the three here and I'll take care of them." He paused and studied the two-by-three-foot-high wooden crates that bobbed on the bow of the boat.

"Aye, they're quite heavy, mate."

Charlie lifted a box, the strain visible on his face.

Igor grabbed the box from him and set it down on land. The boat rocked back and forth, its load lightened.

"You know," Charlie started while he scratched his silver beard, "I've been having a think. I might just open one of these boxes and have me a bottle. You know, giving myself a lil' bonus." A broad, crooked smile spread across his face as he looked at Igor and chuckled.

Igor ignored the man once again and waved his hand for the next box. He didn't have time for small talk. He needed to bring the boxes all the way to Borough Market by car and drop them off.

"You know, I was asking myself, why do you have the wine brought here? I could bring the boat closer to the market. You maybe live over here? That'd account for the early mornings we have, eh?" Charlie took off his dirty cap and used his jacket sleeve to clear the sweat from his face.

"Well, don't ask yourself," Igor growled. "Off-load the crates, and if you're out of here in another five minutes, I'll toss you twenty quid." Igor turned around and glanced towards the vacant parking lot.

"Nah, I got to find me a corner shop. Need some food and a shitter. I'll be on the water all day, ya know, and this'll probably be the only time I'm tied up." Charlie pointed absentmindedly to the rope that hung slack from the short light post. "So, if ya don't mind—and hell if you do—but I'll just be running into town quick."

Igor did mind. No matter how small or trivial the situation, he hated to be told what to do.

"Sure, old man. Let's go with the last crate. You can be off, and I'll load these up."

Igor grabbed the wooden wine crate on the ground; it was much heavier than the previous deliveries, because they didn't have the same contents. He made towards the car, careful not to drop the awkwardly heavy crate. The grass, still slightly frosted, crunched under his feet as he trudged along, leaning backward to counterbalance the weight. He eyed the black Citroën he had called his own for several days now, bought for cash in the East End, and for which he'd overpaid too.

The trunk popped open with a metallic clink, and the newly added weight caused the rear suspension to let out a painful squeak. Igor pushed the crate far enough against the side of the trunk so that the two others could fit in. The crates had taken a beating thanks to their various ports of call—three to be exact—starting in Bordeaux, on the Gironde River, then up the Atlantic coast of France to La Rochelle, then Jersey before they passed through the English Channel and slipped past the white cliffs of Dover before eventually reaching the Thames and Igor.

Igor pushed with his full body weight to ensure the crate was wedged deep in the trunk as the car pitched to and fro. He turned around to see Charlie struggling mightily with a crate, laboring across the frozen grass. He could hear the clinking of the contents inside.

"Put that down! I'll get it," he said tersely, his face red with anger. Igor tried not to raise his voice so early in the morning; he did not want to attract unwanted attention.

Charlie's slender old frame strained with the weight. He leaned further backward as the crate and gravity took hold. Igor hurried towards him and closed the distance between them in seconds.

"Give me that."

Igor grabbed the top and bottom of the crate, while Charlie clung to the sides as if it were a life raft in the middle of the sea.

Both men were determined to get their way. Charlie finally relented and gave a push of frustration that sent all the weight of the crate to Igor, who wasn't expecting it. Spinning with the momentum, Igor was taken to his right and downward, and the corner of the box met the hard ground. There was a thud and a crack as the wooden box splintered.

Igor had caught himself with his hand, and he steadied himself on the ground. He stood and scowled at Charlie, who'd been too helpful for his own good.

Charlie's face was still, his mouth agape, as he stared past Igor towards the cracked crate. Igor turned slowly and saw that it had split diagonally from the corner, revealing its contents. There were several bottles of red wine, with white labels and red foil covering the cork, packed tightly with brown paper. Amongst the wine, several broken bottles revealed wads of cash, neatly rolled and held in place by rubber bands. Between the bottles was a black metallic object that caught a glint of sunlight. A gun, recognizable by the trigger and hammer protruding from the box, had commanded Charlie's attention.

Igor spun, his eyes narrowed as he stared at Charlie. He could see the color drain from the old man's face. A realization appeared to hit Charlie like a tidal wave, sending him hurtling towards the harsh reality that he was most certainly in danger. He blinked in disbelief. He'd transported not only wine but also money and weapons for a man who paid in cash and insisted on discretion. He never had reason to mistrust him, but by the look on Charlie's face, Igor realized how foolish his courier felt. The arrangement was simple enough: transport crates of wine up the Thames for a shop so they could sell a few bottles and promote the incoming shipment before the rest of the product arrived. He'd run worse things up the river before. During over fifty years spent on the water, he'd seen a good deal and carried God knows what.

Charlie made eye contact with Igor, who appeared calmer.

"Listen, I-I-I didn't see nothing, I'm-I'm..." Charlie began, stammering.

Igor held his hand up and shook his head. "Let's just get this in the trunk, eh?"

He held Charlie's wide-eyed gaze and he could feel the old man's fear. Igor collected the crate as best he could, holding the splintered sides together, and marched towards the car. He put the crate on the ground as Charlie followed like a scolded puppy.

Igor took a look around the wharf. It was still early enough that no one was out, the sun not yet fully risen behind the skyline of London. Igor noticed there were no lights on in the windows of the apartments surrounding the wharf.

"Could you lean in the trunk and just make sure that crate is pushed to the side? Need to make sure these three all fit." Igor pointed in the trunk as Charlie nodded and shuffled his feet across the asphalt. He bent at the waist and leaned into the trunk.

Igor pulled his coat up and grabbed the Walther PPK tucked into his jeans. It required one long motion thanks to the extra four inches the silencer added to the short-nosed pistol. He raised it to the back of the old man's head. The gun spat.

Charlie would have never known what happened to him. It would have been as if someone switched off the lights as the bullet entered the back of his head and left a small dot on his forehead. He lay slumped on his stomach, his legs sagging on the ground, as he hung from the back of the trunk.

The legs were heavier than Igor imagined they'd be, partly due to Charlie's waterproof boots. Igor lifted him into the trunk and closed the lid. There were several things he needed to do to buy time. Charlie had been a casualty of trying too hard. *No good deed goes unpunished.*

His main thought now was hiding the boat and the body well enough so that they would not be found until the next day at the earliest. He needed that time or the entire plan would be spoiled, just like it would have been if he let the old man live; he had seen too much.

Igor tucked the PPK back into his waistband and made his way towards the boat, where the last crate was. It would be an easy drop-off at the market, and he'd make contact with Nasir later to explain how to pick the crates up. He would need them, or their plan wouldn't work.

The seagulls had woken with the first break of daylight, their chorus of shrieks announcing to the world a new day had begun as they flew above the bay. The wind picked up, carrying water from off the river, hitting Igor in the face as he marched to the boat. He pulled his jacket collar up tight and put his head down; there was going to be a storm.

26

London

Hart woke up to the sound of heavy rain beating on the windows. His eyes fluttered open to watch the old glass take the pounding rain without a problem, as it had for decades, protecting guests from the English weather.

He rolled over and was greeted by an empty bed, covers halfway down. For a moment, he thought he'd dreamed the night before, a passionate and unbelievable dream, but then he saw the Savoy Hotel stationery on the pillow.

Breakfast when you wake. Bisou, Clara

Hart held the thick notepaper and smiled, replaying the night before in his mind, content to let the memory float around and grow more vivid. He lay still for a time, a strange concoction of contentment and anxiety washing over him.

He showered, put on a pair of chinos and a sweater, then checked his emails. It wasn't until he had read the reply from Roberts that he remembered the football tickets. He shook his head in disbelief. His trip was more of a vacation every day. No auditors or government regulatory agencies watching everything he did, or boss barking orders with the self-confidence of a man who knew he was in charge and liked it.

Hart studied Roberts' email, a lengthy response to his Igor inquiry with two documents attached. Roberts had evidently done a tremendous amount of research on the mysterious Igor.

Paul, hope that you're working hard in London. I'm sure you are... at a pub. Did some research for you and didn't find much, which made me curious. All I found were the documents attached, but this is pretty unusual for a banker. Exposure is usually a good thing.

Anyway, I hope you don't mind, but I had a friend who can be helpful in delicate situations take a look. Turns out Igor is well connected socially as well as financially around London. His company has stakes in numerous companies operating across different countries in the European Union. I've added a list of a few companies that my contact suggested looking further into. Happy hunting.

Hart opened the first attachment and read the small Riverbed Capital description copied from its website. There was Igor's name with no picture, and a short biography, detailing his time at Oxford and how he went through the ranks of firms in London, then became a partner at Riverbed.

Hart had hoped his suspicions would subside, countered by information, but Roberts' email only left him feeling alarmed. He knew Roberts had reached out to a good friend at an international bank, the type where everyone who was someone had money parked there.

He paced the room and rubbed his face. He found himself rationalizing that Igor had to be vetted to protect his own client, Renard. Hart didn't want Calhoun's client, the one he earned more business from, thus saving his career, to be in bed with the wrong people. But maybe, Hart thought, it was just personal.

Hart bent over the desk and opened the second email attachment and saw a list of company names that Igor was associated with via Riverbed Capital or his personal dealings. The names of the majority shareholder, addresses, and business types were listed in neat columns. He scanned the list for no reason other than to look. What for? He didn't know.

He was anxious to head out the door to see Clara for breakfast and began to shut the laptop when he saw a familiar name that rang a distant bell. Whatever he had seen disappeared as quickly as it had flashed before his eyes.

He put his finger on the screen, going line by line, until his memory sparked again. Jean Luc Bichot, Paris, France. Could this be the same Jean Luc that Clara had worked for? He felt his pulse race.

The company listed to his name was Vin Merchants LLC, with an address in London. Hart Google-Mapped it to find that Vin Merchants conducted business in Borough Market. He took a photo of the address as he heard a knock on his door. Hart closed his laptop and made his way to the door, where he paused a moment to brush a hand through his hair. He opened it. The smile Clara gave him as soon as he saw her conveyed everything he needed to know. Her eyes sparkled with the look of a woman who was content and confident, causing his heart to skip a beat. He knew the night before hadn't been a mistake, because they both had wanted it, and there were no regrets the next day.

She had on a dark-blue cardigan over a bright-white oxford shirt, complete with small oval-hooped red earrings that matched her penny loafers.

She kissed him gently on the lips. "*On y va?*"

"Yes. Let's go." His hand found the small of her back as they made towards the elevator and breakfast.

They were seated in the hotel dining room, with black-and-white-checkered tile surrounding the oval bar. A few guests ate quietly, the atmosphere subdued on the rainy morning.

Hart stole a glance at Clara every few moments, looking up from his plate to be greeted by a knowing smile and flirtatious wink. He felt full of energy, unlike before. He had found what he wanted and was content, until he remembered the tickets.

"I meant to bring this up earlier," he began between small bites of toast as he pecked away at his breakfast. "That last night with all the, uh, commotion." He looked up at Clara, who gave a soft smile. Hart cleared his throat. "I forgot to mention that a package was delivered. There were two tickets for us from Igor. We've been invited to the match tomorrow afternoon." He looked up at Clara. Her face gave nothing away.

She spooned up a bite of her yogurt parfait. "I thought you bought those tickets."

Hart was quiet for a moment and set his fork down. "I think it's a miscommunication. I did bring them, as per Renard's request, but I never bought them. I don't know. We might as well go."

Clara nodded. "*Mais pourquoi pas?* Why not? We could use today to relax and tell your boss we're working. Then tomorrow we go back to Paris after the match." She shrugged.

Hart nodded happily, since she'd been keen to stay. However, he silently cursed as his thoughts swirled around Igor and the information about Clara's former boss. Did she know? Was there something more unsaid about Jean Luc? He remembered their first lunch conversation, Clara telling him the story of her boss running away with his mistress and money. Did Clara know more than she let on? Perhaps she didn't even know he had a business in London, or that Igor was even somehow connected with it. Maybe it was bad information; after all, he wasn't a foolproof source but rather a friend of a friend doing research off the books.

Hart's mind was alert and fresh, but his face betrayed consternation as he caught Clara studying him. She knew when something was amiss. *Women always know*, Hart reminded himself.

He bought himself a moment to regroup as Clara watched him. He began to cut his sunny-side-up eggs into more manageable bites. He figured that if he were to tell her about his baseless suspicions about Jean Luc, a man he'd never met before, he'd come off as paranoid. On the other hand, if he were to say nothing, the gap between them would widen, with both people knowing something was being left unsaid.

They ate in silence for a time. Hart consulted his coffee often to match the slower eating pace of Clara. He looked around the room and desperately tried to think of a way to stop his mind from focusing on Igor. On the table was a half-folded copy of the *Guardian*. Small print at the corner read "Perfect winter getaways—See Section G2."

"So, I'm curious," he started, aware of Clara's tension. "Outside of work travel, where do you like to go on holiday?"

Clara wore a puzzled look. She glanced at the newspaper on the table.

"I don't get to travel as much as I'd like—too many cities and not enough beaches. But there are a few places I love to go."

"Such as?" Hart asked.

She grinned. "Well, when I was a young girl, my grandfather had a small fishing home on the Noirmoutier, a small island off the coast of France in the Atlantic."

As she spoke, her eyes grew softer. "This is not an ordinary island. In fact, when I was a young girl there wasn't even a bridge to cross the water. The only way to get there was by boat or to wait for low tide, which revealed a cobbled road called Passage du Gois.

"I loved waiting with my grandfather in his old Renault to cross. Families would drive onto the road that was still covered with shallow water and hunt for seashells amongst other things left behind in the sand by the moving tides." She stopped for a moment and took a sip of her orange juice. She cleared her throat; her voice was straining with emotion. "My grandfather was a fisherman, but only in retirement. He lived on the island all year. Even in the winters, when all the tourists left, he would stay. He was never an artist, but as true Frenchmen do, maybe all people, he grew more philosophical with the passing of time. I still remember what he'd say to me crossing the *passage* for the last time."

She had become melancholy, and Hart regretted asking a simple question about holidays, although he realized he was learning about something dear to her. The emotion in her eyes, her swollen lips, the fondness for days gone past made her all the more attractive.

She pressed on. "He used to say, 'Clara, *belle*, the tide changes with the coming and going of the water, and it will always reveal what we need with time, like the passage to cross. Water is like time, and all things will be revealed with it. Water may rise high and seek different channels, changing directions, but eventually it will find its way out to sea. That is just like the truth; eventually, who we really are in life will be revealed. Like a path that water takes to the ocean, twisting and turning, but in the end the truth will always find its way out. Time is the ultimate truth teller.'"

Hart stared at her a moment, absorbing the enormity of her story, which held deep personal meaning to Clara. Somehow it felt like more than just a memory, as if Clara were speaking directly to him.

"Your grandfather was a wise man. A poet as well."

He smiled softly at her. She smiled back, then lowered her eyes to the table.

"When was the last time you visited there?" he asked.

She spoke with her head down towards her plate. "I haven't been back since my grandfather passed."

"It's a place I'd like to visit with you. Just hearing about it, it seems special." He reached across the table and put his hand on top of hers.

"I've found that in life, when you find something special, you do well to hold on to it."

Other than a quick twitch of her lips resembling a smile, Clara ignored the comment. "So, what are the plans, then, for today?"

Hart leaned back in his chair for a moment. "Have you ever been to Borough Market?"

27

London

Clara and Hart took a cab east towards the Shard, where they had been the previous evening. The ride was quiet, both passengers lost in their thoughts as they watched the scenery pass by. The rain had subsided late in the morning, the sun breaking through the thick gray clouds.

Clara turned towards Hart. "Any interest in walking?"

He responded with a nod.

She asked the driver to pull over just past Blackfriars Bridge, and they walked east, on the south side of the river, passing Shakespeare's Globe theater, built to look like it had been centuries ago, with fake hay-and-mud walls.

Clara walked next to Hart, hands deep in her overcoat pockets. The sun was bright, but a chill could be felt when the wind blew off the river. Hart's head swirled with the information about Jean Luc Bichot, Clara's former boss. The connection between Igor and a former employee of Renard, who left suddenly under mysterious circumstances, was too much to overlook. That, added to the newfound romance with Clara, and everything had gotten quite murky. He decided to focus on the one matter he could address immediately.

He turned towards Clara as they were passed by a group of midmorning joggers in bright neon. "Are you enjoying your morning?"

"*Oui*," she said, her face stern.

Hart nodded, but mostly to himself. He sensed she was not happy.

"Could I ask you if something was wrong?" He raised an eyebrow in anticipation of the response.

"You could."

Hart felt his chest tighten; his questioning could lead to an awkward and unpleasant day.

"So, what is wrong?" he asked as they passed a steady stream of people walking off the Millennium Bridge, a steel walking bridge.

Clara let out a deep breath. "Do you ever start something or do something that before you even begin, you know how it will end?" She looked at Hart for a moment. "Like there's no way it can be different, but then suddenly it is. Without warning, your plans are gone, and instead of things being easy they become painfully difficult."

Hart grunted in affirmation. He knew the feeling. "Specifically, you're talking about...?" His voice trailed off as his mind told him, *Us*.

"The need to change." Her words hung in the air.

He decided to let it rest rather than press her. Clara had mixed feelings over something, or maybe him, and that was a good thing, he reasoned.

They walked in silence for a time, the seagulls cawing and swooping down for bits of breakfast pastries that had been blown away from Zizzi's terrace, which looked over the waterfront. They found themselves off the river and passing through narrow cobbled alleyways until they enjoyed the intoxicating smell of Borough Market before it came into view. The voices from the market carried far, as shopkeepers peddled their goods, with aromas of strong cheese, pies, and fruits mixed with a strong mineral smell from the water used to wash away the previous day's activities. The shops spread as far as they could see, and they stood for a moment, planning where to venture first.

They entered by a Turkish stand selling kebabs and pistachio baklava that caught Clara's attention. Slowly, they strolled from booth to booth, down the rows of shops, occasionally stopping for Clara to pick or point at lavender candles and macaroons, then proceed to explain to Hart how they were French and wonderful. Hart listened carefully. He was glad the market had energized her, but he was uneasy. He constantly looked over his shoulder, just like he had days earlier when he'd found the tracking coin in his pocket. The market seemed eerie, and he half expected to see someone he recognized.

They came to a cheese shop that enticed Clara with its salty musk of Gruyère. The shop was dark and narrow, and it stretched far back to where a glass-case refrigerator protected the more delicate, softer cheeses.

Clara walked further into the store. Her shoes made thuds as she walked across the wooden floorboards until she reached the back wall. Hart followed her across the floor, which groaned under his weight.

He stood watching as Clara pointed to the middle shelf, which housed different products—lavender candles, each wrapped in purple ribbons, bottles of hand lotion, creams, and scent sticks—and picked out a small package.

"Look at what I've found," she said, holding up a bag of salt. "This is sea salt from Noirmoutier! *Sel de mer*. The best in France." Her face beamed with pride.

Hart was handed the small bag complete with a small teal ribbon tied neatly on top. There was a blue label, a picture of a small boy wearing a straw hat and holding a rake while standing in a shallow pool of water, with a sailboat behind him. Reading the label, he remembered this was the place Clara had told him about over breakfast.

"Your grandfather's home. I might have to be a tourist and buy some." He smiled as he took the bag.

Clara took the bag back and studied the label. The shopkeeper looked on from behind the counter to their left, facing the market, uninterested by her patrons.

"*Oui*, it's nice, but expensive. You could find it cheaper in France. We will look when we return?" Her imploring face left him little choice.

"Of course."

He put his hand on her back, gently guiding her in front of him and back towards the market. Hart felt Clara's shoulders relax. Her body felt warm as she led the way out. Hart was looking down while they navigated their way out of the narrow shop and nearly made her topple because she had suddenly stopped near the front of the store.

Hart figured she had spotted something. Her face was pained with confusion as she stared straight ahead.

"What's he doing here?" she said to no one in particular, frozen in place.

Hart followed her gaze and recognized the man carrying a bulky wooden crate into a wine shop. Hart's blood ran ice cold. It was Igor. He stood under the sign that read "Vin Merchants," the same shop that only hours earlier Hart had learned was owned by Jean Luc Bichot, Clara's former boss.

His mind tried to momentarily convince him that this was a coincidence, as he stood paralyzed with confusion. But there was no such thing as coincidences as far as Hart was concerned.

Hart watched Igor for a moment before checking on Clara, who had not moved. He imagined she was thinking the same thing: *Why the hell is Igor loading goods like a deliveryman?* He wore a black jacket and dark pants; certainly not work attire, and it was a Wednesday morning.

Clara looked incredulously at Hart. "You knew he was going to be here, didn't you?"

Hart, taken aback by the accusation, shook his head defensively.

"No. How would I know?" He shrugged.

Clara turned back to look at Igor. Her eyes remained fixed, observing him in the shop talking to the shopkeepers like he knew them. Polite smiles and small talk.

"Something catch your eye?" The shopkeeper in their cheese shop finally moseyed from behind the counter, inspired by their lethargic departure.

"No, we're fine," Hart threw over his shoulder at her, before moving closer to Clara and whispering, "We should move."

Clara's acceptance came in the form of a nod, her feet still cemented to the floor. Hart softly took her upper arm and moved in front of her, shielding her from the view of the wine shop and Igor. A group of passing tourists blocked most of the view, allowing them to exit the shop and turn a quick right in between two shops down a one-person-wide alley.

On the other end of the alley, there was another street full of shops, which made for an easy escape, but Hart couldn't leave without knowing what Igor was doing. Turning around, with Clara behind him, he moved back down the alley they'd come from to ensure they had not been seen. However, the tight angle blocked their view of the wine shop.

"What are we doing? Why not just go say hello to him?"

Clara seemed agitated, her harsh tone breaking through her attempts at whispering as she fought to free herself of Hart's protective hand.

"There's more to this. I'll explain it to you later."

"Later? I knew it. You know him somehow. I knew it."

Hart let out a huff of frustration. "I told you, I've never met him."

He swiveled back towards the shop and stuck his head out of the alley to catch another glimpse of Igor.

"Maybe he is dropping off the wine from the auction last night." Clara sounded more like she was trying to convince herself than anything else.

Hart remained focused on Igor, watching him grab the last box off a trolley. The crate seemed heavy, evident from Igor's backward lean and strained face.

"This is childish. Why are we avoiding him? Paul, tell me what is going on." Clara's voice was tense and demanding.

"I'm not sure who Igor is, and there's things about him that don't add up."

Clara scoffed. "So, we hide like schoolchildren? What has gotten into you?"

"You don't find it a bit odd that he is here, on a weekday, delivering goods to a wine shop?" Hart asked.

"Okay, a bit strange, but we don't know what he is doing until we ask. Let's go and see him. He is probably just returning unused cases from last night."

"No." Hart felt his face getting warm. He was tired of being second-guessed. His gut told him there was something wrong about Igor, and now he had proof. It didn't matter how trivial it was. He had proof that he was right in his conviction: Igor wasn't to be trusted.

Hart and Clara leaned out, to see Igor walking away from them down past the shops they'd originally come from. His head was down and his hands buried in his coat pockets as he glided away unnoticed.

Hart craned his neck, imploring Clara to follow. He took off at a steady pace after Igor, with Clara matching him at his side.

"What are we doing?" she asked as she strained to see Igor, some forty yards ahead of them.

"Following him to see where he goes," Hart said, his eyes not leaving Igor's back.

"His office is across the river. He'll probably take London Bridge or catch a taxi."

"Then we will see."

Igor headed south towards the river but then took a right, back towards the fresh produce area of the market. He walked between stands selling squash and heads of lettuce, navigating towards the middle of the market, where they'd just come from.

Clara touched Hart's shoulder. "Do you think he knows we are following him?"

Hart frowned. "How could he? I haven't seen him turn around yet."

"He seems like he is going in circles," Clara offered.

"That may be the idea."

Clara paused for a moment. "Well, I'm curious. We can't afford to lose him, so I'll go up ahead on the left here and you hang back. This way, if he turns left or right down an alley, I'll be even with him so that we can see where he is going when he turns. Make sense?"

Hart was impressed by her unexpected enthusiasm. "That's not a bad idea. Just don't be seen, and if you are, act—"

"Normally, like I'm surprised to see him." She nodded to herself in affirmation. "Not a problem."

"You seem like you know what you are doing..." Hart's voice trailed off as her green eyes mischievously narrowed.

Clara flipped her raincoat collar up to shield her face and took off ahead.

Hart was surprised she was eager to play along in whatever he was doing, and he wasn't so sure what his own plans were. Maybe Clara was right and there was a simple explanation, but there was only one way to find out.

Clara weaved in and out of shoppers, many carrying large bags or pushing metal folding carts, further up the street. The sweet smell of fruit hung in the air as Hart passed stands full of strawberry crates, oranges, and golden-red apples, one of which had fallen and been trampled on the ground. Hart sidestepped the destroyed fruit and continued following Clara and Igor under a low bridge that separated one part of the market from the other. The overhang was short but dark, and Hart could barely see Igor, still forty yards ahead of him, zigzagging deeper into the market.

Igor unexpectedly stopped at a stand and picked over sausages links. Hart, who had hung well back, had no problem slowing down, and slid behind a group of tourists. Clara, however, was nearly ten yards away from Igor, but on the far side of the street. She ducked into a line of people waiting for fresh potpies.

She looked back at Hart, who deliberately shook his head to signify it was not okay to move. Peering past the group he'd hid behind, Hart saw Igor on the move again. He waited a beat and set off himself, intently watching to see if Igor would turn around again, but he kept going straight ahead, to the pubs and buildings across the street from the edge of the market.

Clara spun away from the line she hid in with the grace of a ballerina exiting the stage and fell back in stride at Hart's side. They crossed Stoney Street, buffering the market and the rest of bustling Southwark, and followed Igor south towards the Thames.

The crowds thinned as they left the market. They kept their distance behind Igor as they came to a stone-arched tunnel. Igor had quickened his pace through the cold and damp tunnel and led them into a series of small streets and narrow cobbled alleys, a far departure from the shoulder-to-shoulder crowds of the market. Clara and Hart were forced to fall even further behind, but their eyes stayed fixed on him.

Igor turned right down Winchester Walk, which twisted, and doubled back the way they'd originally came. Casually, he slowed his pace, then stopped at the corner where the road met Winchester Square. He leaned up against a building on the quiet street, while Hart and Clara ducked into a doorway before Igor could turn around. Clara waited a moment and leaned her head out to watch Igor light a cigarette and nonchalantly puff away.

The street was quiet for several minutes, the only noises the voices of a few lost tourists and waitstaff out back behind a restaurant, enjoying a smoke break.

Clara spoke softly while peering out from behind the recessed doorway. "What should we do? If he comes back this way, we are in trouble, and we can't stay here all day."

"I know." Hart sighed. "I don't know. What do you think? This is so odd."

Clara was about to open her mouth to say something but stopped. She leaned closer towards Hart, who had his back against the side of the doorway, and peered around him down the street.

"A young man just walked past Igor, turned around, and the two are talking. They don't seem to know each other, but I can't be sure." She leaned back out of sight.

Hart grabbed her gently by the shoulders and maneuvered around her, switching places. The back of Igor's head was to him. He was leaning against a building, smoking, talking to a dark-skinned man with white sneakers, black jeans, a long raincoat, and a red hat. The younger-looking man was holding his hands in front of him, nodding along. Both men seemed to not quite know each other, but after a few nods, Igor stood straight up and gave the young man his pack of cigarettes. Igor leaned back against the wall as the young man looked down the road in Hart's general direction. Hart guessed they were some thirty yards from them, but he could still make out the young man's small beady black eyes.

The young man in the red hat nodded at Igor and started walking away from Hart and Clara, continuing south towards the river. Igor waited a moment, then peeled off the wall and took a narrow alleyway that was between them back towards the market, and not in the direction of Hart and Clara.

Hart raised his eyebrows towards Clara. If their adventure being detectives was to continue, they had a choice to make: split up or pick one of them to follow.

"What do you think?" Hart asked Clara, pointing, signaling the subject for debate.

"Let's follow the other one. We can't follow Igor all day," she said with conviction, and took off.

Hart followed closely behind, passing the alley Igor had gone down, but he was nowhere to be seen. Clara's pace quickened, and her footsteps echoed off the old cobblestone streets as she chased down the man in the red hat, who had rounded a corner out of their vision.

Continuing towards the Thames, they emerged from the smaller, narrow streets into an open square. The square was a building site. Apartments were being refurbished, and dumpsters and heavy machinery were scattered about, the old brick buildings surrounding them looking in dire need of repair. Clara's pace kept her ahead, until Hart lengthened his stride to catch up. They crossed the square and, at the corner, found a small underpass, wide enough for a car and some forty yards long. The underpass was dark, with dull fluorescent lights that had long ago lost their luster. At the end of the small tunnel lay a road, where a black Citroën sedan was parked. The area was noisy with the construction on top of the normal rumbles of the city and the distant sounds from the city roadways.

Hart approached the tunnel cautiously, as did Clara, who stayed a few paces behind him, careful not to tip off their prey. They hung to the right side of the wall, wary of walking in the middle of the road. Hart could see the street where the black Citroën was parked more clearly once in the tunnel.

The car had its engine and lights off, and the beige brick buildings towered above the narrow street like a valley coming into view as they moved towards the exit of the tunnel. Hart couldn't see anyone on the street, the light becoming brighter towards the end, the sun peeking out from behind the clouds and directly into their eyes.

Hart looked back to see if Clara was still following. He found her close to him, her eyes alert and cautious. He turned back around, and with no one in sight still, he felt his body relax. Their chase seemed over, their game had gotten away, and in a way Hart felt relieved. He stepped out of the tunnel into the sunlight. The warm air felt welcoming after the dark dampness of the tunnel. The light momentarily blinded his vision as his eyes fought to adjust, and Hart raised his forearm to block the sun.

His world became clearer for a moment, just before he saw sudden darkness as a thick wooden board swung towards him, striking him hard across his head. He fell on his left side, the heavy board splintering over his arm and his head as he heard Clara scream.

He didn't have time to react. His body lay twisted sideways on the ground after the first hit, pain screaming from his head. He staggered to his knee before the second blow of the board smashed across his shoulder and back, but not before he saw the flash of a red hat and beady black eyes.

Hart had just reached the outside end of the tunnel, and the man in the red hat had been waiting for him, hidden from view. Hart's world was shaking and his ears ringing as he put out his hand, grasping for Clara. He felt Clara's arms around his head, holding him, as he heard an engine turn over and the howl of tires tearing away.

28

London

The sky in London changed in the midafternoon, the sun giving way to heavy dark clouds that rolled in and blanketed the city. Rain followed, the type that washed down in waves, an unrelenting pounding. The storm had arrived.

Hart sat on the padded bench in his room by the window overlooking the park. Clara was on the bed, lying on her stomach, her legs intertwined and her chin resting on a pillow. The room was dark, lit up only by the occasional flash of lightning, casting long shadows across the walls. When they'd returned earlier from the market, Hart had taken a shower and ordered room service. He had found out early in life that when stressful situations arose, so did his appetite. He ordered a large pot of coffee and a pastry basket, complete with toast and jam.

Neither of them had spoken. Clara tended to Hart's injuries. Nothing serious. He was lucky to have been shielding his head with his arm when he was struck. Hart had felt the board cracking over him, the old wood made softer by time, having presumably lived in the elements until it had opportunistically been used as a weapon. He had a few cuts on his face and body, but nothing that required stitches. His shoulder was aching, and he had a pounding headache, but his biggest injury was simply to his pride.

He stared out the window to the green courtyard below. The rain left streaks running down the window, but he could see the gravel walkway starting to shift its shape, the stones slowly rising, overwhelmed with the amount of rain washing away onto the grass.

"I don't mind the rain," he said, the first words spoken in quite some time, facing the window. He fleetingly glanced at Clara, because he wasn't able to look at her; his body and pride were too tender for that.

Clara raised her chin slightly from her pillow. "You don't mind the rain?" Her voice was strained, betraying a mixture of cautiousness and confusion.

Hart continued without looking at her, mesmerized by the window and the sway of the trees against the rain, which began lashing sideways. "I think people curse the rain. They think it ruins their day. It's different for me. It's cozy weather. The type that makes you want to lie down with a blanket and read a book. Sleep in, watch a movie." He stopped, took a sip of his coffee, and put it back on the saucer on his lap. "The rain has always come, and always will. It's always going to be there. Nothing can change it. Why not just accept it and enjoy it? Allow yourself to actually like it."

Clara rested her head back on the pillow; she was still before letting out a deep breath. "We can't just ignore today. We need to talk about what happened."

"Talk about what?" Hart said tersely. "We walked into something that frankly I don't want any business with. It was a coincidence and foolish, nothing else to say."

Clara scoffed and sat up. "Nothing else to say? You're clearly not telling me everything."

Hart closed his eyes and told himself to focus on what the hell had happened earlier in the day. He argued with himself: How much should he divulge, and how crazy would she think he was if he told her the truth? He rubbed the bridge of his nose.

"I'm going to be blunt with you, because that's who I am, I tell the truth." He took a deep breath, trying to savor the last moment of innocence in their relationship before it was taken away by circumstance. "I didn't like Igor. Something about him didn't feel right. Everything from Renard asking me to personally deliver the envelope, to his smug black-tie auction, to his manner towards you."

"Towards me? What does that have to do with anything?" Clara raised her eyebrows as her eyes widened.

"It doesn't. Just let me finish."

Their eyes met, and silence reigned for a moment before Hart steadied his courage.

"I asked a friend for a favor, and it was not exactly an ethical one. I asked for him to look into the guy, to learn about his reputation and associations. Maybe I hid behind the fact that he is in business with Renard. But I felt compelled to do my homework because, simply, I don't like the guy. It's why I want to go to the soccer match we were invited to, and why I want to know I was right, that something about him doesn't add up."

"And so what?" Clara's voice was skeptical, as if the pieces to the puzzle were not all on the table yet.

"Well, I was given a list of businesses he is associated with and..." He paused, playing the next part of the conversation in his mind—it didn't go well, but he was already committed. "One of the businesses he was involved with"—he struggled for the words—"it was a wine shop in Borough Market, and the majority owner of that shop was Jean Luc Bichot." He moved his eyes but not his head to watch Clara's reaction. She was motionless. The room was silent for a time until Clara spoke.

"So, you lied to me." She let the words hang in the air for a moment. "You just said you wanted to visit the market at breakfast. Do you have any idea the danger you could have..." She stopped and corrected herself. "That you did put us in today? You can't go around pretending to be some American cowboy and chasing things you don't understand!" Her voice cracked with emotion, taking Hart by surprise.

"I didn't lie. I just didn't tell you because it was stupid. Now that stupidity has caused me to get smacked around and us to have more problems than we need. Let's just pretend we didn't see anything, all right?"

"That is not a possibility." She slid off the edge of the bed and stood looking at the floor as she shook her head.

Hart held up his hands. "What? I apologize for not telling you, but I didn't want you to think I had some crazy vendetta. And it was your old boss whose name I recognized. I figured it would be a sensitive subject."

"You don't understand: this isn't as simple as that."

"Then tell me what is going on. I stumbled across some information that led to me nearly getting killed. I wasn't quite expecting that to happen today." He stood with his arms held out at his sides.

"Don't be dramatic, Paul. You were never in real danger." She rolled her eyes and continued. "My old boss, Jean Luc Bichot. He didn't just run away with his mistress. He embezzled over two million euros of Monsieur Renard's money and fled."

Hart rubbed his face in shock as the words sunk in. He tried to digest the new information, his stomach tightening. "Why didn't you tell me about that type of money?"

Clara paced around the room, barefoot. "Renard never found out. He believed the story I told him about his mistress, because Bichot was a womanizer. But I found out, because Bichot confided in me. I was forced to keep quiet so Renard wouldn't find out or even suspect me of anything. I needed this job."

Hart shook his head and looked back out the window. *What the hell have I gotten myself into?*

Clara continued. "We probably shouldn't speak here. It's getting late, anyway. Let's go for a walk and get dinner."

Hart nodded, happy to end their spat. He put his head in his hands. *Really, what in the hell have I gotten myself into?*

They spent the late afternoon and early evening walking west across London towards Chelsea under a Savoy Hotel umbrella. Hyde Park was quiet in the early twilight as they made their way along the coarse gravel next to the Serpentine lake. Green-and-white-striped lawn chairs lined the path, but their usual guests were taking cover against the stormy day. The sky slowly darkened to night; the sun, not seen since morning, snuck a few last rays of daylight over the buildings.

Since leaving the hotel, Clara had been more amenable than earlier in the day. Hart had noticed she would occasionally grab for his hand and hold it for several paces, as if she were reminding herself he was there.

The walk allowed his mind to dance around thoughts that he could not get rid of. The heightened silence and ambience of the park would have set others at ease, a casual stroll with a new lover, but it made matters worse for Hart. Instead, his mind raced back to Hutchens' offer of the trip that had him running in circles to save his job, and since then his life had only been clouded by confusion and mystery.

Things were supposed to become better with new opportunity, not worse. With the difficulty of his past week, thrust into a new life he thought he wanted, the idea of complacency wasn't so terrible after all. With compliancy came routine, and with routine came consistency. Choices would rarely lead to anything exciting or terrible, but perhaps that was the appeal of it. He was too deep into the dilemma that he found himself in, caught between the expectations of both Hutchens and Renard. But perhaps more importantly, he was keenly aware of his feelings for Clara and the challenges they would bring.

Hart realized he'd made things worse; his own foolish need to prove himself right had only led to a hurt shoulder that screamed with every deep breath. The pain and the distress could be worth it, though, he reasoned. The feelings he had for Clara, while not yet a week old, certainly were there. The relationship's foundation—excitement, intrigue, and novelty—gave him hope that it could work out. That meant something to him, the hope that it could carry on.

The affair earlier in the morning, the childish idea of following someone, had led to danger and fear but had also been oddly exciting. He couldn't over-look that, could he? The situation was bathed in happenstance that couldn't be chalked up to coincidence—Clara's former boss connected to the shop, seeing Igor loading boxes, of what exactly he didn't know. The mischievous and seemingly deliberate route that Igor took them on; the young man on a street with several different exits, and their subsequent ambush were all too much to ignore.

He felt Clara stop and lean in front of his line of sight. "You are deep in thought." Her face was inquisitive, a combination of amusement and deep curiosity. "Where were you exactly?"

Hart shrugged and offered a half smile.

Clara grabbed his hand. "Are you hungry? There's a delicious little restaurant not far from here. I think it's quite cozy. Any interest?"

Hart responded with a smile. "I am always up for dinner with you."

He pushed the concerns he felt, like a pack of wolves circling around weakened prey, from his mind.

Their dinner was smooth, full of light conversation, as if both of them had erased the events of earlier in the day from their memories. They ate at a spot called Burger & Lobster, in Mayfair, a neighborhood with white townhomes and Ferraris and Range Rovers parallel-parked on the street. They split a burger and steamed lobster tail, "classed up," as Hart put it, by ordering a bottle of Laurent-Perrier champagne.

Once back at the hotel, Hart and Clara made their way to their rooms but came to a stop outside Hart's door. Clara held both his hands near his waist and kissed him softly good night, her lips salty from the french fries. She unwound herself from his arms and stepped a few feet back, letting go of his hands.

"I was worried about you today," she said.

Hart tried to laugh. "I'm fine."

"Yes, because I was there to protect you."

"I don't know if that's how it is supposed to go."

Clara hummed. "Why not?" Her green eyes lingered on him as she turned to head down the hall to her room.

He stepped forward, reached for her hand, and gently implored her to stay. She paused and looked back up to his eyes, not staying nor leaving. He brushed the back of his hand down her cheek.

"I might have some trouble getting to sleep. Maybe you could come in," Hart said.

Clara smirked and shook her head. He lifted her chin and kissed her once again while his hand opened the door and they both slipped inside.

29

Paris

Renard woke early and slid himself across the violet silk sheets to the end of the bed. His bedroom was dark, made so by the blackout curtains blocking the windows overlooking the Seventh Arrondissement and, most vividly, the Eiffel Tower. The room was quiet, which was to be expected so high up above the street. Early-morning commuters zipping across the city on their Vespas could not be heard, although he could hear soft breathing. That came from his prize won the night before, an aspiring model from the Besançon region of France. She had soft skin the color of cream, and her curled blond hair spilled out from the covers as she rolled over onto her back, her breasts swaying as Renard left the thousand-thread-count silk sheets.

He looked over his shoulder at her, the makeup she wore from the night before still clinging to her full face, her large eyes the most radiant blue he'd ever seen. She was something he had needed to clear his mind for the day that lay ahead, and she had done her job quite well - twice. He caught himself reminiscing about their evening and reprimanded himself; there were things to do today. He crept across the dark oak floors opposite the windows towards his closet, which was larger than most studio apartments in Paris. He put on a crimson silk robe and his favorite smoking slippers, and shuffled sleepily into the hallway and towards his private office.

The two-thousand-five-hundred-square-foot penthouse was modest for Paris elites, but it served his purposes. There were other homes to boast about, like the hunting estate he'd bought for several million euros, a reasonable price after staunch negotiations. The grounds and home had once been a family estate in some aristocratic family for generations and were about one hour southwest of Paris. It was perfect for chasing birds while wearing expensive Barbour coats and leather boots, only he secretly preferred quiet evenings with a glass of cognac by the large old redbrick fireplace. It was in stark contrast to his ninety-four-foot Pershing yacht, which he kept in Nice, although for tax purposes it was registered out of the Bahamas, where he'd purchased it. The yacht was usually taken with a few younger women, keen on experiencing the white-glove service of the four-man crew, which not only scrubbed the deck but cooked freshly caught seafood or scurried ashore to fetch foie gras and freshly baked baguettes.

The office in his penthouse was smaller than his office at the company headquarters, which was a fifteen-minute drive away with no traffic when he left his home at 7 a.m. every morning. He always found himself motivated by work, led by the desire to make money. The money served its purpose, bought the yachts, the homes, chauffeurs, and made women twenty years his junior fall over themselves to spend the night with him, but money itself had become less fulfilling.

There had come a point over the past years of his life when he'd reached the Mount Olympus of financial success, when it had dawned on him that he wanted more power, not wealth. Unlike most men his age and of the same net worth, he didn't want another few million, or another challenge of building another company; he wanted to leave his mark on the world, as his father had when he'd built Renard Industries. It was around that time that he met Igor.

The relationship between the two men was nefarious from the start. Renard had always been sly, playing the fool in order to put people at ease, but under the surface lurked a cunning fox. It was the trait that helped him notice discrepancies in an account allotted for entertaining clients that was operated by one of his most trusted employees, a Monsieur Jean Luc Bichot.

Renard had invited Bichot and other government officials in the agricultural finance department to a working vacation. Renard had footed most of the bill, extensively planning the event for French bureaucratic officials. They could be quite dense and stubborn behind their desks and regimented schedules, but get them out into the fresh air with the finer things in life—great food, drinks, and women—and they were much easier to conduct business with. It was always good to have friends in high places, and they certainly made Renard's life easier, with tax breaks and less oversight. The long weekend had gone well, and after the subtle twisting of arms, Renard Industries was the winner of a government contract to facilitate the cultivation of new agricultural equipment that would be heavily subsidized.

Many weeks later, a business partner had an ethical dilemma and demanded that he pay his own way for the trip, asking how much he owed to cover his costs. Renard normally would have remained uninterested in the cost, but when a number came back much higher than he expected, his curiosity was piqued.

Renard had personally requested to look at the invoices and ensuing payments to make sure they weren't doubled. But the accountants had added up the payments and numbers correctly. Renard scrutinized the names of the payees, finding three payments of just over fifty thousand euros made to a holding company based out of the United Kingdom. A quick search on the internet identified the company as the parent company of a liquor distributor. Renard had wondered if a few too many bottles of Romanée-Conti had been purchased. Thus, started the secret inquiry into Bichot, who oversaw the entertainment expenses account.

Renard, with his suspicions stirred, set about keeping a watchful eye on the approver on the account, Bichot, who signed off on every expense. He enlisted the help of a younger assistant in the department, a beautiful creature by the name of Clara Nouvelle. She was ambitious and in close proximity to Bichot, which made for the perfect insurance policy. Her weekly reports on her boss' meetings, initiatives, and habits were compelling reading for Renard. It seemed that his chief government consultant had a penchant for visiting London.

Renard summoned an audit team to his office and gave them strict rules, zero context, and specific instructions to verify every transaction out of Bichot's expense account for the year, particularly transactions made in and around London.

What they discovered was staggering and nearly unexplainable.

Bichot had been traveling to London regularly, under the guise of attending dozens of meetings with agricultural ministers and trade representative to look at different ways of conducting business post-Brexit. However, Renard learned, only a few meetings were actually attended, and the rest of Bichot's time was evidently used to embezzle funds.

Renard asked that a quiet internal audit be conducted, and he found nine hundred and twenty thousand euros missing from the account. Further research found the transactions were related to different banks, paid to different accounts under similar names, companies related to wine and other holding companies, giving Renard the impression that something sinister was going on.

However, Renard had a plan. He traveled with Bichot to London and watched his treacherous colleague firsthand before confronting him. He felt confident that Bichot had no idea his scheme had been uncovered, so the activity continued and provided Renard an opportunity.

A discussion took place over cocktails at Duke's Hotel bar, where, fittingly, Ian Fleming, the creator of James Bond, found inspiration for the Vesper Martini. Renard fancied himself a fan of the books, more so than the films, but nevertheless decided to take Bichot there, perhaps for the theatrics. The irony of the clandestine operation was not lost on Renard as he sat at a small table in the corner of the well-lit bar as a barman in a gray vest made a tableside Polish vodka Martini.

Renard had always seen himself as smooth, deliberate, and precise, but the sheer magnetism of learning why Bichot stole from him overpowered his better nature. He barely made it past two sips of his Martini before confronting his subordinate.

The response from Bichot was apathetic, as if he had been waiting to be asked. He let out a huff, took a pull from his silver-colored liquid Martini, and looked at Renard.

"You've finally seen. Now there is someone you should meet."

It was later that same night that Renard met Igor. When Igor arrived, Bichot stood up, to the confusion of Renard, and left, leaving the two alone. Renard's confusion was only replaced by anxiety when the square-jawed, well-dressed man sat down across from him.

Renard had broken the silence first.

"So, you're the *connard* who is stealing my money."

Igor had ignored the comment with a coy smile and wave of his hand as he leaned forward so to speak softly. "Now you know, which means you can't do anything about it, because it would only damage your company. What we have done is frowned upon, but the good news for you is that this is only a taste of what I am capable of."

The audacity of the man was what Renard remembered most, blatantly admitting his transgressions and assuming he would blackmail Renard into approval. Renard bluffed, telling Igor he had already tipped off the police, but Igor just smiled and shook his head.

"Bichot was right about you. He said you were a man who would have to see for himself."

Left without much recourse, Renard went along apprehensively, if only at first to gain understanding of the operations so he could eventually spin his way out of the mess Bichot made. He realized he was putting all those years of his father's hard work building the empire at risk. Was Igor planning a setup or simply extortion? Renard's anger subsided into rationalization as Igor steadily produced profits, which made Renard feel indifferent, corroding every fiber of his being, until he no longer recognized himself. Igor had turned Jean Luc Bichot's small-time embezzling into a full-fledged fraud scheme that utilized the same vehicles of deception, amassing millions over several years.

It wasn't until after a year of working with Igor, requiring frequent weekend trips to London, or Igor visiting Paris, that Renard finally understood

Igor's goal: to change the current state of affairs in Europe. The ambitious goal made sense to Renard, and he was far enough removed from Igor that there was deniability. In fact, he felt himself becoming intrigued with the idea of the sort of peace Igor pursued. But peace wasn't to be sought after but rather won, as Igor had explained. Oftentimes, with blood. Their task wouldn't be easy, and life would become trying, but Renard saw that victory could be his legacy. That was what Renard realized he wanted, and he never knew it until he was shown the possibility. He didn't need the world to know what he did, but he needed to know he affected the world.

Europe had grown inclusive, as Igor saw it, blurring the lines of cultures and markets and, worst of all as far as he was concerned, borders. The global marketplace had been profitable for Renard, but Igor fed the ideology of isolationism to him, making the case that the United Kingdom had recognized the pitfalls of globalism. Brexit was birthed from a country swelling with immigrants, driving out the good tax-paying citizens and replacing them with, according to Igor, people that survived by crime, violence, and above all else had a lack of interest in integrating. For years, the UK had bled opportunity, as countrymen fled for the tax haven of Switzerland, the leisure of Spain, or the opportunity of Germany. Renard saw France as the sufferer of this same disease, and Igor had only shown him the symptoms. The rising production costs of his equipment, the endless need to be paying the government millions in taxes, which were used to make ends meet for people who weren't born in France. Igor had played to Renard's ego and appetite for money, but more importantly to Renard, Igor believed the two of them could change Europe's path by driving divisiveness and isolationism.

Renard didn't take his decision lightly and considered the consequences, which did give him pause, but not enough to stop Igor from charting the course of redemption to restore nationalism to more European countries. Igor had explained to Renard that there was money to be made while exploiting the fear that swept through Europe and the world. Capitalize on the fear of anything different, and then countries would want to banish it. Renard wasn't told how Igor would accomplish this, or what dark place birthed his ambitions, but when growth and higher returns were promised, he went along with it. But when he understood Igor was an idealist, not just a greedy businessman, it was too late.

Igor took it upon himself to conduct operations on behalf of refugees and immigrants who felt their assimilation wasn't being taken seriously enough by their nation-state. Igor would cultivate young men to carry out attacks, promising safety for their families and financial freedom.

But Igor started taking things too far, waging a secret war that Renard didn't have the courage or the foresight to see coming. There was an attack in Brussels, made to appear as if a massive fire swept over a low-income housing block, but really Igor had targeted the building's owner, a Belgian who ran a small manufacturing company. He was forced to close shop due to the high cost of building repairs, putting him in desperate need for liquidity. Igor managed to buy the man's company for pennies and merged it with one of Renard's businesses.

It was a war fought with violence, but also of perception and false realities. Provide enough propaganda to slander a group, Igor explained to Renard, and soon people would view their worlds through the lens that was provided to them. Their views changed, so that slow economic growth was blamed on immigrants who had taken all the jobs. Along with the immigrants— as Igor planned to demonstrate with Renard's financing—came violence. Gone was the relative safety of walking your family around a busy tourist city; every person who looked different became a threat. And in the process, he could make money for Renard and pretend everything was for his success, but Renard always felt like he was being used.

Renard tipped back in his leather office chair and reached to the counter behind his desk, dropping a Nespresso pod into the machine, which rumbled to life, as the display lit up the room. The twenty bars of pressure building up inside the machine grumbled to push espresso into the glass, steam spilling out as Renard marveled at the simple things that could be accomplished by brute force.

On his Bordeaux-colored, leather-topped desk, a Sony laptop sat closed. Renard grabbed his espresso and, with the carefulness of a child playing with their favorite toy, opened the laptop. Renard blew on his hot espresso while he dimmed the brightness of the screen, punching at the keyboard with one finger.

The Wi-Fi connected to his secure encrypted network, and he first allowed himself the indulgence to check *Le Monde* and *Le Parisien*, finding nothing of interest other than Paris Saint-Germain football news and the president's poll numbers. Next he clicked his favorites bar and was immediately brought to YouTube. Having memorized the exact title, he carefully typed the video name, ensuring his spelling was correct. A video of Ronald Reagan's "Tear down this wall" speech popped up on top of the search results. Renard clicked on it, noticing not many people had watched it since the last time he had visited the page. Scrolling down to check the number of comments, 220, he began a scroll from the most recent, looking for the specific name that would signify contact. JawsFan2007, which was Igor's user name, had left a message. *Contact made. The guest has been entertained.*

Renard decided he had to do what he had planned.

He gently opened the long, middle desk drawer by its crystal-jeweled knob and peered inside. On the left-hand side were several glass paperweights, three Montblanc fountain-pen boxes, an old-fashioned accounting calculator, and a small Smythson notebook Igor had recently given him. He scanned the drawer until he found the military-grade encrypted satellite phone, an Iridium Extreme, which had cost him nearly two thousand euros. He had only used it two other times, spending less than forty seconds on the call each time as per the instructions, just in case someone was listening. When a call was placed, via the upgraded software on the phone, thanks to a military contact the signal would bounce off of several satellites before reaching the number it had dialed.

Renard punched the number he had written down in the inside of his small black notebook with "The Devil Is in the Detail" stamped on the front leather cover in gold lettering. The satellite phone, not built for luxury but practicality, was awkward in his hands as it rang three times before a voice came on the other end of the line, managing a groggy, "Hello." The voice seemed coarse on account of a late night, or perhaps because of the early wake up. Renard had called at 7 a.m. in the morning on purpose.

"*Bonjour*, Paul. I hope you slept well. Sorry to wake you."

Renard listened to the static on the other end of the line. He heard the rustling of sheets and imagined Hart was sitting up in bed.

"Uh." Renard heard Hart clear his throat. "Good morning. What can I, um..." He coughed. "Do for you?"

"Ah, Paul, I am terribly sorry, but something urgent has come up in Paris. I must ask you to return immediately. Don't worry about the game, but I need you to make sure Clara stays for it. Very important, because our clients in London are crucial to us, and I would hate to cancel on them." Renard paused to gauge his banker's willingness to follow the directions he'd been given. After a moment of silence, which would have sufficed as Hart's opportunity to protest, he continued. "And unfortunately, you mustn't tell her exactly why you're returning. Just tell her it is for some business issue. Please for the moment don't tell her that I am the reason for your return. I fear she may become upset, jealous perhaps, that I needed your help and not hers. It will not be a problem, though. Okay?"

The silence hung in the air on the line. Renard imagined Hart shifting through the reasons for the request to go back to Paris on such short notice and his options, which were none.

"Okay. I will return to Paris as soon as I can catch a train," Hart said. "I'll check the schedule."

Renard could hear Hart turn on the tableside lamp. "No need for a train. I need you urgently, so I have sent a plane. There's a charter waiting for you at London City Airport. It is about fifteen minutes east of the city, much faster and much more convenient than Heathrow. When you land, feel free to come straight to the office. Thank you, Paul. Goodbye. And remember, discretion will be appreciated. One other thing: Would you mind sending the amount I paid at auction last night? There should be Wi-Fi on the plane, and you can send a wire transfer from my account. That would be wonderful. I'll text you the details. Goodbye."

He hung up the phone before Hart could respond and powered it off. He opened his email and wrote to Clara Nouvelle with "Urgent Business" as the subject line. The email was brief, explaining that Paul Hart was going to return to Paris immediately on urgent business. She should, however, stay and enjoy the game, since Igor invited them.

Renard leaned back in his chair and stared at the wall. The early-morning sunlight was filtering in through the edges of the blackout curtains covering the large windows. With the dull light, Renard could make out the outlines of the ornate gold frame around a dark oil painting. He rose, pressed a button on the wall, and the black shades lifted, exposing the curved architecture and beauty of the Sixteenth Arrondissement.

He drained his espresso and walked slowly around his desk. The room was submerged in early-morning light, in stark contrast to the dark mahogany wood covering his office. He had always savored the immeasurable stillness of a morning, the serene and peaceful way that moments of privacy met the rising sun, bringing on a new day. He stood in front of the oil painting, its gold frame perfectly framing the valor and bravery of hunters on horseback with swords and spears fighting with lions. It was a Ferdinand Victor Eugène Delacroix painting that had been in his collection for many years but had been lent out to the Musée D'Orsay. He lingered over the painting, studying the faces of the men, the fear in their eyes as a lion attacked, roaring with fury.

He'd often pondered the meaning of the painting, and it is why he had to own it. Some days, the lions seemed under attack, thrust into defense by invaders on horseback looking for a kill. But other days, it seemed as though the lions were the aggressors, hunting the men on horseback, the ultimate prey. Perhaps it was all a matter of perspective, but one thing that both the men and lions had in common was the knowledge that victory meant survival, and defeat meant certain death.

30

London to Paris

The Gulfstream G550 climbed higher as sleepy London and the River Thames fell away from Hart's view. The starboard-side wing tipped downwards as the jet broke through the thin layer of silver clouds that blanketed the city.

Hart sunk in the plush leather bucket seat and gripped the armrests. His forehead rested on the cool window as he looked towards darkening clouds off to the east. As the plane sped further towards Paris, Hart couldn't help but think of London and who he was leaving behind.

His goodbye with Clara had been rushed and awkward. He'd knocked on her door, bag by his side and coat on. She'd answered in her white hotel robe, hair wet, and her face flushed from the hot shower needed after their vigorous evening before. They stood in the doorway of her room, one staying and one leaving, the symbolism not lost on Hart, evident by the sick feeling he had had.

The two of them hid behind the roles they played, ignoring the feelings they shared. Hart could tell how she felt the moment she needed to look away, if only to compose herself. Leaving Clara had caused his throat to tighten with sadness and uncertainty. Was it goodbye? Would he see her again before he left for New York? Her eyes had betrayed that she knew too well what the casual goodbye could mean. He was burdened by the guilt of giving Clara his vague reason to leave, as per Renard's request to be discreet, but as he flew away he realized he was more troubled by their unclear future.

Hart didn't know what was ahead for them, just that when he was with her, he felt like he was soaring. Was it the same for her? Or maybe Clara would simply forget about him in a few days, remembering him as an amusing fling. He thought back to the end with Veronica, how he saw it coming like a passenger in a car spinning towards a cliff. Did he feel the same? The empty and nauseous feeling in his stomach certainly felt familiar.

Hart rolled his head back into the leather seat and stared at the beige interior of the plane. The stewardess placed a double espresso on his gold cup holder. Her blond hair was tied neatly up in a bun with a short stick through the middle. The perfume she wore was faint, perhaps left over from the night before. Hart politely nodded, too tired and uneasy for small talk.

"Would you care for some breakfast?"

Hart reflected on the comfort of the Savoy dining room and eating with Clara. The heavy porcelain plates, his piled high with scrambled eggs and breakfast sausage, complete with a French press the size of a football. But that seemed far away. Instead he was sentenced to imprisonment by the five-star luxuries that took him away from her.

"What are my options?" He managed a small smile back.

"We have a few breakfast cereals, oatmeal, or there are some scones and muffins that were delivered right before we took off. I'm afraid we didn't have time to completely stock them up at the last minute."

"Some pastries please. Thank you."

"Just a few moments. I'll warm them. Again, I'm sorry we didn't have many more options. You booked so late. We weren't expecting to fly this morning," she said in her delicate English accent.

Hart was about to correct her and say he didn't book the flight himself but played the conversation in his head and realized questions inevitably would require answers, and he only wanted to think. So instead he turned to take a sip of his espresso. It burned the tip of his tongue, and he clanked the small cup back on its saucer and cursed his impatience. He felt out of sorts, not sure of himself or his current state of affairs. The amusing thing was that no matter what circumstances he found himself in, one thing he could most assuredly count on was his appetite. Hart always welcomed the familiarity that came with one's meals.

He dug into the fresh basket of pastries, which were surprisingly tasty, and offered to share the basket with the flight attendant, who politely declined with a soft giggle. He figured it was likely the least harmful invitation she'd had while working on the jet.

With his morning lethargy combated by coffee and food, he opened his computer and logged into Renard's client portal. He read Renard's text with instructions on where to send the wire transfer and dispatched the large amount Clara had bid at auction. He was feeling more and more like Renard's errand boy.

The plane prepared for descent before Hart had even settled in. He'd finished his breakfast, had another espresso, and was about to open his iPad to read Alan Furst's *Mission to Paris*, which he'd bought because the title seemed too coincidental to pass up.

The Gulfstream dipped back under the silky cloud layer that sat over the green countryside north of Paris. Hart saw the pine trees and rolling hills with roads cut deep into the forests leading to the capital. Le Bourget Airport was the busiest private airport in all of Europe, but the landing was on time, and the plane touched down with a small squeal of the tires hitting the runway. A quick taxi to the terminal, and the stewardess asked Hart if there was anything else she could do. He couldn't think of anything other than going back to pick up Clara, but didn't say. The port-side door opened, and the stairs unfolded. Hart descended, the brisk air hitting his lungs sharply as he fought to catch his breath. He'd realized he might have to go into the terminal and find a car to get him into town, when a black Mercedes pulled up. The driver's door opened, and Maxim appeared.

"*Bonjour*, Paul. Decided the train back wasn't for you, I see," Maxim said, stone-faced.

Hart grunted. *If only he knew.* "So, where are we off to this morning?" Hart asked, trying to change the subject as he got in the back seat.

"I am to take you back to your hotel so you can change and await Monsieur Renard."

Maxim closed the trunk with a press of a button as the power-lift gate started down.

Hart scratched his chin. "Are you sure it's straight to the hotel?"

"*Oui.* Straight to the hotel, and I am to wait with you, per my instructions."

Hart let out a deep breath. "Well, I guess we better hurry up and wait, then."

The black sedan's large bi-turbo engine stirred to life as Maxim drove off the tarmac and back towards Paris.

The hotel room was exactly how he'd left it, apart from the freshly made bed. Hart threw his bag on the floor and sat on the edge of the bed, staring out over the Jardin. It was a view he hadn't gotten tired of, but somehow it felt foreign to him. It was strange, he thought, to be in the city without Clara, as if the only Paris he knew had her in it. A feeling of lethargy came over him, which he shook off by thinking of a way to keep himself busy until whatever crisis Renard had called him back for needed his attention. The wait for Renard could be short or last well into the afternoon; he had no way of knowing. Maxim told him he'd wait in the lobby, having valeted the Mercedes.

Hart went to his desk and flipped open the laptop. He sent a quick email to Hutchens. The old man didn't seem to miss him much, but he wanted to keep up appearances. He said he'd returned to Paris after a successful venture to London, leaving out that he'd flown back on a private chartered aircraft, which probably cost more than his annual salary.

He remembered that he never followed up with Roberts and thanked him for the tip that led to a sore shoulder and bruised ego. Hart logged into his personal email and sent a thank-you, saying the information was appreciated. After sending the emails and sitting in the deafening silence of the room, he decided he needed company. The pastries he had inhaled on the plane felt like a brick in his stomach, which constantly turned in his angst from being apart from Clara. He cursed himself for the lack of patience on both counts and felt he needed a strong, hot cup of coffee to jolt him back to his senses.

After taking the elevator to the lobby, he was surprised at how easy it was to pick out Maxim, who was seated in a chair against the wall, facing the revolving front doors. The chauffeur's uniform—the black suit, white shirt, and black tie—was a stark contrast against the golden-yellow paint of the lobby. He sat with his legs crossed, exposing the rubber soles of his polished shoes. He seemed startled by Hart approaching him.

"Maxim, I could use some company. Want a coffee?" Hart asked.

Maxim shrugged. "Why not?"

They made their way to the bar, which was quiet on a Thursday afternoon, as the hotel guests were shopping on Rue Saint-Honoré or milling about the *Mona Lisa*.

Hart sat on the overstuffed red plush bar stool with his elbows on the dark-brown bar top, worn by time and countless guests. The air smelled of citrus from the freshly cut lemon wedges one of the barmen was preparing.

Maxim ordered two espressos in rapid French. The bartender gave a curt nod, acknowledging the order, but proceeded to finish slicing his last lemon, tossing the neatly cut wedges into a small plastic bin. A subtle French show of force, letting the patrons know who actually was in charge. Maxim's stare lingered on the man.

"Has it been a busy few days for you with us gone? Or did you manage to get some time away?" Hart asked.

Maxim made a *phf* sound with his lips and shook his head. "I never get days off."

The bartender arrived with two small white espresso cups on matching saucers and set down a small tray between the men of packets of sugar and square chocolates. Maxim thoroughly stirred in his cube of white sugar, maneuvering the small spoon with an ease that came after years of practice. The conversation was light and generic. Talk of the weather, the best museums in Paris, the best meal one had ever eaten and where. Maxim went on at great length about a restaurant near the Canal Saint-Martin that served mini-sliders with slices of seared foie gras that melted in your mouth.

Hart was daydreaming about a classic American cheeseburger and decided he would have to swing by the Shake Shack near his office when he got back. *When will that be exactly?* The thought was pushed abruptly from his mind as his cell phone rang. It was a New York area code: Hutchens.

"Hey, boss."

"Don't 'Hey, boss' me. We have some serious shit to talk about here," Hutchens barked. "What in the hell do you think you're doing? I think it's time you came back here. You put a short on some small company, bought a luxury box for forty-five thousand dollars for a soccer match, and just cleared a wire transfer from the account? The concept is for our clients to bring us money, not go around spending it!"

Hart felt his throat tighten. "I can explain. But I'm sure it's a misunderstanding."

"The hell it is. There's no misunderstanding here, Paul. You were sent to do a simple job, and instead you've been running all over Europe wasting time and money! I want you back here immediately so I can fire you in person."

Hart was about to protest when loud murmuring in the bar caught his attention. Hart heard Maxim curse and turned to face him. He had put his open palm on his forehead, his face stricken like he was going to be sick. "*Mon Dieu.*"

The murmuring in the hotel grew as several phones from around the bar and the hotel lobby rang, buzzing and chiming at the same moment. Maxim grabbed Hart by the shoulder and stood staring at the phone, which shook in his unsteady hand.

"I'm going to have to call you later." Hart hung up on a screaming Hutchens.

"What is it?" he asked Maxim.

"There has been an attack in London," Maxim whispered, as if saying it out loud would bring its evil to where they stood.

"An attack? What kind? Where?" Hart felt his stomach turning, the black espresso mixed with fear and regret at leaving Clara.

31

London

The streets of North London were overcrowded by midmorning. The air around Wembley Stadium was filled with football fans' exuberance. England supporters, wearing the Three Lions kit, marched towards Wembley like a conquering army. The Thursday afternoon World Cup qualifier between England and Italy had woken London with gusto.

There was a soft fall breeze that carried the smell of beer and fish and chips as Josh Cornwall and his nine-year-old son, Eric, made their way past the hotels and pubs lining the closed-off streets towards the west gate of Wembley Stadium.

Josh had taken Eric at the imploring of Anna, who had been with Josh at the Riverbed Charity Gala when Igor, their wealth manager, had given them two tickets for the match—a perk of being a client. Anna told Josh to take their son, Eric, even if it meant a day off school. As she put it, "He can always learn. He can't always spend time with his father."

Being the CEO of a company on the brink of a sizable and lucrative merger required Josh to travel often and be away from his family, but he worked hard so he could provide for them. The irony was that his work allowed his family an upper-class lifestyle, living in the west of the city, but his career cost him his presence at the family dinner table—and breakfast table, for that matter.

The start of the match was approaching—there was less than forty minutes until kickoff—but Igor had requested that all his invited guests meet outside the gate twenty minutes before kickoff so they could enter together. Josh didn't know the other couples attending; he had met an American and a Frenchwoman who worked for Renard at the gala—they seemed nice enough and fairly fond of each other—but as for the guests for the match, he hoped they wouldn't mind he brought his son.

But before he worried about the attendees, there was a bit of business to attend to. Josh, still holding his son Eric's hand, scanned the surrounding area, searching. There, about thirty yards before the west gate, down the boulevard, lined with supporters, he saw what he was looking for and smiled. Eric looked up at his dad and gave a quizzical tug on his hand.

"Dad, there are so many people!" Eric said, an astonished look on his face.

"Son, we English always come out to support our boys." Josh looked down, noticing his son had no England gear on. "What do you say we go over there?" He pointed to a merchandise tent. "It isn't right that you don't have any England gear on for your first game!"

Eric's face lit up. "Dad, the scarf, that is what I want! Can I have it please?"

The excitement in his young son's voice melted Josh's heart.

They patiently waited in line. Eric bounced up and down with excitement. Josh tried to soak in the moment; it would be one of the last days of quiet before work became even more demanding. He'd been working on a deal, with the help of Igor's introductions, that would merge his company, Cornwall Limited, with several others across Northern Europe. The deal would boost the company's value tenfold, opening new markets in Russia and China, some of the hardest to break into. The deal was coming together, and he was to take it to the board of directors the following week. The merger would be the finest achievement of his career.

They made it to the cashier in fifteen minutes, and Josh had checked his watch every other minute to ensure they weren't late to meet Igor. He'd also used the time to try and remember if his son had a winter scarf and decided he didn't know. He played the scenario of coming home after the game in his head. *Darling, I bought him a scarf. You can never have too many for winter.* It was worth a shot.

"That'll be thirty pounds," said a young cashier hurriedly, sweat beading off his dark-skinned forehead as he looked past Josh, seemingly towards the long line of people.

Josh reached for his billfold, found a fifty-pound note, and handed it over. His son beamed with happiness and wrapped himself in his souvenir.

"Quite a bargain, eh?" Josh smirked, showing only the best of British sarcasm, passed down from generation to generation.

"Your twenty quid." The young cashier held out the change, ignoring the comment as he gazed past him at the line of supporters standing in long queues. Josh figured the young man was worried about the long queue of customers before the match and felt sorry for him. He squinted and read his name tag. It was a name he wasn't familiar with.

"Cheers, Nasir. Have a nice day," Josh muttered as he grabbed Eric's hand and headed for the west gate.

Nasir stared back with beady black eyes and a blank face.

It was time to find Igor before heading into the match. Josh strained his neck to see over the crowds towards the gate and lifted Eric up onto his shoulders, allowing his son a better vantage point.

Igor didn't mind the crowd but despised the drunks stumbling around. He took solace in knowing they wouldn't be missed, but he needed to focus on what was to be done. Having arrived at Wembley by Tube, as did almost everyone else that morning, he had flashed his VIP ticket and headed towards a merchandise tent. Nasir was working, looking like a fool in the bright-blue oversized jacket worn by the event staff. All staff members were screened and vouched for by their company, and he never caused a whiff of suspicion. He was, to his employer, a quiet young man making a few pounds here and there, as he had been for the past year.

Igor had gone to the tent about forty-five minutes before he was set to meet with the rest of the group and waited in line until he got to Nasir. As Igor had instructed him the day before when they met on the street outside Borough Market, he greeted him in the tent with no acknowledgment. Igor asked to purchase a sweatshirt, and Nasir grabbed the bag that sat wrapped under his cashier stand. Inside the bag were some of the contents of the wine shipment, including a 9mm Beretta and a carbon-fiber Karambit knife that reminded him of a raptor's claw. Igor had dropped off the boxes at Borough Market the day prior and instructed Nasir to go back to the market later that evening. Igor mentioned his suspicions that he was being followed that day, and after losing the couple Nasir had identified were indeed following him, he headed back to Vin Merchants and picked up his package. The shop gave Nasir the wooden crate marked "For Pick-up Only," and he took it back to his apartment to view the contents, ready to smuggle them into the event.

Igor stood by the west gate, per his instructions to Josh Cornwall and Clara Nouvelle, amongst other unimportant guests he'd invited. He wasn't concerned with the others; he only had his instructions from Renard to worry about. Igor heard the man's voice repeating in his head "Make sure Clara and Josh are both there."

He saw Josh, with his son on top of his shoulders, walking towards the gate and gave a small wave, barely raising his arm. A casualty of their plan; Igor thought nothing more of it. He had alerted Renard to the possibility of the merger, the same one he helped create. The merger gave Igor another excuse to cause terror and mayhem while making Renard money, and somewhere along the line he had started enjoying himself. It was addition by subtraction, or, in Josh's case, elimination. He wasn't Igor's first, and he wouldn't be the last.

Igor leaned against a thick cement pillar, where he could shield himself, protected from the storm that was about to be unleashed. From his position, he couldn't see Clara or the American, but he was sure they'd be on time. Nonetheless, Igor couldn't miss his chance to take out Josh, who was the main focus. In operations one has to adapt or die, and Igor didn't plan on dying just yet; the plan would proceed.

It only took a few minutes of waiting before Igor started to hear panic in the air. He peered around from his vantage point and saw police running into a crowd that had gathered around. He closed his eyes and braced for the eruption, but none came. Igor quickly scanned the crowd, his eyes searching for Josh, the specific target. Nasir wouldn't know who he was, but the attack would create enough chaos and damage that Igor could always silently finish the job.

He thought back to his late-night walk with Nasir, the terror in the young man's black eyes about giving his life to a cause he didn't truly believe in. Igor shook his head and grabbed the burner cell from inside his coat pocket. He hurriedly typed the number and without hesitation pressed "Send."

The first yells hadn't warranted Josh's attention. His subconscious slowly tried sorting out what exactly it heard and had deemed them unimportant. But it was the bloodcurdling, piercing scream that caused him to instinctively turn. Josh caught but a glimpse of the commotion in the merchandise tent where they had just been. He was uncertain as to what he was seeing. Did someone fall? Was there a fight? His attention pivoted to his right when he heard several police whistles piercing the air.

It was after the fourth whistle, when the crowd, quieted by the confusion, allowed Josh to focus on the abundant stillness. As if a veil was pulled over the crowd, time seemingly ticked slower. Josh heard a loud shout that jolted him and made his blood run cold, and people began to scream. His adrenaline kicked in, and he picked up Eric.

He watched several uniformed police officers run towards the tent. "Halt!" he heard an officer say, a mix of terror and anger in his voice. There were several gunshots. People began to run, moving in every direction to get away from the gunfire, but it was too late.

The blast was as instantaneous as it was powerful, with a blinding flash and a shock wave that smashed through the crowds. The explosion obliterated everything within a fifteen-yard radius, sending its shock wave another twenty yards, knocking over everything in its path. Several police cars and trailers parked near the gate that were blocking the road flipped over, landing on bystanders.

Shards of glass and brick fell from the stadium; the frayed and burned merchandise tent flapped in the soft breeze. Police sirens wailed across the city. Screams could be heard from both victims and the first responders, cries of fright and action. The air was smudged with thick smoke as small fires burned.

Josh Cornwall's eyes fluttered open to bright light and a piercing ringing in his ears, flooding all of his senses. Everything hurt as he tried to move from his prone position, his mind trying to make sense of what just happened. He looked over to his left, where an England scarf lay tattered and torn, no longer white. It was now stained crimson with blood. He rolled onto his back and felt the crunching of broken glass and pain as it cut through his tattered clothes. His breathing was shallow; his ribs felt like a truck had crushed them. He blinked to try to clear his vision.

He saw Igor standing above him, and Josh put out his hand to the man he knew, begging for help. He felt his eyes swell as his world flooded with pain and fear. Where was his son? Was Eric okay? He opened his mouth to speak as Igor knelt down and jabbed a sinister-looking knife into his throat. The last thing that went through Josh Cornwall's mind was, *Why?*

Igor turned under the cover of the thick smoke and headed into the stadium, ignoring the cries from the victims for help. His ears rung and his pulse raced but he wasn't hurt. The pillar he hid behind had protected him.

Nasir had been weak, Igor thought. He was glad he saw it coming. He'd only rigged up the cell phone detonator after it appeared Nasir had gotten cold feet. The triacetone triperoxide, or TATP, had been perfect and did its job. The peroxide-based explosive had the capability to be 80 percent as deadly at TNT but was much easier to smuggle in, fitting perfectly into a wine bottle. The unstable material had been packed gingerly, so that Nasir, a quiet loner, could transport it easily into the event under the cover of his job.

Terror swept over the stadium as Igor fled towards the north side to make his escape. He had hoped Josh would have been killed during the explosion, but in the end the backup plan of Nasir smuggling weapons to him did the job. He wondered about Clara. Such a shame to waste such beauty, but Renard had requested her death for reasons Igor didn't know or care about.

He found a staircase with people running for their lives and strolled out of the stadium and into the chaos on the street. The news crews would focus on the carnage, the people killed, and the police would investigate the explosives, the young man, and his motives, and Igor would be free. No one would consider why Josh was killed, his body close to the blast and so disfigured that it would take days to sort out what happened.

Igor tucked his chin into his chest and went down the street.

32

London

There were news reports about the attack within minutes of the smoke clearing. The skies over the stadium were closed, so no news helicopters flew, nor did any journalists in the immediate aftermath have their camera feeds up and running; only essential personnel had communication privileges. The Tube stations were shut down, and terrorist assault teams scrambled from their nearby, undisclosed locations.

Within a short time—sooner than veteran journalists were accustomed to—intelligence on the attack was leaked. The blast had claimed many lives, and it had been captured on many of the CCTV cameras placed around the stadium. Soon the name of the attacker spread on social media, and shortly thereafter photos circulated. One of the pictures had the caption, "If you knew this monster, please contact the tip line listed."

Pundits, eager to capitalize on their platform, took to the airwaves to denounce the European Union's immigration policies and their subsequent effects. Later that same day, demonstrations took place in Trafalgar Square, where students in support of migrants had violent clashes with the angry opposition. Some politicians called for peace, others resuscitated their calls for further immigration restrictions across Europe.

Law enforcement in the United Kingdom, namely MI5, called for every resource available as they began to pore over camera footage and evidence from the scene, and collect background information on the attacker—whom he knew, what he liked, where he went. Their investigation would produce results quickly: Nasir had been smuggled into England via a migrant camp, where he originally was detained. Days would elapse before any picture of his life in London could be put together.

The London Stock Exchange trended downwards. Some stocks were hit harder than others, while a select few, namely defense-related industries, rose. The veterans on the floor had seen worse. Usually, after a terrorist attack markets would drop 2 percent but would rebound in a relatively short amount of time.

In Paris, the police increased their presence across the city, with several vans of gendarmes parked along the Champs-Élysées. Commuters cast glances at their fellow passengers on the Metro to gauge their safety.

Igor he made his way back to his office in Canary Wharf, the streets quieter than usual. A strong breeze blew off the Thames, through the old buildings of the somber city, urging people off the already desolate streets. His mission had ostensibly ended. Only time could tell what the benefits would be, but Igor was confident that his planning would pay dividends, both literally and figuratively.

Security had been a concern at the stadium, but Igor had seen past that. There had been security sweeps, security men and women in bright-orange jackets waving wands over the incoming patrons, not knowing that the real danger was already behind them. Nasir had been working on the stadium grounds as a trusted employee with access to and from the merchandise area for almost a year. No one from security thought to look for the fox already inside the henhouse.

The damage from the explosion would not be catastrophic, nor would it warrant any immediate political changes, but it was yet another wound inflicted upon an already mangled country. When Nasir's name appeared in the papers, the general public and boisterous lawmakers would be one step closer to calling for a retreat into further isolation.

Eventually, authorities would trace the simple reason for Nasir's escape from the migrant camp; he'd lost his mother and sister, and sought to find them. Little did he know they had been dead a long time, but Igor didn't mind the lie; he exploited feelings for a living.

The West would be furious that a refugee bit the hand that fed him, and Igor would watch the further destabilization of foreign policy while making his client richer. Renard had canceled his appearance in London for the charity gala, sending Hart in his place. He'd told Igor that Hart would bring tickets to the match and requested that both Hart and Clara be invited. Igor had to admit it did seem a bit strange bringing them so close to the operation. The move was perplexing, but Renard was cunning, and Igor assumed there was a good reason.

It was later than he realized, nearly 4 p.m., when Igor climbed the narrow staircase to his South Kensington flat. He must have been enjoying his walk, a clandestine victory march through the streets of a conquered city. He grabbed his computer to browse the news. The headlines told of the devastation in London. The police said the investigation was "being treated as a terrorist incident." Yet it was so much more to Igor. Small attacks festered in people's minds, creating hatred, and from it, isolation blossomed. Countries would close borders, seizing on the fear of their citizens, dividing and weakening the same powers that once murdered his mother. Divided they would fall; he would see to that.

Igor leaned back in his chair, and Clara's green eyes floated across his mind. He wondered what happened to her, imagining her death, presumably along with the American Hart's—although he didn't have any specific instructions for him. From behind the pillar, he hadn't seen either of them, but he was sure they'd been there, as was requested.

Clara seemed like collateral damage, perhaps a love affair gone wrong or she knew too much, while the American was harder to figure out. Igor had reasoned that she was bait to lure Hart; at least, that was what he would have used her for. She was a beautiful damsel for Hart to latch on to and be eager to impress. While Renard's circle of confidants wasn't endless, Clara certainly wasn't the only person who could have held Hart's hand while he was in Europe. Igor couldn't solve the mystery of why she needed to be bait. His mind hopped around, trying to make connections. He knew he was pumped full of adrenaline and told himself he was thinking too hard.

His cell phone buzzed in his jacket pocket. The number came up as private. He answered, expecting a familiar voice.

"Yes?" Igor said, having sunk into the large couch in his living room.

"Sad day," Renard said purposefully.

"Incredibly sad." Igor checked his watch.

"I need you to come for a visit."

"I don't know if that is a good idea," Igor retorted, confused by the timing of the request. Normally, days if not weeks would go by after a plan before they connected again.

He heard a huff. "Cannot wait. We have a problem."

"What problem?" Igor could feel his temples pound.

"Our house is still in need of cleaning, and I need you for the job. There's a rat."

Igor dropped his head onto his chest and closed his eyes, trying to slow down his breathing. "I understand."

Igor hung up and checked his watch to make sure the call didn't exceed more than twenty seconds. He dropped the phone and stepped on it. His nostrils flared and his chest rose as he sat still for a moment, before rising and smashing his fists into the living room wall.

33

Paris

Maxim raced through the traffic in the Mercedes on Rue La Fayette towards
Gare du Nord. He cut the wheel hard to the right, the bi-turbo V8 engine
swallowing air as it roared, passing a truck and going into the taxi lane. He
cut off a dark-blue Volkswagen Passat cab that came within inches of where
Hart sat in the rear passenger seat. Hart watched through the windshield as
they passed a parked bus with little room to spare while running a red light,
leaving cars scattered about in the intersection.

The Mercedes skid to a stop at the three-way intersection a hundred yards
in front of Gare du Nord.

Maxim turned around to Hart and pointed at the street corner. "I'll wait
there. It's platform number four."

It had been only fifteen minutes since Hart had been sitting in the hotel
bar, nursing his third Dalmore scotch and feeling sorry for himself, when
Maxim had grabbed him by the shoulder. "She's on a train." Hart processed
the words sluggishly; not on account of the alcohol, although it didn't help,
but because he'd been expecting the worst, lost in a daze of self-pity, tortured
by the thought that he left her in danger. He felt he should have been there to
protect her after the day at the market when she protected him.

It had been nine hours since the attack, and he hadn't heard anything
from or about her. The British authorities leaked information, and news
outlets reported upwards of thirty dead and dozens wounded, but instead of
thumbing through the news on his phone, Hart had been rolling the scotch
around in his glass, watching it swirl, numbing his mind from the uncertainty
of her fate.

His first instinct was to ask Maxim if she was dead or alive, but he could
tell from the look in the man's eyes. They'd run from the bar as the barman
yelled for a room number, to which Hart didn't bother to respond.

Inside the train terminal, Hart could sense the fear and anger in the air, with travelers on edge. Armed French commandos stood outside the glass doors at the front of the station, their camouflage battlefield gear, black berets, and submachine guns in stark contrast to the City of Light. It was only normal that the rest of Europe, if not the world for that matter, would be on alert after the attack. Inside, travelers hurriedly brushed past Hart, seeking the shelter of the next hotel or heading home to warm beds and the comfort of family or friends.

Hart ran to the screens showing arrivals. He squinted to find the London St. Pancras train and read "Arrived at 8:17 p.m. on Platform 4." He hurried towards the platform, where passengers were exiting. Hart strained to see over the crowd of comatose passengers, their faces blank with exhaustion, but couldn't find her. He was desperate to see her, to hold her again. He'd told himself that just the sight of her would be enough, but he realized he needed more. Whatever was to happen between them didn't matter; the only thing he hoped for was that she was safe.

He thought he made out her dark-colored hair, tied up in a bun, in the distance. His chest began to pound as shock swept over him, numbing his hands and drying out his mouth. The numbness lingered; it was the only feeling he had apart from the need to run to her. He didn't care what happened next; she was safe and back home. He'd be damned if he was going to let the moment pass.

She exited the platform, passed the throngs of people, and lifted her head up at him. She made no move towards him; rather, her pace slowed and she stopped a few yards short of where he stood. Her face was not how he'd remembered it when he'd last seen her that morning. She had a two-inch scratch above her left cheek, a bruise on her chin, and a vertical cut in the middle of her forehead near her eyebrows. Her green eyes appeared more honey colored, like dark-golden pools, as if she'd been crying. Her somber mood contrasted with her chic khaki raincoat, with the collar turned up, but her burgundy leather tote bag slung over her shoulder was ruined by black soot. Clara played with the straps as she stood staring at Hart.

Hart was the first to move, stepping towards her and putting out his arms. "I'm so happy you're all right."

She recoiled slightly, tucked her chin to her chest, and tightened the hold on her purse. He could feel her body tense as he held her. The perfume she'd put on, with notes of citrus and lavender, clung to her. Hart breathed her in, the taste of his scotch gone, made sober by the adrenaline rush of holding her once more.

Suddenly, Clara pushed away, her eyes swollen and her lips quivering at the corners of her mouth. He didn't know what to do or say. She had had one hell of a terrible day. She looked down for a moment to compose herself, showing the strength of a woman who had no interest in being felt sorry for.

"Tell me it wasn't you." She looked up, her eyes narrowed with anguish.

"What?" Hart said.

She spoke again before he could ask what she meant. "*Non*, Paul, tell me it wasn't you. You know what I am talking about. Tell me!"

Her voice rose as she demanded answers to questions Hart didn't know. More than one passerby turned to watch.

"Clara, I don't know what you're asking me."

His patience was slipping; this was not the reunion he had expected.

She shook her head, as if the question wasn't worth asking anymore. "Where is Maxim?" Her gaze drifted past Hart and she picked out Maxim from the crowd.

"He's parked out front."

He turned, holding his hand out. She brushed past him and his hand, moving towards the exit, but craned her neck over her shoulder. "Come on, we have work to do."

They walked out of the quieting terminal and sought the embrace of the Parisian night sky.

34

Paris

The Mercedes crawled past Place de Vosges, through the narrow streets of Le Marais. Maxim pulled onto Rue de Turenne, perpendicular to the Seine, a few blocks away. The sedan straddled the curb; Maxim put it in park, peering up and down the street. He and Clara spoke in rushed French, the words coming too fast for Hart to distinguish what was said.

Clara opened her door. "Come upstairs please. We have a lot to discuss," she said to no one in particular as she got out.

Both Maxim and Hart exited at the same time. Hart was momentarily confused by the fact that Maxim was getting out, but the day had been too long to question anything. Maybe they were getting some of Clara's things so she could stay the night at his hotel. An appetizing possibility, he thought.

Hart followed her through the large steel gate, which led into an expansive concrete courtyard with a small bench and potted evergreen plants. They passed through two thick wood doors, to a spiral staircase that echoed as they climbed the four flights to Clara's apartment.

Her apartment was on the corner, looking down the *rue* towards the Seine, represented at night by a gap of darkness between the buildings. Across the river, lights from the Fifth Arrondissement flickered like fireflies in the sky. The apartment was bigger than he'd expected, judging by the surrounding neighborhood, its walls pristinely white, with a tufted yellow couch framed by two leather chairs. The wood flooring was oak, worn smooth by age and occupants. The building was quite old but refined, tuned by time, like a vintage Bordeaux. The label might be a bit tired looking, the wine a dark-plum color, but you knew it was expensive, and it would, with time, grow on you to become something loved.

Clara threw her tote on the small butcher block that doubled as her center island. A half-empty bottle of Burgundy sat on the counter near the sink. Hart could tell she hadn't had company drinking it; there was only one dirty glass, with lipstick stains, next to the bottle, the pinot noir crusted and clinging to the bottom of the glass.

He was about to take a closer look at several pictures on the fridge when Clara told him to sit down, pointing to the couch. There was a certain authority to her voice, not the welcoming tone of a host offering their guest a comfortable place. Without a word, he went over to where Maxim sat on one of the leather chairs. Hart chose the middle of the yellow couch. It was plush and sturdy, so much so that he felt he could lie down and be asleep within minutes.

The room was silent except for the faint hum of the fluorescent light in the kitchen and the zip of scooters buzzing down the streets below. He awkwardly fiddled with his pant leg. The suspicion that something was out of the ordinary was confirmed when Clara came back into the room, sat on the chair opposite, and Maxim returned her quick glance with a nod of approval.

"Paul," Clara started, her hands folded in her lap, her blue cable-knit sweater hanging loosely from her shoulder after traveling all day. "We need to be honest with you, and you need to be honest with us. You're being given this chance because—well we..." Clara stopped looking at Hart and found Maxim, who nodded again at the acknowledgment. "Well, we think you have gotten caught up in something that has escaped you. And we really must get to the bottom of it, because there is more to this than just money." Her eyes narrowed, as if she were peering into the mind of Hart.

Hart sat upright and cleared his suddenly tight throat. His gaze shifted to Clara in confusion before he turned to stare at the coffee table. He focused on the hardcover book of Van Gogh paintings, the cover, *The Starry Night*, turned at an angle decoratively in the middle of the walnut table. What was she on about? His mind fought for answers, but nothing connected.

"I have no idea what you're talking about."

His hands were outstretched in innocence. He shrugged to add conviction but couldn't help the feeling of guilt, even though he'd done nothing wrong. He turned to look at Maxim. What was he doing in Clara's apartment and as a part of this conversation? It didn't make sense. Maybe she was mad he left her that morning, but he was too.

"Paul, don't make this complicated. The situation is understandable. I may disagree with it, but I can understand why you do it. But it has spiraled out of control. Now it's gone too far." Clara brushed her hair behind her ear before continuing. "But Maxim and I can help. We can make things better for you." Clara stopped and let out a sigh as Hart's face remained blank with confusion.

Her tactic of getting him to confess to something he was completely unaware of was not working. Before he could ask what exactly he had done, Maxim spoke.

"Paul, I saw how much you care for Clara today. I find it hard to believe you would put her knowingly in danger. Help us find out who is behind these things, and we can help you before this goes too far and you're beyond help."

His accent was thick, but he spoke confidently, more like a businessman than the carefree limousine driver. Hart felt confused and knew he was becoming agitated. What was it that they thought he was involved it?

"Stop. Please stop for one moment. What the hell is going on?" He could hear his voice shaking.

Clara puffed some more air through her lips, a sign of annoyance, as she shook her head and brushed another unruly strand of hair back behind her ear. "Paul, your involvement with Renard extends beyond just managing some accounts in the US. You've been helping him here, and there, moving money behind the scenes, laundering, avoiding detection. We know he is doing it, and now with you in town, the way things have gone"—she paused for a moment to look away, her face strained and her glossy eyes betraying her true emotion—"it's evident that you have a role."

Hart felt like he'd been punched in the gut. "A role in what exactly? I am so confused. What makes you suspicious of me?"

He looked at Maxim for an ally. Maxim looked away towards the humming light of the kitchen and then at Clara, and Hart realized he was on his own.

"Paul, do you remember the story about how I got my job?" Clara had her eyebrow raised in anticipation of his recollection. "My boss—"

Hart cut her off, anxious to show he listened and had a memory to match.

"Jean Luc Bichot..." He paused, his eyebrows jutting in puzzlement, his mind quickly recalling Borough Market, the shops, Igor, the foolish pursuit, and the still-tender bruises.

She bobbed her head in response. "Very good. Yes, well, he didn't actually run away with someone and leave the job by way of stealing money. But I think you already know this. After all, that is why you asked to go to Borough Market, isn't it? Maybe you had a nice thing going with Monsieur Bichot, and next thing you knew, Igor got cut in on it. And you didn't like a piece of your pie being taken—am I close?" She turned her head ever so slightly with contempt and curiosity. The unruly strand of hair fell from behind her ear once again, and she brushed it into place and leaned back in her chair, folded her arms, and held Hart's gaze.

Things were starting to line up for Hart. The Bichot connection was puzzling, and the fact that Clara and Maxim, whatever role he played, were pressing him was because they didn't know the full truth. But what truth were they after? His patience was wearing thin, his curiosity the only thing keeping him from walking out.

"I'm not into playing games. Tell me what it is you think I've done." He pinched the bridge of his nose to compose himself. "Furthermore, I don't have to stay here and be accused of things. I'm okay finding my way back to the hotel. It isn't enjoyable being accused of something I don't understand." His face felt hot, his ears burned, and he spoke to no one in particular, looking at Clara, Maxim, and the coffee table in front of him.

"Should we tell him?" Clara asked Maxim, who gave a dismissive wave and glared at the ceiling.

Maxim stood and began pacing, the heels of his polished dress shoes thudding on the floor. He walked back and forth between the chairs and said nothing apart from making a single plea: "Please be honest with us."

Clara pulled her legs up off the floor and sat further back in her chair.

Maxim stopped and looked over Hart, seemingly less intense, shaped into a person with heavy eyes and sharp creases of fatigue along his cheeks and forehead. He loosened his black tie and undid the top button of his dress shirt, letting out a sigh of relief.

"Paul, where'd you grow up?" he asked, surprising Hart with the change of subject.

"Connecticut."

"There any farms there? In Connecticut?" He sounded out the state's name slowly, repeating how Hart had pronounced it.

"Small ones. But I didn't live on one, if that's what you're asking."

Maxim nodded in appreciation of Hart's answer. He took a pack of Gitanes from inside his jacket pocket and held them up for Clara to see. She shrugged in half-hearted confirmation that he could smoke. Hart was surprised by the exchange. It seemed as though Clara was resigned to Maxim's wishes. The small flicker of annoyance in her eyes, the same look he'd seen from her at Musée D'Orsay when he confessed he didn't know what he was doing in Paris, gave it away.

Maxim strolled to the window, opened the French shutters by turning a lever halfway, and left them slightly ajar.

"I grew up on a farm in the southeast of France, near Italy," Maxim said. "So, I was slightly honest when I told you I was from Marseille. But my family has lived on the same farm, in the same town, for as long as anyone can remember. My grandfather was born and raised in the same home, where he later raised my father, who in turn raised my two older brothers and I with the help of my mother, a beautiful woman from Corsica. My brothers never became farmers, but that is another story for another time." He took a long pull of his cigarette, its strong smoke rolling through the open window, yet it still managed to engulf the apartment with its aroma. "Our farm had sheep, a few dairy cows, chickens. It was nothing special, but it paid the bills, as you say. Generations lived there, as I said, and it was a tradition that the men were always in charge of the sheep, because that was the most dangerous job.

"We would take the sheep to pasture to the rolling hillside above our house through a small forest. Our family always had herding dogs that would nip at the heels of the sheep. These dogs were smart—always a Belgian sheepdog—bred to guard and protect sheep. They would work all day, and at night they would stay in the house, sleeping by the fireplace, or in the summer lying on the cool tiles."

Maxim tapped on his cigarette with his index finger as he held it out the window. His face was pensive, as if he were back at the farm in his mind. Hart could almost see the memories scrolling across Maxim's mind. Hart sat rigid, listening, trying to make sense of why Maxim was apparently in charge.

Maxim continued after blowing smoke out of the window. "When I was a boy, these dogs would sleep in my room. They would play with me when I was just a *gamin*. It always amazed me how docile they were with me, even with the excitement of the running and screaming of a small boy. They did their job tirelessly, and would protect the sheep fiercely, but they could be the sweetest companions any boy could ask for, obedient and gentle." Maxim took another drag and pushed the window open, peering further out down the street, blackened by night.

Hart glanced at Clara, who seemed lost in thought, unengaged by Maxim's story and uninterested in empathizing. Hart's eyes pleaded for understanding, but she ignored him and rose and went to the kitchen, returning with a small metal ashtray, which she put on the coffee table. Hart rubbed the tiredness from his eyes.

Maxim nodded at Clara with a smug smile before continuing. "My grandfather lived on the farm until he was ninety-six years old. He'd stopped working many years earlier, obviously, but he didn't want to leave the place he'd lived all his life. With our family growing, the house had become cramped, but he never wanted to leave. I loved my grandfather, but I remember how he never trusted the dogs. He used them when he worked on the farm for many years, from the early 1920s up until the war and after. But he was always suspicious of them." Maxim flicked his cigarette out of the open window, its orange glow somersaulting in the darkness. He'd lit another before it landed on the street.

"I think this was because of the wolves. There used to be many in France, but they were killed off before World War Two. Now there are none. But when my grandfather herded the sheep as a young man, the dogs were meant for protection. Their job was to guard the sheep, to keep the wolves from the flock. My grandfather used to say that even though they are dogs and live in our houses, for thousands of years they've had wolf in their blood, and that is exactly why they could protect us from them. The wolf in them comes out, ready to defend, to fight. He once told me a story of how the dogs killed a wolf that attacked the flock, and during the fight he couldn't tell what sounds came from the wolf or the dog. The true beast in the dogs was brought out because of the wolf.

"They were gentle, but when they saw a pack of wolves lurking in the woods, they transformed into something else. Something they probably didn't even know they could be. It takes a wolf to protect against a wolf. This is why my grandfather never liked the dogs; he said they were too close to wolves."

Maxim walked back to the table and put out his cigarette with several stabs in the metal ashtray that Clara had brought out. The smoldering ash glowed faintly as it lost its life, the smell rising into the room. Maxim blew the last bit of smoke from his lungs out through his nose.

"There is an expression that was used to describe you to me, and I think it is quite accurate. *Entre chien et loup*. Because, Paul, you were once a dog who got involved with wolves, and now you've ended up becoming one yourself."

35

Paris

The motor whined and then roared with the downshifting. The jet-black Yamaha motorcycle sped up as it wove through the late-evening traffic. The drivers of the small Citroëns, Renaults, and white vans, the unofficial vehicles of Paris, were oblivious to the one of many mad riders zipping through the streets. But unlike the riders of the other motorcycles and Vespas, who might be racing home to a loved one or meeting a group of friends at dinner, Igor was on a kill order.

He had arrived shortly after Clara, by a different means of transportation—a boutique private airline that specialized in discretion. The airline was expensive but practical. If they were ever asked to track down a flight manifest or cargo onboard, the airline usually had organizational problems. *Excuse us for this incredibly foolish lapse. We have misplaced our records of the flight; you know computers these days.* The one-way fare cost twice the amount of a normal private charter, but Igor didn't give a damn, because Renard would pay for it. After all, it was his request that Igor come immediately.

Once he landed, a car took him to an apartment that he rented year round in a thirty-unit building, with floor-to-ceiling bay windows. The five-floor building had been renovated and doubled as a home away from home for men who kept a mistress or two, along with several couples. The building was perfect cover, as its rich inhabitants kept to themselves, not interested in the comings and goings of others, unlike inquisitive retirees.

The apartment worked perfectly for Igor. The layout was simple: a small gray kitchen, a living room with a single sofa, along with a table with four matching chairs. The walls were bright white, painted once and never given another thought. A clock hung above the couch. Its ticking was the apartment's only noise, thanks to soundproofing, another feature Igor loved. There was one bedroom, with a queen-sized bed, although he'd never spent a night there, but the apartment had been lived in and had some secret upgrades of its own thanks to the main former tenant, a Jean Luc Bichot.

In the bedroom, beneath the wooden floorboards to the right of the headboard, if one were to stomp down hard enough a hinge would pop up slightly, revealing a shallow black safe with a silver dial. Enter the correct eight-digit sequence, and the safe revealed cash, euros, pounds, and lira, along with three new small burner phones in their plastic casings, an Italian-made Beretta pistol, a small flashlight, and two sets of keys.

When Igor had stopped by the apartment, he'd grabbed the key for the Yamaha in the garage and the Beretta. He stashed the pistol under his black leather riding jacket. It would do a messy and loud job, but there was little time for preparation. Sometimes people got in the way and had to be dealt with. Curiosity killed the cat, and it surely killed the boat captain, who saw too much. Now he was coming for Clara and Hart.

The traffic thinned considerably once Igor was inside the Third Arrondissement, where the roads shrunk to cobblestone walkways. He shifted the bike into neutral and rolled past the iron gates of closed *boulangeries*, shops, and chocolatiers. For a moment, he wondered what it would be like waking up, baking bread, selling to customers all day, and then locking the doors and heading home for the evening. A simpler life, but he scoffed at even thinking of the possibility. Not for him; he knew that and accepted it. A deceitful life was what he lived, and he had a job to do.

The address had been provided to him, but not much else. Renard had left instructions via an envelope that was waiting for him on the airplane. It was a handwritten note on thick white paper, folded several times. On it was an address, along with a four-digit number Igor assumed was the door code, the apartment number, and one line.

Your guests, both he and she, await your presence.

Igor cursed his stupidity. He should have ensured Clara and Hart were there before the attack, but instead he had his own mess to clean up. He recognized he couldn't wait a day. By then, the truth might come out, and with it, answers to questions neither Hart nor Clara knew existed. Renard had entrusted Igor with a job, and he was intent on seeing it through. The hit would have to look like a robbery gone wrong, a random burglary in a quiet neighborhood ending in senseless death, but the story would hold long enough for Igor to escape.

Hart was already over at Clara's house, probably consoling her after the painful day, Igor thought to himself as he looked up and found the street he was searching for. The small blue sign with a green frame affixed to the white stucco of the building said "Rue de Turenne." Clara's driver had dropped them both off, according to Renard, who, acting as a concerned employer, asked the driver to notify him via text when Clara was returned home.

The street was empty, apart from an old man who walked his beagle, which sniffed every inch of sidewalk before raising a leg against the wall at the furthest end of the street. There was a garbage bin on the corner of the street closest to him, its contents spilling over the sides. A yellow plastic bag overhung from the bin and lazily blew in the evening breeze. Igor grabbed it and stuffed some rumpled-up napkins and a discarded falafel wrapper in the bag, so if he were spotted in the building, he would be a man bringing home a late dinner.

He walked to the doorway, gave one final glance down the street, saw a large black Mercedes parked halfway on the sidewalk, and thought nothing of it. *Another wealthy Parisian creating their own rules.* He punched the code in and slipped into the building.

36

Paris

"I'm a what?"

Hart sat dumbfounded, glaring at Maxim. He could feel Clara's eyes sweeping over him and turned to catch her gazing at his hands. Hart's right hand was curled into a fist, the left resting on top, rubbing his thumb back and forth. She looked up at him as if she had read something written on his skin.

Maxim huffed and stood. "Paul, there isn't an easy way to say this, and you're obviously not forthcoming with us, so let's cut through the crap, shall we?"

His tone was even, but his words jolted Hart further into confusion, which his face tried to hide with little success.

Clara held her hand up for Maxim to stop. She pursed her lips and nodded, accepting what she had to do. She looked at the ceiling and then at Hart before speaking.

"Paul, I'm not just an employee of Monsieur Renard. I am currently an undercover agent for the Direction Générale de la Sécurité Intérieure, the DGSI, as part of their financial crimes unit. We've suspected Renard has been avoiding taxes through various offshore companies and pass-through accounts scattered about Europe and perhaps the United States, costing France and the European Union hundreds of millions of dollars in fraudulent tax filings."

Hart felt his throat tighten as the room began to spin. He strained to get oxygen, like he was walking into a hurricane with gale-force winds stealing the breath his lungs couldn't catch. His mouth became dry, but his eyes remained alert, darting from Clara to the floor, to Maxim, and finally back to her. She sat on the chair, her right leg tucked up under her, her other one dangling, not quite touching the floor. Hart took her in as if for the first time.

Just moments ago, she seemed so innocent and beautiful, but now Hart saw an agent on a mission—and who had lied to him.

He covered his face in disbelief as he grappled with the revelation. *Who is this woman?* His first instinct was to ask for an attorney, but before he could say the words they disappeared, chased away by the reality that he'd done nothing wrong.

His mind moved slowly, like a tractor-trailer hauling a heavy load up a steep hill, its engine straining, and when it was time to shift gears for more power, all momentum was lost as it lurched to a stop.

"You're who?" Hart retorted, the words all he could manage to spit out.

"Not just me, Maxim is too." She nodded in the direction of the man whom Hart had come to know as the driver Maxim. "He's my commanding officer."

Hart swiveled his head to Maxim, who sat, expressionless, on his chair. Because of his new title, Maxim was more menacing than he had been mere minutes ago. Hart tried to slow his breathing and not look like he'd seen a ghost, but with little success.

"What does this have to do with me?" Hart's delivery was purposeful.

Maxim smacked the coffee table with his fist and stood, causing the metal ashtray to jump in the air and land with a loud clank. His face became severe, his jaw muscles tensing. The ashtray flipped around, the metal ringing throughout the apartment, the noise barely covering Maxim's heavy breathing. He turned to walk away, stopped, and spun back towards Hart.

Maxim pointed at Hart. "We can help if you're honest with us. Tell us what you know, how long you've been helping him, and we'll make things easier for you, for your company."

Clara sat up, stretching her legs and sitting on the edge of her chair. "We've always known that Renard had help from outside his company. When Bichot left, we lost our only lead. We knew he conspired several different ways, laundering money and evading taxes, but we didn't know to what extent. What's the purpose of hiding hundreds of millions of dollars if you are already a multibillion-dollar company? We caught Bichot, giving him the option of going to jail for a long time as the sole person responsible, or pointing us in the direction of those who were and go away quietly. He gave up Renard, but the information was vague, incomplete. Before we could get the entire story or even more factual evidence, Bichot disappeared, we think killed."

Hart held up his hand for her to stop and shook his head. "You told me he ran away. Now you're telling me not only was he laundering money or whatever it was you're saying he did, but that he was killed." His eyes widened when he said the last word; the talk of murder made him feel like he'd been kicked in the gut.

Clara solemnly nodded. "We believe he was killed. He was never found, but we find it hard to believe he was skilled enough to evade us."

Hart scoffed. "So, you don't actually know if he even was killed? I am getting the impression there are a lot of accusations being thrown around on some pretty thin evidence. Because I'm a banker and met with Renard I suddenly become a suspect? I don't appreciate this. I was just doing as my company told me to do. Nothing more, nothing less."

He slumped back into the plush couch. His mind raced through his options—what he could do, where he could go—until the ugly thought raised its head again that Clara had lied to him. Neatly and professionally, from the moment he'd met her.

He hadn't realized he'd fallen for her when he saw her in the restaurant. Their conversation flowed smoothly as they drank red wine, their interest in one another genuine, and their smiles real. *Or so I thought.* Maybe he'd fallen for the woman she pretended to be.

The room began to swirl around him. *She lied.* He began to feel nauseous, as if someone had cracked an egg over his head, the broken yolk rolling down to cover his head as the numb tingling took over. He realized he was having an anxiety attack.

Being accused of criminal activities and being with people he thought he knew but didn't were the reasons for the torment he felt, but the realization that the woman he had fallen for lied to him was devastating. He'd fallen for the lie, and the newfound truth put the past in a different light, lit by the explosion of his former reality.

Hart pinched the bridge of his nose and laughed quietly, suddenly finding hilarity in his predicament. He'd been helping a man he'd met only a week ago commit tax evasion by two undercover French DGSI agents, yet his concern was that the woman he'd been falling for, and sleeping with, lied to him.

Hart shook his head. "Why bring this up tonight? What caused this sudden confrontation? And"—he held up his hand to Maxim, who opened his mouth before closing it—"why aren't we at your offices, in some kind of government building, rather than Clara's apartment?"

Hart thought he'd brought up valid points, reassuring himself that he had this all wrong and he wasn't in nearly as much trouble as alleged.

Maxim lit up with delight. "Ah, but now you've asked the right questions." He tapped his temple. "Smart, Paul. We have you here because my agent"—he tilted his head towards Clara and held his hand in her direction like a waiter offering the *plat du jour*—"managed to compromise the investigation by, how do you say, screwing the suspect?"

Clara's face flushed a shade of crimson. She uncrossed her legs and folded them over again, her right ankle on the opposite leg, unable to sit still. Hart saw her look of sadness and resignation managed to hide the flicker of anger behind her eyes.

Hart pursed his lips and chewed on the predicament they both had stumbled into. Perhaps Clara's uneasiness at times with him was explained by her career, the constant reluctant tango between desire and contempt—the feelings she showed and the job she had to do. She often seemed to dance between the two. He thought of her betrayal, the events leading up to the lie making more sense, the questioning of him at the museum, and the night at the Savoy, when she came to his room late; her anger when he'd gotten her from the train station. *Was it all a ploy?*

She stood. The strand of unruly hair once again fell down, as did her defenses, betrayed by a swift exhale and her raising her chin towards Maxim. She seemed to brush herself off, straighten her jeans, and remained standing.

"As I've said in my report, and with my years of experience, I do not believe Paul was the mastermind behind all of this but rather caught up in Renard's businesses."

Maxim's brow furrowed in disgust before he feigned surprise. "Oh, I guess this American is okay because the woman he is screwing says so." He mockingly pouted as he shrugged. "Okay, we can forget the last-minute business trip Paul took to meet with Renard with no known purpose other than gaining complete access to review all of Renard's accounts, the mysterious envelope brought to the banker in London, and the auction, which was so clearly a front, they might as well have a sign on the door. Shall I continue?"

Clara shook her head. "If his meeting with Renard was so secret, why did Renard insist he meet me beforehand?" she retorted. "Paul said that Renard gave him the envelope without any further instructions, and I was the one bidding at the auction, with the help of Igor, not Paul."

Hart could see her chest heaving with her labored breathing and for a moment felt she was protecting him, unlike she had when she lied to him.

"Well"—Maxim wagged his finger and made a *tsk-tsk-tsk* noise with his tongue—"you don't get to decide what is worth investigating. Maybe Renard was losing money somewhere and needed the mastermind to come help. Shake a few trees and see what falls out. Or maybe you and he decided to take some off the top for yourselves and run away." Maxim pointed at both Hart and Clara. "He has access to the money, and Clara, you clearly don't see his guilt, because you've accepted it and moved on. *Je sais pas.*"

Hart's fight-or-flight instinct had never been truly tested, but he felt compelled to defend not only himself but also Clara. He'd known he had always erred on the side of taking direction from others, but the injustice of seeing Clara's work and personal life being questioned fueled him with rage.

Hart stood and faced Maxim. "You better be damn careful about what the hell it is you're going to accuse us of doing. Because as far as I'm concerned"— Hart jabbed at his own chest and then towards Clara—"you're accusing both of us of some pretty bad shit. And on top of that, you've got no concrete evidence."

Clara sat still, her eyes wide, and a small trace of a smile spread across her lips as she anxiously studied Maxim.

Maxim nodded before smirking. "*Bon*, you seem to be getting a bit defensive here, so I will tell you what it is we know for certain. One, we saw you two exiting a bar quite intimately, and rather tipsy I might add, on your first evening here. I have photos that were taken from my car down the street. And your movements the following day, when you mysteriously had the day to yourself, spending lots of money shopping. We had an agent slip you a tracking device in a small euro coin, and my goodness you sure got around. It was almost as if you figured you were being tailed and tried to lose us, because you even dumped the coin in a garbage bin." Maxim rolled his eyes. "Then you spent the entire day in Renard's office poring over accounts and statements. What was that about? Not to mention your curious departure from London just before a terror attack. Odd timing? Or are you that lucky? Perhaps, but it was you who booked a private charter late last night and lied to Clara, saying Renard requested your return for urgent business, and you who delivered the tickets to the match, no? We might not have the whole picture, but we have pieces to the puzzle."

Hart finally recognized the further betrayal. Instinctively, he realized that he was a pawn in a much grander game—a real and dangerous one. So, the odd device he'd found was a clue—one that could have prevented him from being involved in the mess completely, that he missed. So much for smooth French security services, Hart thought, but then he remembered they had actually found their way into his bed, quite literally.

Hart began to panic, searching for a way out. "I think my government would love to know you had surveillance on an American citizen, because I'm assuming this wasn't something you asked permission for." Hart's eyes were intense, like a hawk that had spotted a field mouse.

Maxim shrugged. "You Americans always try to hide behind your flag, like the big, bad papa who will protect his children from mean people." He laughed.

Hart was running out of ideas. What was he missing? His anger had begun to trump logic, his thoughts made murky by confusion and anger. The connection he found between Bichot and Igor was distressing, and he'd hidden it out of fear that it would expose his unethical behavior, but it could be the card to play to prove his innocence.

He calculated the risk. If he told them of his suspicions of Igor, it could heighten their suspicions of him, as though he was passing the blame. But it also could prove he wasn't unaware of Bichot's actions, since he wanted to check out the small wine shop in Borough Market. He was, after all, assaulted, and evidently Clara had left that out of her debriefing, or they hadn't covered it yet.

Maxim continued. "You see, Monsieur Hart, you either help me, and in return I can save your girlfriend's career, and maybe even save both of you jail time, or we destroy you, Renard, and your company in a dramatic way. Would you like to cooperate? Or shall we do this the difficult way?"

"It's Igor." Hart's eyes were moving about the room as his head remained frozen in place. His eyes darted back and forth between Clara and Maxim, who had begun pacing. "And I can prove his involvement with Bichot. I have documents on my computer, but not because of my involvement. I was suspicious of Igor when Renard asked me to bring him some letter, and not Clara. Didn't like the guy and wanted to find out more. That's all."

A wide grin spread across Maxim's taut face. "Well, finally we have some cooperation. You see, Clara, I knew he was involved." His dark eyes glimmered with pride. "But you two shouldn't worry. I've already sent the report of my suspicions to the head of the DGSI financial crimes unit. I figured Hart would come around like a good old American cowboy and save the girl in deep trouble. Clara, your indiscretions have been left out of my report. But you should be ashamed, and I suggest you look for another line of work immediately."

Clara dropped her head onto her chest, unable to look at Hart or Maxim.

Hart stared at Maxim with fire in his eyes. "Clara has done nothing wrong, you arrogant prick."

"Yes, Paul, you've gotten your way with that. She'll be spared much hardship." Maxim shook his head. "But I'm afraid that you're under arrest by order of the Republic of France on conspiracy to commit tax evasion, wire fraud, and money laundering."

37

Paris

The orange lights from adjacent buildings and streetlamps spilled across the wooden floors of the apartment, giving off a fiery glow. A cool breeze entered through the open French shutters, cooling the sweat on Hart's forehead. He had only begun processing what was happening, his mind shutting down to save him the pain, the words, "You're under arrest," going off in his head as if shot out of a cannon.

He was jolted upright by someone seizing his forearm and twisting it behind his back. Maxim smirked while he clasped the cold steel handcuffs on Hart's wrists.

"You can't! You promised me you wouldn't."

Clara's body shook with a volatile mix of anger and fear. She was several feet from Hart, unable to look at him, but instead glared daggers at Maxim. Her eyes were watery, without tears, but swelled with emotion, looking at a man whom she'd clearly trusted and who'd betrayed her.

Maxim growled. "He isn't cooperating! I have the authority to hold him for further questioning. Perhaps being inside an interrogation room will restart his memory," he said, shaking Hart.

Hart swayed momentarily, but his legs gave out. He flopped back onto the couch. An inner voice pleaded his innocence, but Hart's mouth was prisoner to his confusion and fear.

Maxim lifted Hart back up. Clara stormed across the creaky old floors and stopped between Maxim and the door. She crossed her arms and spread her feet, fire in her eyes.

"Clara, out of the way. He isn't going to talk here. Look at him." Maxim pointed to Hart, who wobbled in a daze. "This is the man you're so fond of protecting? He looks like he is going to be sick. Hardly an impressive man, wouldn't you say?" Maxim scoffed and gave a quizzical look at Clara: *This is the man you're risking everything for?*

"I'll go with him," Clara said, stepping towards Hart and grabbing his arm. "You're hurting him. I'll take him."

Hart watched the two of them fighting over who got to lead him downstairs and, presumably, into the police station, where he figured there was a long night ahead of him. Paralyzed by the surreal world he found himself in, he retreated inwards, resigned to the fact that Maxim wasn't interested in the truth. He only wanted what fit his agenda, to pin everything on the profit-seeking American.

Clara threw her arms around Hart, pulling him from Maxim, who finally relented. Hart found himself looking at her lips, which were swollen with emotion. She looked even more beautiful when passionate and, curiously, made him want her at that very moment. The anger he'd felt about her lying to him was exchanged for appreciation of her refusal to believe in his absolute guilt. Clara caught him gazing at her as they stood near the door. With a soft glance they expressed what only their eyes could. *I'm sorry. Yes, I know.*

Clara grabbed her trench coat and bag off the coat hanger next to the door and stood to the left of Hart, who was directly in front of the door, with Maxim on his other arm. Clara pivoted forward as she reached for the handle and looked across at Maxim before she opened the door, silently pleading for one last chance, but Maxim turned away from her with an exasperated huff. Clara opened the door, and the stairwell motion detector caused a bright flash as harsh light spilled into the darkened apartment.

Hart took half a step forward with a nudge from Maxim as Clara held the door. He stepped onto the small landing with his chin on his chest, defeated. He was barely halfway out of the doorway when he felt the violent force of a boot kicking him in the chest. The shock of it barely had time to register in his brain as he was thrust backward into the apartment, landing hard on his shoulder. His head bounced off the floor as he skidded back into the room. The door flew open, smacking into Clara, who fell behind it and under the fallen coatrack. Hart saw a massive figure in the entryway, his face familiar and tense. Igor calmly raised a black pistol and took aim at Maxim.

Maxim had lost his balance when Hart was sent sprawling. Hart watched as a staggered Maxim fought to regain his footing and draw his weapon. His face was ashen with shock when he saw he wasn't going to be quick enough. Igor's pistol boomed three times, hitting Maxim in the stomach, then twice in the upper chest. He landed with a heavy thud on the floor several feet from Hart, his eyes wide, crystallized in shock.

Hart rolled hard to his left, kicking off the ground as bullets ripped into the floorboards where he'd lain. He scrambled to his knees and dove for the kitchen opening awkwardly. With his back against the kitchen wall, he tried to see Clara, who had remained hidden behind the open front door. He watched her give the door a kick, slamming it into the side of Igor, who let out a muffled grunt. The door bounced hard off him, swinging back towards Clara, who gave it another kick. She pushed herself backward on the floor, sliding away from the door. As she slid, she pulled a small handgun from her bag and fired at Igor. Four loud rounds hit the doorframe as Igor dove to avoid the gunfire.

Clara rolled onto her stomach and crawled into the kitchen as two more shots smacked into the other side of the wall, where Hart had propped himself. His hands were still cuffed behind his back, and he lunged awkwardly further into the kitchen to make space for Clara.

"You got to get these cuffs off me!"

"The keys are on Maxim." Clara's voice was calm, her breathing smooth as she swept her gun across the apartment. They stayed silent for a moment; Hart's ears were ringing from the deafening noise of Clara's gun.

Clara poked her pistol around the doorframe, her head following, searching low under the chairs and coffee table. The apartment was still, apart from the sound of brass casings rolling across the floor. She waited a moment and crossed the room, opening the bedroom door, and then ran towards the front door, stepping over Maxim and out into the hallway. She leaned over the iron railing, listening, before spinning back into the apartment.

"He's gone."

She knelt down at Maxim's side. His eyes were void of life, his hands empty and spread out at his sides.

Clara dropped her head onto her chest and covered her mouth and whispered, "So is Maxim."

She reached into the inside jacket pocket of the dead man. She found the small key and undid Hart's restraints.

"What are you doing? Where did Igor go? What are we going to do?" Hart mumbled as he rubbed his wrists and fought the urge to vomit.

"*Merde.*" She stood and held her head as she searched the floor around Maxim.

"What?" Hart could hear the high and low pitch of police sirens from a distance, fast approaching.

"We have to go *now.*" She made it over to Hart in three strides and yanked him towards the door.

Hart dug his heels into the ground, confused. He was startled by the fury in Clara's eyes.

"Paul, we have to go now. There's no time to explain!"

She tried to pull him into the hallway, but Hart held on to the splintered doorframe and looked down at Maxim, dark-red blood pooling around his body.

"We can't just leave him. They'll think we did this!" Hart could feel himself slipping back into shock.

"Paul!" Clara shook him by the shoulders. "They are going to think we did this. There's one way we get out of this, and it's by leaving right now. Igor took Maxim's gun. He is going to frame us."

The police sirens grew closer.

Hart nodded to appease her angry tone and followed her up the stairs before glancing one last time at Maxim. They bounded up two flights before Hart could hear heavy footsteps running up the stairs from the lobby. The iron railing shook from the police, who were shouting orders, running up to Clara's apartment.

Clara smacked Hart on the shoulder, and he stopped to peer over the railing down the spiral staircase below. She placed a finger over her lips: *Be quiet.* They reached the top of the staircase and a door with *Sortie de Secours* in red letters. Clara carefully opened the door, paused for a split second as if waiting for the alarm to sound, and then they climbed through, up onto the roof.

It was nearly midnight, but Paris lay awake with her lights on. Hart could see Place des Vosges ahead of him, surrounded by the orange glow of streetlamps, and across the slanted rooftops to Notre-Dame, its white towers bright from spotlights. The curved, dark rooftops stretched until he could see the red blinking light atop the Eiffel Tower. Blue police lights danced off the buildings from the street below.

He realized he'd just nearly been killed and saw a man gunned down. Perhaps worse was knowing he was on the run. *But to where? And for how long?* He wasn't an expert at this, whatever *this* was.

Clara tugged at his arm again and pointed out where to carefully walk across the narrow wooden planks that spanned the top of the building. She took his cell phone and dropped it, along with her own, down a storm pipe. He could hear voices below, shouts of "*Allez!*" and the crackle of radio transmissions. He wondered if they'd caught Igor, but he doubted it.

Clara crossed first, jumping a three-foot gap that connected her building with another. She stepped off the ledge and dropped the last two feet onto the gravel of the building's roof before motioning for Hart to follow.

They crossed two more buildings on the same side of the street and ducked into an emergency exit door that led down five flights of stairs, crossed a courtyard, and headed out onto the street through a service entrance. They walked four blocks, heading in a staircase pattern south towards Bastille, where crowds of people spilling from the restaurants and bars provided cover. Once south of Bastille, they headed east, on a quiet march along the river.

Clara led Hart to a white stone building with wide maroon-colored doors fitted with brass knockers in the shape of a lion. She punched in a four-digit code, and the keypad lit up cobalt blue as the doors opened. They took the back staircase and proceeded up three levels. Clara gave a tepid knock on apartment number 312. There was stirring inside before the door was cracked open. Hart could make out a single brown eye, protected by the door chain, inspecting him and Clara. The door shut and reopened.

Justine stood in a blue terry-cloth robe, her hair pulled back. She wore a worried look, but before Clara could say anything, she waved them inside and shut the door.

The caller had dialed the emergency services number, 17, while walking west, further into the heart of Le Marais. The French operator answered halfway into the first ring.

"There's been several gunshots in the building. I heard an American shouting, definitely English, and I think he was shooting too," he'd said in rusty French.

The operator asked for the building number, at which Igor supplied the apartment floor as well.

Was there anyone hurt? How many did he think? Was anything still happening? Please stay in a safe place. Authorities will be there soon. Your name and address, please? Hello? Hello?

Igor ended the call, took out the battery, and dropped it in a gutter on Rue de Escouffes, then tucked the sim card into his front pocket. He took the plastic burner phone, dropped it on the street, and broke it in half with the heel of his boot, partly out of anger, partly out of necessity.

He had timed his entrance poorly, hoping to have the element of surprise. But instead he was the one caught off guard. The handcuffs were surprising, and the man he'd killed wasn't the American. Perhaps it was the chauffeur. He seemed to be the driver, but why the handcuffs and gun? He didn't expect anyone else to have a gun there, but two people did. Clara had decent aim, her shots tightly clustered around the door, the mark of a pro.

It wasn't in his best interests to stick around, and when he'd seen the dead man's gun lying on the floor after dodging Clara's fire, he'd taken it and improvised. Thinking creatively, he'd decided to try and set them up. With the dead man's gun gone, it might look like a murder. A messy murder, ill thought out and poorly covered up, but a murder that could take a day or two to figure out. Plenty of time to get out of the country and go somewhere new—London was too rainy, anyway. There were several banks in Europe where he had accounts, all outside the United Kingdom, so what did he care if he never returned there again?

But as Igor crossed through the narrow streets, heading towards the river, a thought floated into his mind like a loose thread that, once pulled, began unraveling everything. What if Renard had set *him* up? Yes, go to Clara's apartment; it's only her and Hart there. You'll take them both out, like a lovers' murder-suicide, lovers who'd done one too many wrongs. Had Renard known who Clara was? She certainly wasn't simply a subordinate at his company.

There was only one way to scratch the itch he had. He'd always trusted his instincts, and they were telling him what to do, because nothing was adding up. He needed to find Renard.

He pulled his other phone and dialed the secure satellite number he memorized. Renard answered on the second ring.

"Is it done?" he inquired.

"No." Igor fought to control his rage. "We need to meet."

Renard hummed. "Very well. Tomorrow I have my monthly massage at the Mandarin. See you then."

Igor hung up the phone. He didn't have a good feeling about any of it.

38

Paris

The voices were soft but animated, but he couldn't make out what they were saying. He regained his senses and woke, momentarily forgetting where he was and what had happened the night before. Hart rubbed the sleep from his eyes and looked around the small apartment, the sun trickling through the closed wooden shutters. He sat up on the couch where he slept and strained to hear the voices coming from the kitchen. Rising to stand, he bumped into the glass coffee table, knocking over several candles. The voices in the kitchen stopped, and Clara peered out from behind the wall.

"You're up." She gave a faint smile.

"Thought I'd let you know," Hart said as he picked up the candles that fell onto the floor.

"*Bonjour*, Paul." Justine stepped out into the living room and smiled, more dressed since their late-night drop-in, wearing a white-collared black sweater and jeans. She exchanged a quick glance with Clara. "I am going to the *boulangerie. À tout de suite.*" She grabbed her purse and jacket, waved, and went out the front door.

Clara leaned against the doorframe in an outfit borrowed from Justine. She looked pensive, as if she was waiting for Hart to explode in anger, but the truth was he didn't know how he felt.

"I could go for some coffee." He clapped his hands softly, his body ridding itself of its nervous energy.

Clara disappeared into the kitchen. He found her at a small kitchen table with a laptop open, scrolling through the news of the attack. The pictures were graphic, but mixed in were smiling faces, pictures of the deceased in happier times.

Hart poured himself a coffee and drank in silence for a moment. It was as if neither of them had the words nor will to speak.

Hart finally broke the silence. "Why did we leave last night?" The question was simple, but it carried the weight of the world from Hart's chest. If he were to go on the run in a foreign country, he wanted to know exactly why.

Clara pursed her lips, then let out a deep breath. "Maxim thought you were guilty of helping Renard from the moment he met you. But I knew you had nothing to do with it the day we met at the museum. No offense, Paul, but you are a pawn in a game that even we don't understand. Maxim was too nearsighted to see it and only wanted to see what he was looking for. There were no other suspects, and he wanted to clear the case. But I was with you at the market. I saw Igor. Maybe I recognized your contempt for the man and doubted you for a moment, but I knew who you were, what you're capable of, and it isn't sinister."

She looked up from the inside of her coffee mug, the one she seemed to have been talking to. Their eyes met, Hart could almost see Clara searching for a sign of forgiveness or understanding from him.

"But that doesn't explain why we fled the scene of a crime. If you're a cop, why didn't we just stay?" Hart shook his head.

"Igor took Maxim's gun, and they wouldn't have believed there was some-one else who escaped. Igor is not even on our radar, and by the time things could have been cleared up, we would lose days. But most importantly, if Maxim had reported that you and I became intimate..." She had a sip of coffee before continuing. "He despised that, because a long time ago I turned him down. Men and their egos. He wanted to find you guilty. You think the police would overlook that? You and I found in an apartment with the man, murdered in cold blood, who wanted to arrest you, my new lover? By the time the ballistics report was done and everything was figured out, Igor would be long gone, and I cannot accept that." Her tone was resolute, and her eyes fierce. "We have a chance now. We owe it to Maxim to find out the truth. If we stayed, we would've lost that chance. I am sorry I've gotten you into this, but now we have to find a way to get the truth out. We are both innocent, but more importantly, we need to find Igor and understand what it is he's done."

Hart sat back in the chair, exhaling forcefully through his nostrils. Part of him was angry with Clara, because she'd made life-changing choices for him. But there was another part of him that felt admiration for her. She was brave and resourceful, and he understood why she'd made the choices she did. Oddly enough, he found himself trusting her, even agreeing with her actions. He let Clara know with a nod that he was with her.

"So, tell me how you can connect Igor and Bichot. This is crucial to understand."

"Well," Hart started, taking another sip of his coffee, "I asked a friend who has access to bank information in the UK to run a simple search related to Igor. He sent me a list of people who were associated with Igor, either by helping create the business account, being an owner, or preparing the actual documents establishing a business. At first, I was curious, but then I became suspicious because on the list I recognized the name Jean Luc Bichot. It had him listed as a part owner with Igor of a small wine shop in Borough Market. Then I thought this was pretty odd considering you'd say Bichot had run away when we first met. So, the day we visited the market to see this shop they shared an interest in, we ended up seeing Igor there."

Clara nodded and looked out the small kitchen window to the plane trees partially blocking the view to the Seine. "So, since Bichot was working with Igor, we need to operate under the assumption that Igor is behind this. And because last night was more than just moving money around, and Igor's invitation to the match, he is much more dangerous than a money launderer." Clara squinted and shook her head. "The man murdered Maxim, who for his faults was a good man. Igor has to be getting help from someone else. This morning I tried to think of how he could learn my address. There are only two people at Renard Industries that know it: the payroll clerk, who is an old lady, and Renard. We take our privacy quite seriously in France."

"What are we going to do?" Hart asked, half to himself.

"I don't know." Clara drummed her fingers on the table.

Justine entered the apartment, gently shutting the door behind her. She placed a brown paper bag on the small kitchen table. The aroma of freshly baked croissants and pain au chocolat filled the apartment.

"*Bon*, we should eat breakfast," Clara said as she dug into the bag. "*Merci*, Justine."

"There's always time for chocolatine," Justine said with a shrug as she reached into the bag and pulled out a pastry.

Hart, surprisingly, found himself not in the mood to eat.

Clara began scrolling the news on Justine's laptop; Hart leaned in close. He hadn't seen any photos or heard anything new since he picked up Clara the day before. But the first picture online jolted him.

"Scroll back up," he said, his heart pounding.

"What is it?" Clara's face knotted in confusion.

Hart pointed to a photo of a man with blond hair and a blue suit and tie. "I recognize him."

Clara studied the photo. "My God, that's Josh Cornwall. We met at the auction. He sat at our table with his wife. He was Igor's client." Clara turned to look at Hart. "He's dead."

Hart felt his blood run ice cold. He'd forgotten about the trade he'd been asked to make for Renard. He had been so caught up in the pandemonium of the past days he hadn't made the connection. How could he have been so naïve? So blind? His mind started to race through the next days and weeks. Where would he end up, and how bad would it be before the truth was known? He felt nauseous.

"This man in the photo, the one th-th-that died yesterday," Hart stammered as he pointed at the screen. "Renard asked me to make a trade against Cornwall's company before I went to London with you. He asked me to short the company's stock. Basically, buying it low so that if the price of the stock fell after bad news, the value of the company would go down, but the short position actually adds value. You make money on someone else losing it." Hart grabbed the computer and Googled the company stock symbol; the results hit him in the gut. "When he was killed, the stock slipped nearly forty percent before trading was halted on the news its CEO died, but I know Renard made money before that. But I didn't even know anything about this, Clara." Hart sat back down, his face white. "I'm being framed. I swear." His words were drawn out, as if he didn't believe what he was saying.

He took the computer and scrolled the article, trying to learn as much as he could, when he found two beady eyes staring back at him from the screen. The same beady eyes he'd seen just before he'd been clocked in the head after following Igor's contact that day in Borough Market.

"There." Hart spun the computer for Clara to see.

Justine leaned over her shoulder, reading the description. "This is a photo of the attacker? He looks so young."

Clara swore. "It's the man from the market."

"It is. I will never forget those eyes." Hart slumped in the kitchen chair.

"Paul, this is bigger than money. I think we're the only ones who know how big this really is." Clara looked at Justine and back at Hart. "We need to get to Renard. He's either entirely behind this or in real danger, but whichever way, we have to talk to him."

Hart shook his head. "We can't just walk into the office. There's police and security cameras. By now, they will be looking for us. As a matter of fact, how come they haven't thought to look for us at Justine's?"

Clara waved the question away. "Because we met on a trip to Malaysia in college years ago, and there's no record of us on social media or anything. We're safe. Trust me."

The room sat silent for a moment. The coffee pot beeped three times and shut off. Hart could hear the bustling morning work traffic outside, commuters eager to get to the office so they could start their weekend early.

"It's Friday, right?" Hart looked at his watch and read the date, his mind running at a thousand miles per hour. He remembered the massage story from Renard that day in the glass conference room. Hart couldn't recall the name of the masseuse, but he remembered everything else. "I know where Renard will be today."

39

Paris

Justine found Hart a change of clothes, left behind by an old boyfriend. Clara had asked to borrow the Renault, and Justine had graciously agreed because of concerns that the mile-and-a-half walk to the Mandarin Oriental would put Clara and Hart at risk of being recognized. The same went for the Metro and the taxi stands. Better to drive and find a parking spot; easier said than done in Paris, but safer.

The ten-minute ride across the arrondissement was easy, and with divine intervention Clara found parking on Rue Daunou. They walked south towards Place Vendôme and past the glittering fine jewelry shops and five-star hotels, Charvet and the Ritz, before turning east on Rue Saint-Honoré. The late-morning crowds overflowed from the narrow sidewalks as Clara and Hart made their way towards the Mandarin Oriental and Renard.

Hart felt a numb tingling that he recognized as fear. "Even if he's there and we get to him, what exactly is our plan?" he asked.

Clara glanced into the stores as they passed a small mannequin in a gray turtleneck, hand under its chin, the thinking-man position. "Well, we try and have him confess. Tell him that we know about Bichot and Igor. If we can get his confession, he can help us find Igor, and once we do that we are cleared. It's the only way."

Hart frowned. "Seems like a long shot."

"Do you have any other ideas?" Her head craned to the side.

"We have Justine's car. We could get out of Paris. Maybe go to that island your grandpa lived on. Only for a little while, so we could explain our story. Just you and me. We could leave right now." His mind played out the two of them driving away, lovers on the run, but he couldn't picture any more than a few days, though it was something. He pleaded with his eyes: *Think about it. Just us.*

They walked in silence for a few paces before Clara responded. "We have to do this. We can't go, we have to do this." They both knew it wasn't an option, but somewhere deep down Hart wished she had agreed.

She waited a moment before she spoke again. "But after this is over, we'll go there. To the beach and the Bois de la Chaise, a pier where we can watch the days drift by." She managed a soft smile: *We can't, not now, but one day.*

They walked hand in hand, and Clara squeezed his three times and spun towards him, coming to a stop. She grabbed Hart by the back of the neck and pulled him in. Their lips touched, and his world melted away, if only for the briefest moment. She pulled back and looked into his eyes, and he met her gaze and nodded. The corners of her mouth turned upwards into a smile. They continued on to the hotel, Hart silently committing himself to his only option, which was to fight to clear their names and bring Igor to justice.

The hotel was tucked slightly off the street, guarded by two doormen. Clara had decided that Hart should enter first to sit in the lobby. He would wait until he saw Renard and watch him head downstairs to the spa, where his monthly massage would occur. Once Renard was out of sight, Clara, who would be watching from across the street, would enter and find Hart. Together they would make their way downstairs. Clara decided it was best to talk their way past the reception desk by acting like an angry girlfriend of Renard's, which wouldn't be hard, she'd said, "Because he has so many, and I am pretty enough to be one. Those girls try too hard." Hart would lend credence by pretending to be additional security and saying he'd take Clara back to Renard's spa room.

Hart had positioned himself on a purple velour chair facing the front door of the lobby and used a magazine to shield his face. He sat for only fifteen minutes before he saw Renard sauntering in for his 1 p.m. appointment with two large men dressed casually compared to the other guests. It wasn't difficult to guess why they had on oversized track jackets, Hart thought to himself. A rich client with a penchant for associating with criminals needed protection. They would, however, make getting to Renard more difficult.

Renard strode across the white marble floor and was greeted by several hotel employees, who stopped to offer a hello to their regular guest. He wore boat shoes, red pants, an ice-blue dress shirt, and blue zip-up sweater, looking more like he was ready to go yachting than enjoy a massage. The three men disappeared down the staircase just off the lobby that led to the spa. Hart waited for a few moments while Clara entered the hotel, and when they made eye contact, he got up and followed her down to the spa.

Downstairs, a young woman at the front desk dressed in a white tunic with turquoise piping smiled politely at Hart and Clara. The spa entrance was flanked by a small waiting room, furnished with crème-colored leather chairs, deep-red burgundy carpet, and black wallpaper with leafy gold flowers. The attendant asked for the name of the appointment, at which Clara sprung into character, spewing angry words at her lover, Renard, who'd apparently done her wrong. The look of fright on the young attendant's face was promising, Hart thought as he stood back, trying to look like one of Renard's hired security. His clothes, borrowed from Justine's boyfriend—dark jeans, a white dress shirt, and a surprisingly well-fitting navy blazer— didn't exactly make him feel like a menacing bodyguard. Clara had commanded she be allowed to see Renard and leaned over the counter to find out his room number.

The young attendant was uninterested in attempting to calm a scorned lover and did not want to create a scene in the tranquil spa. Hart didn't even need to intervene. He simply followed Clara through the smoked-glass doors and into the inner spa area and towards suite number two. They walked down the narrow hallway and hadn't thought of a plan to deal with the two armed bodyguards, who came into clear view, straddling the door to Renard's suite.

"What are we going to do? We can't just wait out here," Hart whispered in Clara's ear as she marched down the long hallway, making no attempt to quiet the noise of her boots.

"Just follow me," Clara said out of the side of her mouth. She swung her purse, which was draped diagonally across her body, off her hip and slid her hand into it.

The guards recognized Clara and then shifted their eyes towards Hart, immediately becoming rigid and tense. Clara was within three paces of them when she sprung. She lifted off the floor and pulled a Taser from her purse, which she stuck in the neck of the first guard. The Taser clicked loudly, sending over a thousand volts of electricity through his body. The man's teeth clenched, his body constricted, and he fell. The second guard, a shorter man with a bald head, moved towards Clara as she administered the final Taser jolt to his unconscious partner.

Hart watched Clara with awe until he realized she wasn't going to be able to use the Taser on the second guard, who was nearly on top of her. Hart pushed off the ground and sprinted at him, aiming to put himself between him and Clara to buy her time. The man was quicker than Hart thought he would be, and they arrived at the spot with Hart crashing into the man, propelling both of them, thudding, into the wall. The guard gave a quick rabbit punch to Hart's kidney, causing pain to shoot down his back and into his legs.

Hart felt the rage from his past twenty hours build inside him as he pushed off the wall and grabbed the guard's jacket collar with one hand, holding him away from Clara. Hart gave two jabs to the man's face, the first landing squarely while the second grazed the man's cheek. The guard spun and threw a right cross as if it'd been fired from a cannon. Hart ducked, pulling the man down, because his hand still had a firm grip on the jacket collar. Hart, from a crouched position, sprung back upwards and swung his elbow crashing through the man's chin, spinning him around. He landed against the wall.

The guard grabbed the wall with one hand and knelt with his back turned to Hart. He got up slowly, turning back around, revealing his bloodied face. He stood with his arms at his sides the as blood dripped. But the guard didn't move forward; he simply reached into his jacket and gripped his gun. Hart cursed. *Don't forget to bring something to a gunfight.* The guard almost had the black grip of the pistol out from his jacket when Clara stuck the Taser in the back of his neck. She'd snuck around him as he got up, through the dark shadows of the dimly lit hallway. The guard dropped to his knees and then lay face down, drooling, on the floor.

Clara dropped the Taser into her purse, brushed the hair that had fallen on her face, and nodded towards the suite door. "I'd say our plan is working out quite well so far."

40

Paris

Zen music chimed in the dark and humid room. The walls, covered in sheer black tile, glittered with yellow light from the Jacuzzi, and the massage table lay perpendicular to the door. Straight ahead was a vanity mirror, its shelf full of products for clients' indulgences—coconut oil, lavender cream, apricot body scrubs—and smooth, hot stones were laid out on the counter.

Renard sat in a small leather chair in the corner opposite the door in a white terry-cloth robe. Neither Clara nor Hart had seen him upon entering, but when they were both completely in the room, he spoke.

"Yvette, please go. This doesn't concern you, and I appreciate your discretion. Please close the spa off to guests for the time being," Renard said to the ashen-faced masseuse, visibly trembling behind the door. "Please." He pointed his hand towards the door and smiled.

Hart stepped aside as she scampered out, her rubber-soled shoes squeaking as she sprinted towards the lobby and shut the glass doors with a bang.

"That was kind of you to let her go. She is dear to me." Renard's right leg was tucked neatly over his left, with his bare ankle dangling as he sat. "You two have had quite the week," he said, chuckling, examining them.

Holding the Taser, Clara and stepped further into the room. She hovered over Renard, creating space between her and Hart, as a lioness does before pouncing on her prey. Hart, however, was too impatient for the silent drama to play out.

He snapped at Renard without thinking twice. "Why the hell are you doing all of this?" He took a step forward, his fists clenched.

The smile that Renard wore grew while he shook his head from side to side gently and looked at Clara.

"This is who you choose? This excitable American?" He wagged his finger at her and clicked his tongue in disapproval.

"What did I do to you, Monsieur Hart? Well, you are here, so obviously you've surmised some things about me. But really, what did I do to you besides gift you a beautiful opportunity? A nice business trip to dreary old Paris—yes, how terrible of me." He pouted out his bottom lip and looked to the floor in taunting melancholy. "How horrible of me. Demanding you go to London with a beautiful woman who would sleep with you for her own cause? Oh, the unimaginable things you must have done, the dirty things, all for your job. Yes, there must be some sinister reason to this." He raised a mocking eyebrow.

Clara spoke, her voice even, as if she'd been rehearsing the line for quite some time. "Claude, we have the evidence to convict you on charges of tax evasion, wire fraud, and extortion for your role in Renard Industries funneling money out of France." She stood with her chin held high but was breathing heavily, and Hart caught a glimpse of her lip twitching.

The room was silent besides the chimes of the zen music. Renard sat upright, causing the leather to squeak. He squinted at Clara, shock spreading across his face, before he burst into laughter and clapped. Clara and Hart exchanged glances: *He isn't taking us very seriously.*

Hart's fatigued mind had a terrifying thought that caused his heart to pound. What if Renard was clean? Maybe Maxim and Clara were duped into wasting time, catching Hart in a web of lies, bureaucracy, and happenstance. Or more likely, maybe Renard was guilty but unrelenting to the end. Either scenario scared the hell out of Hart, because it wouldn't be easy to prove his or Clara's innocence without Renard's confession.

The realization that life would not go back to the way it was hit Hart. There would be no Air France premium cabin seating for him, he wasn't going to return to his apartment in New York City anytime soon, nor was his company in dire need of him. The one thing he'd been hopeful about, his relationship with Clara, was now clouded in complexity and had forever changed. He felt scared, thrown into a deep abyss of danger. The harsh reality was that unless people started telling the truth, his head would be on the block.

Renard scoffed at Clara's accusation. "Is this some theory you and your little boyfriend over here thought of after one of your romps? Is he that quick that you need to talk so much and come up with crazy plans?" Renard cackled at the thought. "He's the one taking the money, Clara." He burst into laughter once again, doubling over in amusement. "So, you're a cop but still a stupid woman next to a dumber man. You still don't get it."

Hart crossed the room towards Renard in two steps before the man had the chance to look up, Hart punched him in the side of the face. Renard's skin felt warm and his beard oily from the spa, or was it nerves? Hart grabbed Renard's robe collar and jerked him forward in his chair.

Hart sneered. "Tell me what the hell it is you're up to, or, God help me, I'll use that Taser on your balls so many times they'll fall off, asshole." Hart threw him back into the chair like a doll.

Renard's smile disappeared. "Bravo, Paul." His face was stoic. "I never thought you'd have that in you. In fact, that was the reason we picked you." He reached up, straightening his robe to ensure his modesty.

"We?" Hart felt a pang of anxiety.

"Hutchens didn't tell you? That sly old dog. I asked him to send me someone for a project. In return, I said I would expand my relationship with his company but"—he held his index finger up in the air—"I wanted someone who was going to be easy to control. A yes-man, someone who would be happy to get out of the office to feel important, and someone to follow directions and not their curiosity. Perhaps, some would say, a stupid man. I guess both of us had you pegged wrong, didn't we, Paul? But he hated you from the moment you screwed his daughter—can't blame him for that. He traded your services for more money from me."

Hart's eyes narrowed, and his head began to spin. "What do you mean, you and Hutchens picked me? For what?" Layers of his predicament kept piling up. He turned to Clara, who returned his look with a blank stare.

Renard sighed and smacked his legs with both hands. "Both of you are dull. Only because I know you'll never make it out of this hotel alive, I will tell you the entire truth. Even if by some miracle you did escape, no one would believe the undercover cop whose partner turned up dead and then ran away with the suspect. That, my love, was a bad way to do business. It is a modest story, but I'd be happy to share it, because the paradox of my brilliance is that my story will never be known. Well, except by the two of you, but this will sadly only be short-lived knowledge. Anyway, the story is about one man being manipulated by another's greed."

Renard sat back down in his chair before continuing. "Clara, your former boss, Bichot, was the spark that started the fire. The fool, stealing money and laundering it out of the country with help of a gluttonous banker. For purposes of making my life easier, Paul, you've been scapegoated to be that greedy, corrupt banker!" Renard pointed to Hart and clapped. "Congratulations. We didn't think you were cunning enough, but we set you up perfectly for it, better than you could have done yourself." Renard beamed as he once again straightened out his robe, taking his time, as if he were savoring the moment.

"I'd caught Bichot stealing from me years ago. But before I stopped him, I was curious why he was doing it. I paid him handsomely and he had a nice life. But I guess greed always lurks just around the corner, tempting us to follow it down mysterious and dangerous alleys. So, I watched Bichot—with your help, Clara. You reported to me his movements up until the day he vanished, by my own doing. But Bichot was foolish. Stealing money from his travel account, he ended up leading me to my destiny when I found the man who'd been helping him all along.

"Igor always had a way about him, a mission that went way beyond making more money. But Bichot was nothing but a pawn to him, discarded as soon as the next move was set up. We began somewhat small—a few decimal points of a percentage here and there—but Igor had grander plans. We opened a small wine shop under Bichot's name, who did all the necessary paperwork, and it became the base of our operation. It's amazing how simple it is to move money across countries and hemispheres by pretending to buy products. Then the plan started where we would purchase wine from distributors, say for a thousand euros a case, and then sell that same wine for two thousand euros a case. But the important thing was that we were the ones buying and selling, under different business names and as different people, but it was our own money all along. Tourists would come and pay two hundred percent over the market price for our wine, but most of the time all the purchases we made were entirely made up!" Renard paused to marvel at the scheme.

Clara glanced at her watch. "We don't have all day. Get on with it." Hart realized the spa could only be private so long.

"*Bien sûr*." Renard scratched his beard absentmindedly. "Well, we were bribing government officials and hiding the illicit sales, making more money than we could have imagined. But money was only going to satisfy us for so long. For Igor, oddly enough, it was never was about money. Beating the system gave him the biggest thrill."

"We said, what if we could have an effect on the day-to-day business of companies? Competitors, influencers, powerful companies that perhaps were not as visible in our everyday world but nonetheless held true power. Igor's ideas at first involved some information we'd stumble across, or even maybe a tragic accident, a shipment being misplaced that would cripple a small company. Specific companies would be targeted, and then in some way, either by holding a financial position that worked to our benefit, or entering a suddenly open marketplace, we profited from our own designs." Renard held up his hands, rubbing his thumbs on his fingers: *money.* "But I must say that somewhere along the line, Igor decided to get more ambitious with the operation."

Renard was being coy but perhaps speaking enough so it wasn't evident he was stalling. Clara again looked at her watch and at Hart, who stood with his hands on his hips, utterly confused. The powerful business titan that Hart had flown over the Atlantic to meet with was sitting in a bathrobe explaining how he set him up for some sinister plan.

Hart tried to work out the details. "Yeah, but you set me up perfectly for what? You've managed to hide some money and cleverly launder, what, probably millions by now? But why frame me?"

"I'm getting to that, you impatient peasant. *Mon Dieu.*" Renard shook his head in disgust at Hart interrupting him. "As I said, my partner became too ambitious. He started exploiting other areas that didn't have to do with money; rather, he leveraged fear and used it for his own purposes. Where money was once the ruler in his life, politics took over. He wanted to create fear, for one's family, for lives to be changed forever, companies destroyed, and ultimately countries changed. He took things too far. Used people to kill for him, like the London attack. He said it was for us, but it was always for him." Renard put his head in his hands and stared at the floor, private memories flashing in front of his eyes as Clara and Hart watched on.

"Things got carried away. We were ambitious, but we forgot why we started and we went too far. But I was cornered, trapped by the invention of my own game. Igor wanted to exploit a fear of differences, assimilation, and he thought that two birds could be killed with one stone. Josh Cornwall was just another example of violence in exchange for profit, but I saw it as my opportunity to get out. I framed you for this, Paul, because I need to start over, to get away."

Hart rubbed his temples and heard a small noise outside the closed door. It was probably one of the guards stirring awake, falling about on the cold tile.

He turned his attention back to Clara. "So, we've got what we need, right? This confession can make things work? Clear both our names?"

Clara pursed her lips "We'll need it in writing and in front of other DGSI personnel, I'm afraid." Clara looked at her watch. "I think we better take Monsieur Renard in and explain everything. There are good people in the organization we can trust like Directeur Pierre-Emmanuel. He's known me since my training. He knows I couldn't do any of this." She'd said this nearly as much to herself as to Hart.

Renard held up a finger. "But you're both missing two critically important pieces of information. Don't you care to know? The first being that I've set up Mr. Paul Hart so well that no matter what kind of confession you think you've gotten, he still looks guilty as sin. It would take weeks, months, if not years, to uncover. By that time, I will be long gone." He beamed, seemingly unfazed by his interrogators.

"After all is said and done, the only evidence that will remain will be that Paul flew to Paris, spent a few days combing over accounts, then flew off to

London, where he handed over tickets—very visible on the hotel's security cameras, mind you—to Igor, my partner in crime. Then with the help of his newfound lover, Clara, who overspent outrageously on some wine at auction, Hart sent the money himself, from the account only he had access to, on the plane he booked to return to Paris. He used the perfect laundering scheme: a charity auction where no one would think twice about overspending." He let the phrase hang in the air for a second. "Strangely Monsieur Hart books the private plane at the last minute without telling his lover, whom he lies to and tells he was summoned back to Paris. But the odd thing is that Hart himself booked the flight. Well, actually I booked the flight but pretended to be you, Paul. But most critically, don't forget the short position in the unforeseen downfall of a company whose CEO gets murdered at a match, where Hart was to attend. You even invited the man with tickets you brought!

"Paul, I purchased the tickets from the account you created for me and of course used your name. It's your word versus mine, but I didn't leave a paper trail. Then on top of it all, two undercover agents go to arrest the alleged mastermind of the plot—that's you, Paul—and one of them dies in a shoot-out. But thankfully, the other, who happens to be his lover, remains alive. Convenient?"

Renard stood and clapped his hands together in mock congratulation. "Well done, you two. Even if you were to get someone to listen to your version of the story, who would believe the two lovers who ran away from a murder? No one! But you won't get the chance to speak, because the second crucial piece of the puzzle is that Igor, the doer of dirty deeds, is here to say hello." Renard looked towards the door to the suite.

Behind Hart, the door handle jiggled, and the door opened slowly. The muzzle of a Beretta entered the room. Hart took a step in between the door and Clara as Igor strode in calmly, blocking Igor's view of her Taser. He stood near the door; Hart figured it was too far away for her to make a move.

Igor wore a dark-blue car coat over a navy pinstripe suit, black driving gloves, and black lace-ups. He had several cuts on his face and his eyes were severe, darting from Clara to Hart and finally to Renard.

"Speak of the devil and he shall appear!" Renard clapped his hands in excitement. "I was just telling these two lovers about my plan to frame them for our own little adventures. I think it's time we close up shop and let the heat die down a bit. Figured it better to ask forgiveness than beg for your permission to do so."

Igor's face turned rigid, his jaw clenched, and eyes narrowed as he shot a look at Renard, careful to keep watch of Clara at the same time. "Our adventures, you say? So that's the game you were playing with them."

His English was good, Hart knew from the charity gala, but mix in a bit of stress, and a hint of an accent came through. Hart took a step back from Igor, trying to give Clara more cover.

Renard was irrationally happy while Hart and Clara watched the scene unfold. Igor carried an aura of evil, and Hart could nearly feel the danger. His mind cried out that he should run. He'd seen Igor murder in cold blood the night before without hesitation, and Hart assumed the worst was to come.

Renard's smile flickered before he answered Igor. "*Oui*, our adventures. The amazing things we've accomplished. What we've done together. It wasn't easy, but we should be proud. This guy yesterday, Josh; you sure made Paul look rich for a few moments." Renard stood in his robe, hands out to his sides as if searching his audience for reassurance. "Right, we've done some amazing things, and now we are free, let's quit while we are ahead." He pointed at Hart with his index finger. "We've set him up for the ultimate frame job. So, Igor, shoot them here, and let's, you and I, take off somewhere. How does Croatia sound?"

Igor stood with his gun trained on Hart's chest. He slowly turned his head to look at Renard, then glanced back to Hart. "So, you were the fall guy. Didn't work out nicely for you." He steadied his gun with both hands.

Hart backed up and stretched his arms out behind him, blocking Clara, not that it would do much good, he thought, his heart stricken as shock took hold. Igor stared down the barrel, while Renard started giggling.

"I had Igor come and, Paul, when I saw you sitting in the lobby like an idiot, I couldn't have planned this better. You're not trained or clever enough to hunt me; you were not a wolf in sheep's clothing. *Au revoir*," he said with a wave.

"Yes, *au revoir*," Igor said as his square face tightened, his eyebrows burrowing as he clenched his jaw. With a quick turn, he pointed the gun at Renard, who gave him a quizzical look. Igor smirked and stared at Renard. "You should always talk to your business partners before making decisions; otherwise, that's just bad business."

He fired three shots, hitting Renard in the forehead and twice in the chest. His body fell backward, landing in the small chair. A glazed look of confusion spread across his face as he slid down the squeaking leather.

Igor turned the gun towards Clara. Hart recoiled, then stepped in front of her to shield her. He never imagined he'd meet his end like this, at the hands of a lunatic in a Parisian hotel spa. He felt Clara put her hand flat against his back as he braced.

For a moment, Igor stared at them, swiveling his head like a dog trying to understand a familiar word. He dropped the gun, which swung around on the index finger of his gloved hand, the weight of the gun toppling the barrel over. He let it dangle for a second before tossing it in the air towards Hart.

Hart caught the gun with both hands and, confused, raised it towards Igor, who sprinted out through the doorway. He pulled the trigger, but the gun didn't fire.

Igor had vanished. Hart looked at his hands in confusion and then at Clara.

"The safety is on, and now your prints are on the gun. He was wearing gloves! We have to get after him!"

She grabbed Hart by his sleeve, causing him to drop the gun, and hauled him out into the hallway. They raced towards the emergency exit at the back of the spa, where the door hung limp from its hinges. Down the hallway, the raised voices of hotel security echoed after them.

Clara burst through the exit door, leading up to a concrete staircase stacked with plastic bins and cardboard boxes. Hart tripped over a box containing plastic wrapped slippers for spa guests and proceeded to kick the box down the staircase. They sprinted up two flights and pushed open another door, leading to the service entrance in the back alley. Clara spun around, searching for Igor, but apart from several green dumpsters and a large puddle of water, the alley was vacant.

Clara made towards the street. "We need to get to the car."

Hart ran after her. "I am tired of leaving! We just left a room with a dead man and my prints on the gun. It looks like we're on a murder spree!" His face was red, and he struggled to keep pace with Clara, who was walking with purpose.

She spoke out of the side of her mouth as they approaching a side street that would lead back to Rue Saint-Honoré. "We don't have time for your feelings, don't you get it? We need to prove our innocence, and all our options are dead besides Igor, who got away!" She bit her lip in frustration and marched into the pedestrian traffic heading west towards Place Vendôme and Justine's parked Renault.

They wove their way through the midday lunch crowd in the First Arrondissement as police sirens howled across the city. Hart and Clara constantly checked over their shoulders until they reached the Renault and climbed into the car, out of breath and, seemingly, ideas.

"What's the plan now?" Hart looked at Clara as she sat with her arms braced on the steering wheel.

She shook her head slowly. "Why am I always the one having to come up with a plan? What do you think we should do? Tell me, you're always asking others for ideas and doing what you're told, but tell me, what great ideas have you offered?" She glared at him. Her eyes searched his, and they betrayed her true emotion, which to Hart wasn't anger but sadness. But, Hart thought, she probably wasn't wrong; he'd been reliant on others for so much, and now his fate seemed out of his hands.

"Let's get out of here and catch our breath. Head south across the river."

Clara nodded. "That was my plan."

41

Paris

Clara drove south across Place de la Concorde. Hart stared out the window, remembering the innocence of his first few days in Paris. They crossed the Seine and went towards the Sixth Arrondissement, where even on a Friday afternoon the tree-lined streets and cafés were quieter than in the bustling First. The sky began to darken as the winds picked up. A late-afternoon storm was creeping closer, just in time for the early commuters' trip home.

Clara pulled to a stop at the four-way intersection where Boulevard Raspail, Boulevard Saint-Germain, and Rue de Bac met. Hart had no idea where they were going but kept staring out the window, trying to calm himself.

A loud rev from a motorcycle behind them caused Hart to look in his side mirror as the light flicked green. Clara turned right down Rue de Bac, past the small pharmacies and chocolate shops of the residential Saint-Germain-dés-Pres neighborhood, and stopped at another light to let pedestrians cross the one-way street. Clara tapped the steering wheel until the light changed.

They passed Le Bon Marché, at the end of Rue de Bac, and continued south further down a side street, where traffic thinned, and Hart told himself they were safe.

Clara lifted her hand up and snapped her fingers. "I have a plan, and I think it could work."

She smiled. Hart momentarily felt relief as the corner of his mouth rounded into a smile, but he caught sight of her eyes widening with fright while she gazed past him out his passenger-side window. Hart turned to see a motorcycle rider with a black helmet raise a pistol and fire several shots into the car. The glass shattered on Hart as he held out his left arm to press Clara back into her seat, out of the line of fire.

Clara slammed on the brakes as the motorcycle sped ahead of the car.

The ear-piercing gunshots had temporarily deafened Hart. He had cuts over his arms and felt his face sliced from the exploding glass window. The black motorcycle screeched to a stop diagonally across the one-way road, some twenty yards ahead of them. The tinted glass of the helmet was raised, revealing Igor's square face. He lifted his gun and fired off two shots towards the Renault that pierced the windshield.

Clara slammed the car into first gear and stomped on the gas, causing the tires to scream in protest. Igor cranked the throttle of the bike and kicked its rear wheel around, hopping the curb, barely avoiding the passing Renault.

An elderly couple on the sidewalk shuffled as fast as they could into a vacant doorway, dropping a grocery bag full of oranges as the bike sped past, chasing down Clara and Hart. Clara smoothly shifted into third and knifed into oncoming traffic at Rue de Sevres, heading westbound across the Left Bank of Paris. She tucked into traffic behind a tall gray van and a red Nissan and quickly became boxed in.

"It's Igor." Hart strained over the passenger seat to get a view of the bike weaving through traffic behind them. His head was blurry from the gunshots, the broken-glass cuts, and the wind as it whipped through the window frame as Clara sped along.

Clara was bent over at the wheel, trying to see through the windshield, which was badly cracked.

"There's a police station and military barracks at Les Invalides. We can make it there. I can't risk innocent lives in a gunfight and a wild chase."

She squinted to see the traffic and pushed the Renault into fourth gear, passing a car on the right, causing a confused and angry gesture from the slower van driver. She swerved back in front of the van, blocking Igor's approach. Hart could hear the high-pitch cry from the motorcycle as it darted into the side mirror, like a lion chasing down its prey on an open plain.

The road opened up as they sped by Hôpital Neckar on their left. Clara cut the wheel to the right, slicing down a side street, Avenue de Saxe, where a wide central reservation with parked cars split the road. They raced towards an expansive roundabout. Igor pulled his pistol and fired. Clara ducked, and Hart spun low in his seat to see the back window explode in a shower of glass.

Clara dropped the car down a gear and the engine cried out at over four thousand RPMs as a three-lane roundabout approached. She pushed the Renault through several lanes, cutting through the flow of traffic like a knife through butter, causing a silver Peugeot to skid sideways to a stop and several horns to be blared in protest. Beyond the roundabout, Hart could see the Eiffel Tower in the distance, the tall icon blending into the stormy clouds as a flash of horizontal lightning lit up the sky.

The Renault's tires yowled in disapproval as Clara pushed the car to its limits. A Mercedes taxi cut across the left side of their car, clipping its front fender. Hart desperately held on to the roof handle as the car shook violently from the hit, wobbling back and forth, before Clara caught its unruly back end. She maneuvered the damaged car to the first exit, down Avenue de Breteuil towards Invalides and the tomb of Napoleon.

"Why is he chasing us if he let us leave the hotel?" Hart screamed over the noise of the engine and wind whipping through the shattered windows.

"He tried to set us up! He figured we would stay, but he tailed us when he saw we chased him from the hotel. He's good. I never saw him!" Clara shouted, cutting the wheel hard to the left, zipping by a car attempting to parallel-park.

Hart could see pedestrians down the road looking up briefly before refocusing on the portion of sidewalk in front of them with Parisian indifference.

Igor crossed through the traffic of the roundabout, trailing behind the Renault, weaving in and out of vehicles much more easily than the lumbering Renault, which was badly damaged from gunfire and the abuse it'd taken. He cranked the throttle and attempted to pull up alongside the passenger-side window once more.

Hart could see Invalides growing closer, its massive golden dome bright in the ever-darkening sky. The storm had rolled in with vigor from the west, and a few drops of rain fell on the cracked windshield.

Hart looked away from Invalides and to his right, and found a black helmet staring back at him. Clara screamed, "Get down!" but Hart didn't listen, his eyes swelling with rage. He opened the car door with as much might as he could against the resistance of the wind and with the restraint of his seat belt his only safety measure. He shoved the door as hard as he could into the motorcycle. Igor kicked back at the door, which slammed shut with a great deal of force, causing the Renault to swerve. Igor flipped the tinted visor up and stared at them with spiteful gray eyes, as if shocked by Hart's brashness.

Clara seized on Hart's initiative and grabbed him by the arm and yelled, "Hold on!"

She swerved the car hard to the right, pinning the motorcycle to the parked cars that lined the street. The Renault's front end hit the middle of a Peugeot hatchback, cutting the motorcycle off and pinning Igor to the parked cars. Igor's motorcycle fought for grip to stay upright, but he was thrown sprawling across the hood of the Renault and disappeared from sight. The collision sent the front end of their Renault scraping down the row of parked cars, until it hit the back of the parked van, causing the Renault to violently spin with the impact. The mangled car settled perpendicularly across the road.

Hart was jolted awake to the smell of gasoline and the horn sounding flatly as Clara's head rested on the steering wheel. The cracked radiator hissed, with steam pouring from the crinkled hood. There was a distant wail of sirens and crack of thunder as rain began to fall, finding its way through the broken windows onto his face.

He undid his seat belt gingerly. His body ached from the awkward force of the crash, and he found it painful to breathe. He reached over to put a hand on Clara's shoulder, brushed her dark hair back softly, and leaned over to check on her. Her breathing was labored, her eyes were closed, and there was a pained expression across her face and a gash on her forehead. He shook her gently by the shoulder and said her name softly, and she stirred. Her eyes fluttered once, then shut.

Hart heard the sound of glass scraping on the ground. Igor. He realized that he was half-glad Igor wasn't dead but half-afraid as well. Hart fought to open his broken door. He gave a firm kick and it gave way, the bent metal groaning in displeasure. He told Clara he'd be right back and lumbered out of the car, leaning against it for support as he rolled around the back side to the driver's side to find only broken glass on the ground—no Igor.

He began to turn around when he was smacked across his back. He doubled over, pain shooting through his back. Igor stood, helmet in hand, and swung it hard over his unsuspecting victim once again. Hart blocked the blow with his shoulder, protecting his head, and tackled Igor, trying to drive him to the ground, but instead it felt like trying to tackle a tree. Hart's body was sore from the crash and no match for the strong, boxy frame of his would-be assassin. Igor rolled with the momentum of Hart's attempted tackle and crashed him against the side of the smoking car. The rain had begun to fall steadily, the car slippery as they both fell to the ground, Hart landing on top of Igor. He pinned Igor against the wheel of the car and tried to keep him pressed against it.

Hart reached for Igor's thick neck, managing to grab it and squeeze before Igor countered with two quick punches, hitting him in the kidney and ribs, the sharp pain screaming down his back. Hart gasped for air and swung his right elbow across Igor's face, catching him squarely on the chin. Igor pushed off the wheel with his back and used his body weight to bulldoze Hart over. Once on top of Hart, and holding him by his jacket collar, Igor slammed him into the ground. Hart felt the side of the car with his feet and kicked hard off of it, landing his knee on Igor's back, forcing the air out of his lungs with an audible gush as Igor straightened upright and winced in pain.

Hart sat up and swung both his arms over to the side of Igor and tried to get the bigger man off him. Igor thrashed sideways and threw a punch that connected with Hart's right temple, knocking him back down. Igor lunged, landing on top of Hart, who felt the air leaving his lungs. Hart's arms were outstretched and pinned under Igor's thick legs, which remained straddled on top of him. Igor's meaty hands reached for Hart's neck and began to squeeze, slowly at first, then tighter, his eyes wild and bloodthirsty. Hart gasped for air and felt raindrops falling on his face, the hard, cold asphalt below him, and then gradually the life being taken from him.

He tried to swing his arms and legs with all the power he could muster into Igor to break his grip, but the man was too strong. Hart saw the fire in his would-be killer's eyes. Both men knew the inevitable outcome: Hart had lost. The raindrops continued to fall, but none were felt by Hart, who only sensed a chilling cold and numbness washing over him, his eyes heavy.

The dark sky turned black. The noisy cracks of thunder, the wailing sirens, and scraping of broken glass by his writhing feet were replaced by a piercing silence as death came to Hart. He managed to look towards the car for Clara, who was still slumped over the wheel, her eyes fluttering as she tried to sit up. Hart tried to call for her, but no sound came. He locked eyes with her for a moment, wishing to express things that couldn't go unsaid. Hart said a silent goodbye. Igor looked at Clara, then back at Hart, and smiling, he leaned in close to him.

"I will kill her after you." He leaned in closer, inches away from Hart's ear. "I'll take my time to make sure she feels death coming."

Igor sat back upright and pressed down on Hart's throat with more force. Hart felt his limbs go numb, trapped under his killer.

Hart didn't know what happened next. He thought there was some final stage in which death would pass before him and reveal itself. He felt the thud of the shots more than he heard them, a thunderous clap he first mistook for the storm. Hart saw Igor squirm upright as his hands relaxed from Hart's throat, allowing him to gasp for air, his lungs finding fresh oxygen. Igor's eyes widened in shock, and pain smeared his face.

Igor turned to face Clara, who fired another shot into his chest. She was still slumped in the front seat, with her gun held below the steering wheel, her right arm draped across her legs. Hart sat up and pushed Igor, who toppled over, motionless, on the pavement. The blue raincoat Igor wore bled into a dark red. The man's gray eyes were vacant, reflecting the dark clouds above, a disbelieving look on his face as he felt about his chest.

Hart grabbed Igor's collar, lifting him off the ground. He grimaced as he spoke through his teeth. "Why did you do it all? Tell me!"

Igor looked up at Hart and dismissed him by turning his head towards Clara, staring for several seconds before turning back to Hart with a wide and bloody smile. His gray eyes rolled back into his head and he fell limp.

Hart threw him to the ground and crawled to the Renault and Clara, who sat slumped in the driver's seat, her gun having fallen onto the ground. He staggered to his feet and could see flashing lights and hear the high-pitched sirens racing to them from every direction.

"We're okay, it's over."

He brushed the hair back behind Clara's ear as her eyes struggled to open. He could see her eyelids fluttering, but it was the only response he was getting. Gently, he lifted her off the steering wheel and tried to sit her upright, but she left out a painful sigh, causing him to stop. He looked down at her lap, stained a dark red. He saw her hand pressed to her stomach, covered in blood. She had been shot.

He called her name and gently stroked her face. She was barely conscious, her breathing short and labored, her pulse faint.

"No, no, no! Please, God, no, stay with me! Clara, I'm here. *Je suis là.*" He stroked her cheek, which had lost its color and was cold. "You can't, you can't."

Two large green military jeeps screamed to a stop yards from their car. A dozen camouflaged men jumped out and surrounded them, with their black automatic rifles pointed at them. Four police cars slid to a stop as officers with red police armbands jumped out, pistols raised, yelling orders in French to Hart. His mind couldn't process what he heard, but it didn't matter. All he wanted was for Clara to get medical attention.

Hart stood with his arms raised. He began screaming, pleading for help like a mortally wounded animal howling at the injustice of its destiny. He turned to look at his would-be captors, their faces tense, guns at the ready.

"She needs help, please!"

He collapsed to his knees as the rain began to fall harder.

42

Paris

The sky darkened as day turned to night; the storm clouds rolled further inland, bringing with them more rain and cracks of heavy thunder. Angry winds swept across the office buildings and apartments of the Seventh Arrondissement as the Eiffel Tower watched on like the stoic guardian of Paris. *Another storm, and this one, too, shall pass.* Flashes of white lightning scorched the black sky as rain lashed against the small window that Hart stared out of.

He sat handcuffed to a steel table in a dimly lit room on the third floor of the DGSI building. It was next door to Les Invalides, where its eternal captor, the resting Napoleon, stayed like Hart, confined to a small box, surrounded by guards, with no hope of escape.

Hart had sat comatose alone for nearly three hours. Finally, a tall man with flowing dark hair, a thin nose, pointed chin, and a light-gray Prince of Wales suit had visited him. The man seemed important, carrying with him the elegance of an aristocrat who knew he had power yet wielded it sparingly, knowing full well the damage he could cause. He had a light-blue silk pocket square that matched his dress shirt and dark-navy tie, with golden French cuffs in the shape of the fleur-de-lis. He'd come into Hart's room three times and spoken fluent English, but spoke deliberately, sounding out the syllables. He asked pointed questions to Hart, who sat stupefied, lost in his own thoughts.

When the man had first come into the room, he'd introduced himself as Pierre-Emmanuel. He didn't give his title or position, but Hart could reasonably surmise from the manner in which he carried himself that he was in the business of intelligence, and at a high level. Pierre-Emmanuel had a large black-pebbled-leather notebook with leafy gold pages that fluttered when he rapidly flipped through them, and he never asked a question he didn't already have an answer to with which to cross-check it against. He had produced a pen and proceeded to ask Hart a series of short questions, referencing back to his small notebook as he listened. *Your name? Nationality? Occupation? Reason for your visit to France? What type of business? And whom did you meet with? Had you met him before? How about the girl? How many days? Which hotel? Maxim: know of him? You know he's dead? How? One word is enough, thank you.*

Hart had barely the strength to think, his mind shutting down completely as if to spare him from reliving the day. The pain from not knowing how Clara was, if she was even alive, corroded his thoughts. Everything had changed in a blink of an eye. More trivially, what was to become of him? He thought of the new life that stared him in the face and how alone he felt. The only things he had to keep him company were the small window with thick glass, and the cold steel table where he sat.

The second time Pierre-Emmanuel came in, Hart was more attentive; perhaps he could make an ally. He figured Pierre-Emmanuel to be in his early forties. His long fingers, when not writing or holding the ever-present notebook, tapped slowly on any surface they could find. Hart first noticed the habit when he was asked to describe his business relationship with Claude Renard and Clara Nouvelle. As Hart tried to piece together what he'd been asked to do by his own boss, Pierre-Emmanuel tapped his index and middle fingers softly on his left temple as he took notes, a repetitive *one, two*. Again, Hart noticed the tapping when he was asked to describe his relationship with Maxim, the first time they'd met, and how often they talked. With the eyes of a hawk—alert and a golden brown—his interrogator would give him a cursory glance before squinting back at the notebook. The glances caused Hart to question the authenticity of whatever he was saying. He realized he looked guilty, and he certainly felt guilty. Guilty he was alive; others had not been as fortunate.

The defense he offered was the truth, but he knew it could only be told with time, and he had very little available. The only hope of surviving the catastrophe was Clara, whom he kept asking about every chance he got, pleading to Pierre-Emmanuel that he be told her status. His response was tactful, a quid pro quo, told with a tilt of the head and squint of his hawkish eyes: *You tell me something, I'll share something with you.*

Hart shared everything he knew, the key people he'd met or knew about, Igor, Jean Luc Bichot, Renard, Clara, Maxim, but every time his interrogator would pout, exhale a deep breath, and gently drum with his fingers on the steel table. *One, two; one, two.* With an exasperated breath, Pierre-Emmanuel said he would see what he could find out about Clara and left.

It had been several hours, after Hart had been brought a small plastic tray for dinner consisting of a ham sandwich, a few slices of apple, and a cup of coffee, before he returned. Hart didn't touch the food but drank the coffee, leaning close to the table to drink because his handcuffs didn't allow otherwise.

Pierre-Emmanuel sat across the table and stared at him intently, studying his prisoner, and folded his hands neatly over the notebook.

"I am afraid that I do not have good news," he started, observing Hart closely before continuing. "Your friend Clara has lost a tremendous amount of blood. She sustained a gunshot wound to her abdomen. Furthermore, the trauma her head received in the car accident gave her a severe concussion. That combined with a large blood loss has put her health in grave danger, with her organs struggling to keep her alive on their own. She is currently still in surgery to remove the bullet, but to reduce brain swelling after surgery she will most likely be induced into a medical coma. Her recovery will be left up to her own body's ability to heal, I am afraid."

Hart bowed his head and let his chin fall on his chest. His face didn't flinch, but several tears swelled in his eyes and fell into his lap. Pierre-Emmanuel stood and turned to face the window and the black Parisian night sky. He allowed Hart a quiet moment before turning back to him and crossed his arms. His mouth opened for several seconds before he spoke.

"I've been in this job for years," he said, looking at the ceiling as if recalling memories. "The thing that has always baffled me is that the people who commit crimes—big crimes: extortion, embezzling, fraud, murder"—he looked at Hart when he said the words as if to gauge his reaction, but Hart sat motionless, his head still resting on his chest—"they all try desperately to hold on to some variance of innocence. They'll say, 'It wasn't my fault,' 'They asked for it,' 'I had no choice,' or my personal favorite, 'I didn't do it.' But the thing they don't realize is that they are already here, in this room. The very room in which you sit, which means we know that you have committed a crime, and you were caught for it. Yet criminals insist on clawing and scraping for a few last moments of their perceived innocence."

He gently pulled the other metal chair out from under the table, scraping the metal on the floor before he sat. "The thing is, Monsieur Hart, over time the truth catches up with us all. The only honest thing I've ever known in my life is time. With it, everything is eventually revealed. Please think about this when I come back in the morning."

He stood and left Hart alone with his thoughts.

43

Paris

The shuffling of heavy-soled shoes and raised voices in the hallway woke Hart from a dazed stupor. The voices grew from a hushed discourse to animated shouting. He could hear people arguing back and forth, then hurried footsteps before the shouting would resume. Hart didn't allow his mind to think on it, but instead he stared out his small window at the brightening blue sky as the sun rose on a new day.

He'd sat up nearly all night, visited twice by a guard bringing him a cup of water and oatmeal in addition to a piece of paper, translated into English, that explained he was being held under the French National Security and Anti-Terrorism Act of 2017. He read and signed it but gave his detention no further thought. Instead, he could only think about Clara, and if he'd ever see her again.

Hart replayed their memories: their first meeting over lunch, her casual laugh and seductive half smile, their tipsy walk home after drinks, the perfume lingering on him during his lonely walk back to his hotel. The ignorance he had just days prior was bliss, as he recalled London, the happier moments, where he learned about her and the island where her grandfather lived and the Passage du Gois. Hart bowed his head and rubbed his eyes. He'd give anything for another chance to do it over. They would have run away, taken the car, and hid out on that island, safe for only a little while, but long enough to know freedom, her warm skin under the sheets, a soft hand to hold on a quiet beach.

Hart was stirred from his memories by voices shouting loudly in the hall before the door to his room burst open. A wide-set man in a gray suit that matched his hair and thick silver beard curtly nodded at Hart. He made his way around the table and plopped down in the opposite chair and laid on the table a bottle of Mountain Dew, along with a thick leather zipper portfolio. He pushed his steel-framed glasses further up his nose and took a swig from his bottle. Hart guessed he was mid-fifties, clearly not French, and if the Mountain Dew didn't give it away, his tailoring did. He wore a dense suit jacket that fit, but not especially well, a large blue zigzag tie and a Tag Heuer watch, which he consulted quickly before scribbling a few notes in his portfolio. He cleared his throat and looked Hart in the eyes.

"My name is Stephen Palmer. I am a delegate of the United States Embassy in Paris."

He undid the cap to his Mountain Dew and took another sip before consulting his notes, flipping through the pages of an official-looking report. Hart sat quietly, cursing the eventuality he knew would come: the United States had become involved.

Palmer cleared his throat, leaned back in his chair, and tapped his glasses back onto the bridge of his nose. "So, I have an elementary understanding of your time in Europe over the past week or so, but why don't you take me through it slowly, and we'll see what we learn?"

Hart shook his head. "I first want to know the status of Clara Nouvelle. She was in the accident with me and—"

Palmer cut Hart off by holding up a thick and callused hand. "I already checked. The DGSI isn't too happy their agent is fighting for her life, but she is out of surgery. I don't have a prognosis, and nothing else has been communicated. Now, please, Mr. Hart, can we start? We're in for a long day."

Hart couldn't decide if Palmer was trying to play the good cop to Pierre-Emmanuel's bad cop, but he didn't care. What he did care about was Clara and the truth, wherever it lay in the abyss where Renard and Igor had hidden it. He hoped it would see the light of day in time.

Palmer took notes but didn't show any sign of intrigue or offer any confirmations. Hart had told his story thoroughly to make sure he didn't leave anything out, but he knew there would still be questions. Probing questions; the type where a simple yes or no wouldn't do. Palmer asked him questions that were phrased as inquisitive conversation starters, open-ended in style to encourage Hart to chat. *Tell me about your boss? What is your position at your company? How did you get your job?* They spoke at length about where he'd worked before, how he got the job, and what he did every day. Palmer consulted his notes often, adjusting his glasses absentmindedly while looking on with indifference as he listened. He excused himself and left the room for several moments before bringing back a cup of coffee with some hard breakfast pastries for Hart.

Palmer then shifted the speed of his questions and asked Hart to go back over his trips to Paris and London. He keyed on small bits of information that Hart didn't view as important, but Palmer was his only chance at having any semblance of an ally or friend, so he answered as thoughtfully as he could. He detailed his days spent at Renard's office with files in the cramped glass conference room, where everyone walked by, and the last-minute trip up to London with Clara. It was so unexpected that he needed to go shopping for a tuxedo hours before the gala. He described the envelope, along with Igor's reaction at the auction and the following day's adventure in Borough Market.

A few nods here and there were all the feedback Palmer gave. He would stop writing every few minutes, stretch his hand, and continue listening with a blank stare. Palmer asked several times for Hart to explain how he booked the flight back to Paris, who was on the flight, what type of plane it was, where he took off from and landed, and at what time. *Renard called you? Where is your phone? What were his instructions? How did you feel about the request?*

Palmer closed his leather portfolio, leaned back in his chair, took off his glasses, and produced a white handkerchief. He meticulously cleaned the lenses while paying no attention to Hart, who watched in silence.

Hart leaned his head over the table. "So, who exactly are you?"

"Like I said earlier, an embassy delegate." Palmer gruffly curled his lips into a toothless smile, his beard bushing upwards on his face. "And an ally."

"How did you know I was here?"

Palmer chuckled and then cleared his throat. "Paul, we're the United States government."

"So, why are you here?"

"I can leave you to the French if you'd like. However, the implications if this escalates into an international incident, and the ripples that it will cause if it does, are huge. We prefer to keep the troublesome fish in our own pond. More easily controlled that way. Less ripples, if you will."

Palmer grabbed his things, stood, walked to the door, and gave three knocks, and the door opened. He spoke in French with the guard rapidly, saying, "*Si'l vous plaît,*" several times to the indifference of a shrug, a small flap of the lips, and a point down the hallway from the guard. Hart heard more French down the hall, a chorus of three or four voices volleying back and forth with Palmer, who leaned out of the doorway. Finally, Palmer gave a *merci* and a polite wave as he turned in the doorway, holding his portfolio with both hands.

"Good news. These fine gentlemen have agreed to take the handcuffs off of you and allow you some lunch. I'll have something dropped off, because otherwise, with French bureaucracy and their lunch breaks, you wouldn't eat for hours. I'll be back, but I need to get some things done before I return tonight."

Hart nodded and began to speak. The only need he had was to hear about Clara. He managed to get the words, "Can you—" out before Palmer held up his meaty hand, and a reassuring look spread across his face.

"I will give you a full update on Mademoiselle Nouvelle when I return." He paused to see if that was what Hart had wanted, and Hart nodded in solemn appreciation. Palmer gave a small nod in return before he turned on his heel vanished out into the hallway.

The day passed as fast as it could for a man imprisoned in a small room. The walls were thick, and except for the occasional voice heard by the door, his thoughts remained his only companion. Outside of the small window, the sky turned a brighter blue, the sun strong until late in the day, when it crept by his window, pouring sunlight and heat through the thick glass. Hart had eaten a sandwich and drank a bottle of water. He was escorted twice to a small restroom down the hallway. But most of all he waited.

Late in the evening—or at least he guessed it was late, since the small window had long since turned to the night sky—the door to his room opened, but it was Pierre-Emmanuel who entered. He wore a black sweater over a white dress shirt and dark-gray trousers, and cut a more casual figure than the previous day.

"*Bonsoir.*"

He walked around the table, placed a manila envelope on it, and leaned against the far wall. Hart had been stretching his legs but took a seat and nodded at his captor.

"How did your visit with Mr. Palmer go?" Pierre-Emmanuel inclined his head.

"I told him the truth, same as I told you."

The answer seemed to please Pierre-Emmanuel. He leaned back on the far wall and sighed. "I have some news for you, and perhaps it will spark a discussion for us. It's important for you, and then afterwards we can get to Mademoiselle Nouvelle. Is this agreeable?"

Hart nodded apprehensively then stopped. "Maybe it's best to have Palmer here."

This precipitated a small chuckle. "Contrary to what you may think, we are both on the same side, Mr. Palmer and I. We want the truth and to make sure the threat is over. We are working together on this, as France and America have done and will always do."

Hart nodded. "What have the two of you learned?"

"We have both reached somewhat of a similar conclusion about you." He glanced up at the ceiling, his face unchanging. "There are things that don't add up."

Hart felt his stomach twist. *They think I had a role in all of this*, he thought to himself. Maybe Hutchens could help. It was required compliance to ensure clients' identities; at least that was the original purpose of his trip, until he'd been distracted by Renard's promises and Clara. But he realized that maybe he didn't know his boss as well as he thought, and he might never find out if he was sent out of maliciousness or simply naivety.

Hart understood his situation: Clara was his only hope if he wanted to clear his name. But more importantly to him and his innocence, he hoped she would recover. But he understood their relationship compromised her integrity and alibi, at least according to the late Maxim. Hart rubbed his brow as he tried to stay engaged with Pierre-Emmanuel.

"As you know, you're being held under the 2017 Terrorist Act. The document you signed outlines our governments' internal security laws. This means that we have great discretion over how long we can hold you, what for, and even where." He watched Hart as his words lingered in the air for a moment.

"Look, I didn't do anything wrong. I was doing what I was told and—" Hart started before Pierre-Emmanuel left the wall and sat down at the table, drumming his fingers.

"I think that, after reviewing some of the information you provided to both myself and Mr. Palmer, further investigation is required. Some of these things you'd like us to look into, such as the Borough Market wine shop, the chartered plane, the ballistics of the shooting in Clara's apartment—they are going to take time." Pierre-Emmanuel spread his arms out to his sides: *It cannot be helped.* "It seems we need more time, and unfortunately for you and Mademoiselle Nouvelle, it is not a luxury we have. But I think there is a way that everyone can be slightly appeased. Care to hear my idea?"

"Yes," Hart responded curtly without breaking eye contact.

"Well, as I said, there are things that don't add up. Both Mr. Palmer and I agree that there is much more to the story than you can offer. On one hand, it is entirely possible that someone of your background and resources could have an active role in financial crimes that somehow spun off into excessive violence, maybe a deal gone bad." He pushed his bottom lip up into his top in a pout and shrugged. "On the other hand, maybe a guy such as yourself, willing to please and follow your superiors' directions, got involved in a dangerous game well beyond your understanding and you simply were curious or naïve enough to play along. Either way, there is some negligence on your part and your company's, but that is for Mr. Palmer to deal with.

"However, this is highly concerning to both our countries, particularly

France, where you have had shoot-outs and car chases. The illogical notion that only one person, this Igor, who currently resides on a medical examiner's table, did all of this on his own—I am not sure I believe this. Where there is one there are many, and perhaps even your safety could still be at risk—if you are telling us the truth, that is."

The room was silent for a moment. Pierre-Emmanuel picked at a bit of lint on his right sleeve and looked at his watch.

Hart scoffed. "Of course, I am telling you the truth!" He gripped the cold steel of the table, his knuckles turning white.

Pierre-Emmanuel glanced at Hart's hands and looked back up towards him.

"Potentially, you could be in danger. If Igor and/or Monsieur Renard made attempts on your life and went to all of this trouble to frame you, there's something grander at play. Of course, we don't know what that is, but for all parties concerned—your government, the Republic of France, Mr. Palmer, myself, and you..." His voice trailed off for a moment as his eyes found the floor. It was as if he was searching for words. Hart saw a flicker of inspiration behind the man's steel eyes. "We think it is best if you're placed under a certain form of house arrest. You cannot leave the country until we've completed the investigation, and for your protection, you'll be placed with armed guards in a discreet location while we get to the bottom of all of this." A toothless smile: *This is the best deal you'll get, and I didn't want to give it to you.*

Hart sat still, his mouth slightly ajar, as he processed the news. His initial reaction was joy at leaving this cramped room, but then the reality of house arrest set in. He chewed on the subject for a while as he tried to work out what exactly that arrangement entailed.

"So, house arrest with armed guards. Is that for my protection, or to make sure I can't leave?" His tone was flat and dry; he knew the answer.

"Think of this arrangement as a mutual insurance policy. You are protected and have some liberties, while we rest easy knowing you're safe under our guard. It also gives us time to complete an investigation in a judicious manner. It was not my original idea, but your government persuaded me when they produced a staggering amount of evidence just this evening supporting you. Regardless, Paul, this is your only option besides staying in the French prison system for the foreseeable future. I'd like an answer as to what you'd like."

"Where would I stay?"

"Well, I suspect you have a limited knowledge of our country, but we'd provide you a location. It won't be the Ritz in Paris, but I'm sure you'll be able to make do. I'll have someone pick a location, and we'll go from there. It would have to be somewhere discreet and remote." He stood and produced paper from the envelope and a pen, sliding them across the table to Hart. "If you'll sign this, we can begin the process of moving you."

Hart spoke as if on reflex. "I know where I want to go."

Pierre-Emmanuel suppressed a smile and folded his arms across his chest. He leaned forward in skepticism. "Please do tell."

"I'd like to go to an island, Noirmoutier. I think it's near Nantes."

Pierre-Emmanuel gave a small nod, allowing only the slightest bit of satisfaction for Hart. He pushed the paper towards him on the table with a pen. "I'll see what can be done. No promises."

Hart read the paper quickly and signed the acknowledgment that he was subject to certain laws he had nonverbally agreed to when he cleared customs more than a week ago. Pierre-Emmanuel took the paper, and left without another word, only the sound of his shoes clicking determinedly down the hallway.

44

Noirmoutier

The white Peugeot SUV took up most of the narrow road that floated through the low-lying countryside. The route was framed by tall wispy grass, drawing a distinction between the neglected asphalt and the salt farm fields. There was a dark-brown donkey with gray, old eyes meandering through the narrow strips of grass between the salt pools, as it'd presumably done its whole life, nibbling away. The road curved and fell towards tall old oak trees that stretched into a dark-green tunnel that one had to travel through to reach a coastal town full of white stucco homes with bright-blue shutters.

Hart stared out the passenger-side window, recognizing a hair salon and a pizza parlor, the only businesses in the quaint town. Everyone deserved a chance to look good and eat well, he reasoned. The Peugeot navigated the town's roundabout with ease, merging into the sparse traffic.

Hart had met the two agents that sat in the front seats only earlier that day. He'd been told by a guard to put on the new clothes provided and be ready to travel. Hart finally left the building he'd been imprisoned in. He was fitted with a microchip in his right wrist for added insurance. The doctor had told Hart "not to dig around looking for it with a sharp object, as it would most assuredly lead to death." He'd been taken to the basement of the building and escorted out the rear service entrance to an awaiting van, where he'd met the guards who were currently driving him.

Before climbing into the van, with no idea where he was being taken, Hart had glanced up at his former prison. The building looked serene from the outside, its white façade beaming on another sunny fall day in Paris, a far cry from the silent torment he would remember it for. He thought he'd seen a figure in the third-story glass window, perhaps the long dark hair and hawkish eyes of Pierre-Emmanuel, but he couldn't be sure.

Hart's new acquaintances had been cordial and professional for the several hours they'd known each other. The navigator, Antoine, was dark skinned and stout, with thick black stubble, short, dark, wiry hair, brown eyes, and a large crooked smile. He had been talkative to Hart on their ride from Paris to Nantes via the TGV. He started asking about American sport, namely the NBA, and listed his favorite players. Antoine, apparently capitalizing on an opportunity to practice his English, carried the conversation. He came from Toulouse, a city in the southwest of France where rugby, relaxing, and partying were the cornerstones of life. His mother was Spanish, hence his darker skin, and his father was a police officer. Antoine followed in the family business, ultimately landing in the DGSI. His eyes were sharp and vigilant, and, Hart assumed, Antoine's casual nature towards him was intended to make Hart's guard come down.

The driver of the Peugeot, who'd been receiving a fair amount of directions from Antoine, sometimes well past the needed exit or road, did his best to keep his temper in check. He'd introduced himself as Lucas. He was tall with a neatly trimmed beard, and his dark hair was shaved short. He had a quiet assertiveness about him and was the senior DGSI agent, often scolding Antoine during their ride. He was distant and reserved with Hart.

The day had been tiresome—the travel, the new people—but the distress for Clara remained with him through it all, like a loyal companion born out of familiarity. His thoughts stayed with her, what was to become of him, and what his life would end up becoming without her. He would make a deal with the devil, anything to be able to hold her close once again, even if it was to say goodbye. He shook his head absentmindedly as he thought of her saving his life, Igor squeezing the breath from him, the numbness, the thuds of the shots, her last act. No, *Damn that*, he thought; not her last act. *Far from it*, he told himself sternly. He would see her again.

Wouldn't he?

Hart forced himself to stare out the window as Antoine and Lucas had an animated discussion. The road opened, flanked by restaurants and parking lots, before straight ahead of them was a wide-open expanse with a narrow cobble road: Passage du Gois.

Hart sat on the edge of his seat and gazed out the windshield. The dark-grayish plain was sprinkled with jutting coarse gray rocks and seaweed left behind by the ocean. The openness stretched as far as he could see to the left and the right, with four wooden lookout posts sitting stoically next to the road, which was lined with parked SUVs and cars. People climbed out of the cars, equipped with yellow rubber boots, and waded onto the wet sand and stone, searching for seashells or other lost treasures left behind by the receding tide.

Lucas wrestled the car over the slick stones of the passage that only hours earlier had been covered with ocean water. Hart cracked the back window, and a cold sea breeze rushed into the car, bringing with it the taste of salt and the sharp smell of the sea. The wind stung his face, forcing him to close his eyes. He focused on the seagulls' cries of delight from the fresh buffet the ocean had left when the tide rolled back out to sea.

They crossed the divide between the continent and the island, forgoing the Pont de Noirmoutier, built in 1970, when the island became more frequently visited. The island would be his home for an indefinite amount of time, he a prisoner to its beauty and his own thoughts.

Once over the Passage du Gois, they took a narrow road to the north end of the island, near the Château de Noirmoutier. Lucas swerved, honked, and gestured at the leisurely pace of the local drivers.

Oyster farms and sea salt fields flanked the road until Lucas finally turned down what seemed more like a walkway, which ran parallel to a canal. The canal was subject to the massive tides of the island, too, evident by the fishing boats and sailboats lying on the hard-caked mud at the bottom of the empty waterway.

Lucas parked at the end of the road in front of a gray, stucco, two-story building with white-painted window frames displaying France's ministry of tourism's four-star rating under the name "Le Général d'Elbée." Antoine waved Hart out of the car, and the three headed inside, each of them carrying a piece of luggage. Pierre-Emmanuel had been kind enough to allow some of Hart's belongings from his Paris hotel to be returned—a few articles of clothing and his toiletries. His passport and computer were not amongst them.

Inside the hotel, the men were greeted with a cheery, "*Bonjour,*" from the young receptionist, who led them up a marble flight of stairs to their adjoining rooms. She said they were the only guests for the first few nights of their stay because it was the low season. But their rooms were the best the hotel had to offer, overlooking the château on one side and the canal on the other.

Hart was given the room that overlooked the château, because, he figured, that room had large, expansive windows but no balcony to escape from, or was it to not let anyone climb through? Hart's apartment was spacious, comprising of a bedroom and a separate sitting room with a couch and flat-screen TV, compared to the previous French government hospitality. Lucas checked the room over, looking at the windows and peering down at the two-story drop.

"This will work," Lucas said as he continued combing Hart's room.

"It's great. How long do you think—?"

Lucas put up his hands and shook his head. "I don't know these things, so don't ask. But if you want to leave the hotel, ask. If you want food or need to buy something, ask. Otherwise, don't bother, because we don't have the answers."

Silence filled the room as the appeal of house arrest suddenly seemed to wear off, seemingly for everyone.

There was a light tap on the door, then several seconds' later two more, followed by a forceful third. Hart rose from his couch and opened the door to find Lucas and Antoine in the hallway.

"You have a visitor downstairs in the dining room," Antoine said with a smile, while Lucas scowled.

Hart was escorted down the marble stairs and through the foyer. He had been at the hotel for five days, and outside of Lucas and Antoine allowing him a few walks along the canal towards beaches facing the continent, he hadn't eaten or done much. The island was a tourist destination during summer, but during winter it slowed down considerably. There was CNN International to watch on the TV, but there were no longer the constant updates about the investigation into the London attack; the news cycle had moved on. He had anxiously watched the news to learn about Igor and Renard and the mayhem he left behind in Paris, but it was never mentioned.

Hart didn't know who he expected to see, but when he turned the corner and saw Stephen Palmer, his heart sunk. Palmer sat in the corner of the empty dining room, close to the windows overlooking the covered pool. He stood to greet Hart with a firm handshake and a soft pat on the shoulder. The same receptionist who showed Hart to his room the first day brought over another cup for the silver pitcher of coffee that sat on the table. Palmer waved at Lucas and Antoine, who took a table several yards away.

"How are you holding up?" Palmer asked, sipping his coffee, his glasses fogging from the steam. He wore a dark-brown turtleneck and a gruff face.

Hart shrugged and said nothing. Palmer paused for a moment, pulled out his leather portfolio, and looked out to the covered pool. The sky was gray, thick clouds covered the island, and a chilly sea breeze whisked leaves around the courtyard. Palmer licked his fingers and flipped a few pages over as he looked for some specific note.

"Ah, here we are." Palmer tilted the portfolio away from Hart and placed it on his lap, reading intently.

Hart poured himself coffee and scratched his week-old beard. Patient—or perhaps indifferent—he waited for his visitor to speak. Finally, Palmer sat upright, closed the notebook, and leaned forward, glancing over Hart's shoulder at his chaperones.

"I'm glad we've gotten to speak where there's more privacy than Paris. I am sorry you've been dragged into this."

"Into what exactly?" Hart asked.

"There have been concerns with regards to Renard's companies for quite a while, to be frank. A source told us a little over a year ago that DGSI had stumbled across someone in the organization being mischievous, and an undercover investigation was launched into the practices of the company, along with anyone doing business with them."

Hart shook his head. "I assume this is standard stuff for, what did you call yourself? An embassy delegate?"

Palmer smiled and spread out his hands. "Unfortunately, while I can't get much into specifics, know that you were never seriously considered a suspect by the United States with regard to any of these allegations of money laundering or tax evasion. I even talked our friend Pierre-Emmanuel into letting us help with the investigation. We talked to your boss, Hutchens. The guy is scared shitless, let me tell you." Palmer laughed and took a bite of a croissant, the flaky pastry getting stuck in his beard. "He broke like a leaky dam when agents started questioning him. Said he sent you because he thought it was a meaningless trip, and he didn't like having you in the office. Something about screwing his daughter's life up, and Renard asked him for a yes-man. Hutchens said he was promised money if Renard was appeased by the associate he was sent. So, Hutchens thought to feed you to the wolves. I don't think that speaks well about your career prospects. But apparently he is eager to work out a monetary settlement for your troubles."

Palmer shrugged and took another sip of coffee before continuing. Hart cast a glance at Lucas and Antoine, who were drinking some orange juice and reading the newspaper.

"But anyway, as far as the United States is concerned, and our good friend and ally France, you are no longer considered a subject of interest for illicit monetary transactions."

Hart felt his spirits rise, but it seemed too good to be true. He waited for the bad news.

Palmer winced before adding, "But the relationship you had with the agent has complicated—"

"Her name is Clara."

Palmer huffed. "Yes, Clara." He cleared his throat. "Has complicated things, because now there's motive to some of the crimes, namely Maxim's death, and it seems plausible you both tried to cover things up. I am sorry to tell you, but this is just the way it is. The police are still investigating, looking at cameras from all over the neighborhood of the shooting, the hotel, and the car chase. Jesus, Paul, you're a glorified accountant, not James Bond. What were you thinking? The French will not take your word alone. You'll need Clara to either come to and back your story up, or you could think about pinning this on her." Palmer shook his head, as if saddened by the thought. "The investigation will be thorough. For instance, the woman who helped you hide out and lent you her car isn't saying anything until she speaks with Clara, I'm afraid to say, but who knows when that could or would even be? They haven't charged"—Palmer opened his notebook and scanned the page—"a Justine Bruel yet with aiding and abetting, but it's only a matter of time until they threaten or do that. You need to start thinking about making a deal. There's a dead cop, and they'll want blood, you have to understand that."

Hart exhaled through his nose and clenched his jaw. He had accepted his fate days ago, sitting in his empty interrogation room, as if a spark had caught fire, torching any notion of a normal life, leaving it charred and ashen in the past. There were other people to be considered, and he'd be damned if he would let Justine risk her future because of her willingness to help Clara. Or worse, allow Clara to take the fall for running from Maxim's murder. Furthermore, he'd reasoned, he had no career or normal life to return to.

Palmer looked him over with a hint of sadness. "I think you should seriously consider your options of cooperating with the French government by admitting fault, and maybe they'll go easy on you. A few years in prison for your role in fleeing a murder, negligence, and public endangerment, amongst other things."

Hart turned to face the window and the overcast sky. He believed against all odds that Clara would come to, make a full recovery, and save him again. But, he thought, if she wasn't to be in his future, he simply didn't care about it. He needed time, but he didn't have any. She would save him once again, just like when Igor had him on the edge of death. Hope was a dangerous notion, but as far as he was concerned the strongest feeling worth living for.

Hart finally spoke. "I need time. Clara will recover and tell the truth. If that doesn't happen, I'll do what is best for everyone."

Palmer took off his glasses and vigorously rubbed the bridge of his nose. He put them back on and gave Hart a solemn look. "Paul, you don't have any time." He folded his portfolio, put it in his bag, and stood. "There's probably less than a week of goodwill left between our countries. Then things will move fast. If the investigation doesn't outright clear you, your only hope is Clara, and we still don't have any update on her health."

Hart leaned back in his chair and folded his arms. "Stephen, why are you trying to help me?"

Palmer slung his bag over his shoulder before jutting his lower lip out and looking up at the ceiling. "Sometimes things don't appear to be what they are, while other times everything is as it seems. I wish I could tell you more, but there's much more to this story involving other players and even an entirely different game. But I know a good person when I see one, probably more so because I know the bad ones too well." He gave Hart a toothless smile and extended his hand. "Good day, Paul. I'll see you around."

Palmer turned and headed out of the restaurant past Lucas and Antoine, who watched him leave with indifference. Hart sat silent for a time, replaying the answer in his mind and mulling its cryptic nature. Somewhere deep inside him he had an unsettling feeling that all along he had been caught in a game bigger than he, or even Clara, realized. He thought about another sip of coffee, but instead he made a silent pact with himself. He would do what was best for everyone in time.

45

Noirmoutier

It had been three days since Palmer visited, but Hart still didn't have an update on Clara. He sat in his hotel room and watched the late-morning fog that slowly lifted from the island and disappeared out to sea. The weather had decided to show its different forms the past few days—rain, sun, fog, and wind all made an appearance. Some days, the weather mirrored his pain, while the unseasonably warm weather, like a sign from above, gave him hope.

Hart passed his time the best he could, being escorted around the small town, managing to eat more out of necessity than joy, and reading anything he could find. Just off the lobby of the hotel there was a room, ornately decorated with leather sofas and vintage globes amongst the bookcases, filled with books in French, English, and Spanish. Hart had tried to improve his French by reading, but it only caused him to think of her, consumed by uncertainty. Oftentimes, he found it impossible to sleep; instead, he lay awake, thinking of what he'd do to save everyone the pain of his predicament.

Hart heard a soft knock on the door and turned his attention from the gloomy window. He was surprised to find Lucas standing outside his door. Normally, Antoine was sent to get him for meals and walks.

"The weather will be nice later today. The front desk suggested we visit a beach this afternoon. We will go at 2 p.m."

Lucas said it as an instruction and less of an idea, but still it was a good excuse to leave the room. Hart closed the door and began to stare out the window to watch the outside world lazily pass by but decided he'd rather check the news. He turned on the BBC and caught the end of the weather forecast. The shot cut back to the anchor shuffling papers in the studio.

"News today from France with implications for the European economy as the private business tycoon Claude Renard, who was found murdered in Paris over

a week ago, appears to have been killed by one of his employees. Authorities have provided a clearer story about what happened the week before last in Paris.

"According to our sources, a man who worked closely with Monsieur Renard had allegedly been embezzling millions through various charities and businesses. Sources inside the Paris police department say that Claude Renard was a victim of this convoluted crime that took place over many years through multiple companies. Allegedly, Monsieur. Renard confronted the man who perpetrated the crimes in a Parisian hotel, which escalated into violence that took Monsieur Renard's life.

"During the shoot-out, a Parisian police officer who attempted to de-escalate the situation was also killed. The gunman was killed in the shoot-out before authorities could take him into custody. Monsieur Renard's estate has donated an undisclosed amount to migrant relocation charities, as his will wished.

"In other news, airfares are getting cheaper thanks to small carriers cutting the cost to fly in exchange for stronger loyalty programs..."

Hart sat back and leaned his head against the wall, staring up at the ceiling. The image of Pierre-Emmanuel, his French cuffs and hawkish eyes, talking to Palmer about what story to give the press played out in his mind. Events were now so far beyond his knowledge and understanding, but there was assuredly more. Maybe Palmer reported back to Pierre-Emmanuel that Hart would in time confess and wrap up the affair in a neat bow. But somehow it didn't surprise Hart that Renard was made out to be the victim, and that they'd turned Maxim's death into an act of bravery. Hart couldn't help but wonder if that meant he was off the hook. His current situation didn't indicate so.

Lucas and Antoine walked Hart downstairs to the Peugeot. The sun was high and unseasonably warm, easily burning off the early-morning fog that had settled over the island. A cool breeze came off the ocean, but it was subdued, as if obediently performing its duties without conviction, lazily pushing the few large white clouds across the blue sky.

They drove through a village of white homes with clay tiles clustered together, windows shuttered. Past the maze of homes, the Peugeot rose up an inclined road flanked by picket fences and private-home gates. The road was lined with massive trees, whose branches seemed to reach to the sky, blocking out the sun. A harsh westerly swept across the sandstone earth of the northwestern part of the island.

Lucas parked the car towards the end of the road, where the tree canopy gave way to an expansive view of the ocean. Two buildings framed the walkway to the beach—on the left, a small tourist shop selling beach toys and seashells, and on the right, a two-story white hotel. At the front of the hotel there was a terrace facing the beach, where umbrellas, wooden chairs, and tables sat. Hart squinted in the bright sunlight and read a blue sign welcoming them to Bois de la Chaise.

The beach was crescent shaped, with a rock jetty flanking its right side, and on the left a long wooden pier, which seemed to materialize from the woods, jutted out into the ocean. Hart walked past the hotel terrace and stood overlooking the beach. The weather had given the island an unexpected gift that the locals seemed prepared for. Dressed in light sweaters, but out on the beach, several sat on blankets and lawn chairs reading, while children played soccer. Hart smelled the sea, felt the sun sting his face, and listened to the unbridled laughter from the beach.

He turned to see Lucas and Antoine off to his left, and behind them the forest that led towards the pier. They motioned for him to follow and began to walk up the gentle slopes that led into the trees. A dusting of pine straw covered the firm ground, made of rock and tree roots, which allowed the trees to grow at impossible angles. Hart could see the ocean and the pier through the trees to their right as the three of them made their way deeper into the forest.

The pier appeared behind a small rock formation and under an old bent tree, its trunk made thick by time. Hart would have missed it if not for the small sign that read "*L'Estacade*." There were two fishermen casting long rods and hauling square nets up. Sailboats bobbed just off to the right side in the cove. Lucas and Antoine meandered on the pier, looking down at the water, the rocks, and pointing out things to one another. Hart, off ahead of them, made his way towards the furthest point of the pier out over the water.

He reached the end of the pier and looked out across the choppy waves sparkling as the ocean caught the sunlight. He stared at the water, its color a deep emerald-green that produced a twisted feeling in his stomach. He closed his eyes and pictured Clara at the gala in London, her dress the same color as the ocean, and the soft silk that draped her. He thought of her smile, and the soft accent she had when she whispered to him made him realize the helplessness he felt without her.

He stood on the pier for some time, watching the waves roll into the cove, lost in thought and coming to peace with what he had to do. He knew the serenity of the beach would give him solace and show him the right decision. He looked across the water back to the beach, where a man played fetch with a black labrador, its shiny coat catching the sun as it galloped into the water. A large plane flew high overhead, just a white speck in the sky. Hart wondered where it was going and who traveled on it, longing for the freedom he'd lost, and he couldn't help but think it would be a while before he ever got it back.

He hung his head and listened to the waves hit the pier, the water rushing in and going out from under him. A soft breeze wrestled its way through the forest, the leaves and branches swaying as the wind swept out over the pier and onto the ocean. The breeze carried a familiar scent as Hart drew a breath. He slowly turned to look over his shoulder.

She stood with hands deep in the pockets of her coat, dark hair blowing in the sea breeze, her green eyes soft and fixed on his.

Her lips moved ever so slightly. "*Bonjour*, Paul."

A Note from the Author

Minneapolis, Minnesota, Spring 2019

I sincerely hope you have enjoyed *Where the Wolf Lies*. This work would not have been possible without the support of so many people.

To my wife Marie, who gracefully supported my ambitions, challenged me, dreamed with me, and listened to me endlessly narrate my thoughts on Paul and Clara. *Merci, mon amour.*

For Tim and Susan, my parents, who have always encouraged me, loved unconditionally, while being steady voices of reason in my head, thank you. I hope I've made you proud.

To my sister Laura, who's been a confidant, agent, staunch supporter, all while juggling raising my godson Jordan, thank you. The seemingly endless phone calls and emails did not go unappreciated.

There are first readers I'd like to thank, including author Stanley Trollip, whose sound advice and feedback had been of great reassurance. Phillip Wagener for his keen eye on the details, Jim Johnson for his reinforcement that becoming a writer was perfect for me; Fred Philpot for his thoughtful feedback; and Rory Veraducci who read my book while traveling, as the way it should be, and gave me the compliment: "I forgot I was reading you." Thank you Rory.

To Justine Gambard, who was the first person to read my book at a Parisian café, a dream of mine, and kind enough to send me a photo of the event. *Merci beaucoup.*

My editor Marcus Trower, based in the United Kingdom, who provided me with fantastic guidance, and made sure the characters, and settings were culturally accurate, I can't thank you enough. It was a pleasure to work with you.

In addition, many thanks are necessary to my proofreader Rebecca Millar who did an incredible job providing thoughtful feedback, and kind encouragement to help bring the novel over the finish line.

I would be remiss if I were not to thank my Scottish Terrier Mac, and our rescue cat Gaia. At the time I started writing, Gaia was a kitten, and she would wake me, along with Mac, at 5 a.m. as if imploring me to write. We would all head downstairs, not to wake the Mrs., and I'd write for two hours before going to work. Those early mornings with Mac and Gaia curled up at my feet are when Paul and Clara came to be.

To Noirmoutier, and France for that matter, for making me feel at home. If you ever have the opportunity, Noirmoutier is a must visit. Every place in the novel is based on a real setting where I've visited, and loved, I'd recommend visiting them all.

Finally, but perhaps most importantly, I'd like to thank you, the reader. I hope this story inspires you to travel, hope, explore, and be open-minded to adventure and different cultures.

Many thanks, and Paul Hart will return.

Tyler

CPSIA information can be obtained
at www.ICGtesting.com
Printed in the USA
LVHW091711150120
643721LV00003B/326